THE GOSPELS
for
ALL CHRISTIANS

THE GOSPELS
for
ALL CHRISTIANS

Rethinking the Gospel Audiences

Edited by

RICHARD BAUCKHAM

WILLIAM B. EERDMANS PUBLISHING COMPANY
GRAND RAPIDS, MICHIGAN / CAMBRIDGE, U.K.

© 1998 Wm. B. Eerdmans Publishing Co.
255 Jefferson Ave. S.E., Grand Rapids, Michigan 49503 /
P.O. Box 163, Cambridge CB3 9PU U.K.

Printed in the United States of America

03 02 01 00 99 98   7 6 5 4 3 2 1

Library of Congress Cataloging-in-Publication Data

The Gospels for all Christians : rethinking the Gospel audiences /
edited by Richard Bauckham.
p.   cm.
Includes bibliographical references.
ISBN 0-8028-4444-8 (alk. paper)
1. Bible. N.T. Gospels—Social scientific criticism.
2. Sociology, Christian—History—Early church, ca. 30-600.
I. Bauckham, Richard.
BS2555.2.G626 1998
226'.066—dc21   97-30621
                                              CIP

Contents

Introduction

RICHARD BAUCKHAM

The aim of this book is to challenge and to refute the current consensus in Gospels scholarship which assumes that each of the Gospels was written for a specific church or group of churches: the so-called Matthean community, Markan community, Lukan community, and Johannine community. It is a remarkable feature of the history of New Testament scholarship in this century that this consensus about the original intended audiences of the Gospels has come about without any substantial argument. Nearly all scholars writing about the Gospels now treat it as virtually self-evident that each evangelist addressed the specific context and concerns of his own community, and a large and increasingly sophisticated edifice of scholarly reconstruction has been erected on this basic assumption. It is widely used as the major hermeneutical key for reading the Gospels. But this view of the Gospels' intended audiences has never been justified by argument and discussion, and still less has it been established in debate with the other obvious possibility: that the Gospels were written with the intention that they should circulate around all the churches (and thence even outside the churches).

The present book challenges the consensus by arguing that it is probable that the Gospels were written for general circulation around the churches and so envisaged a very general Christian audience. Their implied readership is not specific but indefinite: any and every Christian community in the late-first-century Roman Empire. Many aspects of

1

the Gospels and of early Christianity are relevant here. Of great importance is the extensive evidence that the early Christian movement was not, as the consensus in Gospels scholarship has increasingly assumed, a scattering of relatively isolated, introverted communities, but a network of communities in constant, close communication with each other. What we know of the "publication" and circulation of books in general in this period is relevant to the case of the Gospels. The question of Gospel genre, especially the strong recent trend to see the Gospels as belonging to the genre of ancient biography, has important implications that have not been appreciated by the consensus, which tends to read the Gospels as though they were Pauline letters. The reading strategies employed by the consensus to reconstruct the community each Gospel allegedly addresses from the Gospel texts need to be examined to see whether alternative reading strategies may not do better justice to the text. Finally, the hermeneutical implications for contemporary reading of the Gospels are considerable if the Gospels are recognized as (in Umberto Eco's terminology) "open" texts that leave their implied readership relatively open, rather than, as the consensus assumes, "closed" texts that define their implied readership very specifically. In the end, the hermeneutical issue is whether a Gospel should be read as a narrative about Jesus or as a narrative about a hypothetical Christian community that scholars can reconstruct behind the Gospel.

Thus the thesis of this book — that the Gospels were written for all Christians, not specific churches — has very wide ramifications both for the historical study and for the contemporary reading of the Gospels, and closely relates to the way the whole of the early Christian movement should be understood. By putting in question not only some key assumptions that are almost universally accepted in contemporary Gospels scholarship, but also a large body of conclusions that work based on those assumptions has reached, the book raises an issue of central importance for current New Testament scholarship. It aims to initiate a debate that will do justice to the importance of this issue. If its challenge to the consensus is successful, the direction of much current work on the Gospels will have to change and much work will need to be done again from a quite new perspective.

The book is a collaborative effort, resulting from a lecture given by Richard Bauckham at the British New Testament Conference in Bangor (Wales) in September 1995.[1] Other British scholars who found that the thesis he presented converged with the direction their own thought had been taking agreed to contribute to a book. An expanded version of Bauckham's lecture forms the first chapter of the book ("For Whom Were Gospels Written?"). This chapter sets out the thesis of the book, puts it in the context of the way the current consensus in Gospels scholarship has developed, presents the main arguments for the thesis, and introduces the main areas of evidence and discussion. It argues that, since all the evidence we have for the early Christian movement shows it to have been a network of communities in constant, close communication with each other, and since all the evidence we have for early Christian leaders (the kind of people who might have written Gospels) shows them to have been typically people who traveled widely and worked in more than one community at different times, the outlook and concerns of neither the early Christian communities nor their teachers would have been locally confined. Both had a strong, lively, and informed sense of participation in a worldwide movement. Even rivalry and conflict between early Christian leaders took place across the general network of Christian communication: it did not produce exclusive enclaves of churches out of communication with others. Moreover, the evidence we have shows that Christian literature did in fact circulate around the churches very rapidly, while some evidence shows the deliberate launching of literature produced in one major church into general circulation around other churches.

That someone should write one of the most sophisticated and carefully composed of early Christian literary works — a Gospel — simply for the members of the community in which he was then living, with its specific, local issues in view, thus becomes a quite implausible

---

1. An earlier version was read as a paper to seminars in the University of St. Andrews, the University of Oxford, and the University of Glasgow. I am grateful to many who heard it on those occasions and made valuable comments and engaged in vigorous debate about its thesis. I am especially grateful to my St. Andrews colleague Philip Esler, whose responses helped to sharpen my thinking in several ways.

hypothesis. Knowing that his work was bound very quickly to reach many other churches, the audience he would address would be the Christians in any and every church to which his Gospel might circulate. His intended readership would be, not a specific community or even a defined group of communities, however large, but an open and indefinite category: any and every Christian community of his time in which Greek was understood. In envisaging an open category as their readership, the Gospels are like most literature of both that period and others. Since a Gospel does not address a specific community, we cannot expect to learn much from it about the evangelist's own community (even assuming he had only one, rather than a succession of very different ones), but in any case the enterprise of reconstructing such a community is hermeneutically irrelevant. The Matthean, Markan, Lukan, and Johannine communities should disappear from the terminology of Gospels scholarship.

Other chapters in the book presuppose the argument presented in the first chapter. They explore in more detail particular areas of discussion which that argument opens up and develop further implications of the argument.

Michael Thompson's chapter ("The Holy Internet: Communication Between Churches in the First Christian Generation") explores in detail one of the topics sketched in the opening chapter: communication between churches in the early Christian period. The current consensus in Gospels scholarship often works with an implicit assumption that the various Christian communities or groups of communities for which Gospels were allegedly written lived in relative isolation from each other and from the early Christian movement in general. Thompson shows that, on the contrary, the churches had both the motivation and the means to communicate often and in depth with each other. The abundant evidence for seeing the early Christian movement as a constantly and closely intercommunicating network makes it "less likely that the Gospels were produced for a select few, and more likely that they were written with an eye to their dissemination."

Loveday Alexander's chapter ("Ancient Book Production and the Circulation of the Gospels") sets the issue of the circulation of Gospels in the context of what we know about the production and circulation

4

of books in general in the Greco-Roman world. Since the commercial book trade played only a small role in the copying and circulation of books, the circulation of any kind of literature depended on the prior existence of social networks through which it could spread. The circulation of Christian literature through the network of communication between Christian communities would be no more than one example of the common pattern. What the material evidence for early Christian book production shows to have been distinctive about the Christian movement is its "remarkable preference for the new technology of the codex." This probably indicates a more pragmatic attitude to books than that of the literary establishment. Along with other features characteristic of the earliest Christian texts, it reveals "a group that used books intensively and professionally from very early on in its existence" and had "robust and vigorous intercommunity connections."

Richard Burridge's chapter ("About People, by People, for People: Gospel Genre and Audiences") takes up the argument of his own earlier study, which is also now quite widely accepted: that the genre of the Gospels is that of ancient biography. This means that they must be interpreted as about a person, not about community ideas or problems. Their four creative authors each portrayed Jesus in his own particular way in the manner of ancient biography. Ancient *bioi* provide no parallel to the idea of a biography written for a specific community. More fruitful for Gospels studies is the recognition that the authors of biographies might well have certain types of people in mind, which is more analogous to the modern concept of "target audience" or "market niche" than to the notion of a specific community as the intended audience. A particular evangelist might have a category of Christians especially in mind, but they would be a category to be found throughout the churches, not a specific community. Study of the various social functions of ancient biographies and the social levels at which they might be read can also provide more relevant clues to the intended audiences of the Gospels than the community hypothesis does.

Richard Bauckham's second chapter ("John for Readers of Mark") provides a preliminary example of the way in which the relationships between the Gospels might be explored in the light of this volume's proposal. If all the Gospels were written for general circulation around the churches, then (assuming Markan priority) the later evangelists must have expected many of their readers already to know Mark. This raises the question of the relationship of John to Mark in a different way from that in which it has usually been discussed in recent scholarship, where the question has been the source-critical one of John's possible dependence on Mark. The question which is rarely asked is: Does the Fourth Gospel presuppose that its readers already know some Gospel traditions, and, if so, which? The argument of this chapter is that, whereas the Gospel clearly does not presuppose that its readers already know specifically Johannine Gospel traditions, as it ought to do if it were written for the "Johannine community," there are indications that it has readers of Mark in view, while not presupposing that all its readers will necessarily know Mark. Though it is wholly intelligible to readers who do not know Mark, when one asks how it would be read by readers who did know Mark, the Fourth Gospel proves surprisingly complementary to Mark's narrative.

Stephen Barton's chapter ("Can We Identify the Gospel Audiences?") returns to the heart of the issue discussed in this volume: the enterprise of reconstructing the Gospel communities and the strategies employed to do so. With social-scientific criticism especially at the forefront of his treatment, he asks some candid questions about the motivation and methodology of the quest for Gospel communities. Taking each of the four Gospels in turn, he throws doubt on the strategies employed in each case to reconstruct the alleged community of the Gospel. He also highlights the hermeneutical deficiencies of the quest for Gospel communities in its tendency to reduce the text to a product of community interests and to distract attention from the theological witness of the text. Instead of the methodologically dubious attempt to reconstruct a community behind the Gospel text, a more appropriate aim of social-scientific methods might be to illuminate the world portrayed within the text.

The concluding chapter by Francis Watson ("Toward a Literal Reading of the Gospels") focuses more fully on the hermeneutical — and hence also theological — issues involved in the issue between the current consensus and its critique in the present volume. The current consensus, which reads the Gospels as narratives about the community to which they were allegedly addressed, practices "an allegorical reading strategy . . . that systematically downplays and circumvents the literal sense of the text," an "allegorical interpretation [that] effaces the past for the sake of presence." Using Marxsen's work on Mark as a seminal instance of this strategy, Watson shows that this allegorical reading strategy is not a theologically neutral historical or literary approach, but has strong theological implications that derive from Bultmann's privileging the presence of the Word over any real relationship of faith to the history of Jesus. Although much recent work on the Gospels as community texts seems innocent of the theological background to its own presuppositions, it cannot successfully extricate itself from theology. Its reading of the Gospels as texts about their communities rather than as texts about the historically particular human Jesus implies a "denial that the Word became flesh." Thus the consensus must be subject not only to the historical critique that is pursued in much of the present volume but also to a theological critique. Both require a return to the literal sense of the Gospels — not to a naive assumption that the Gospels are direct transcripts of historical reality, but to a recognition that their primary intention is to narrate the history of Jesus in the ultimate and universal meaning it has for Christian faith.

For Whom Were Gospels Written?

RICHARD BAUCKHAM

I

The title of this chapter could be analyzed into two distinct questions, only one of which it will attempt to answer. One of these questions is: Were Gospels written for Christians or for non-Christians? This question has sometimes been discussed, particularly in the case of the Gospels of Luke and John, since a minority of scholars have argued that those Gospels, or all four Gospels, were written as apologetic or evangelistic works, not for Christians but for outsiders.[1] On this question the present chapter takes for granted, without arguing the point,

---

1. For this argument with reference to all four Gospels, see C. F. D. Moule, *The Phenomenon of the New Testament*, Studies in Biblical Theology 2/1 (London: SCM, 1967), 101-14 (113: "all four Gospels alike are to be interpreted as more than anything else evangelistic and apologetic in purpose"); and cf. H. Y. Gamble, *Books and Readers in the Early Church* (New Haven and London: Yale University Press, 1995), 103 ("missionary and propagandist aspects" as well as "important functions within Christian communities"). For Luke, see C. F. Evans, *Saint Luke*, Trinity Press International New Testament Commentaries (London: SCM; Philadelphia: Trinity Press International, 1990), 104-11. For John, see D. A. Carson, *The Gospel According to John* (Leicester: Inter-Varsity Press; Grand Rapids: Eerdmans, 1991), 87-95. M. A. Tolbert, *Sowing the Gospel: Mark's World in Literary-Historical Perspective* (Minneapolis: Fortress, 1989), 304, takes the view that Mark was written for two categories of individuals (not groups): Christians experiencing persecution and interested outsiders.

9

the answer given by the scholarly consensus: that all Gospels were intended to reach, in the first place, a Christian audience. For the purposes of the argument of this chapter, it needs only to be observed that, if any of the evangelists did envisage reaching non-Christian readers, they would surely have had to envisage reaching them via Christian readers, who could pass on copies of Gospels to interested outsiders through personal contact.[2] So the Christian audience would in any case remain primary.

The second question, which this chapter does address, is: Were the Gospels written for a specific Christian audience or for a general Christian audience? Was, for example, Matthew written for Matthew's own church, the so-called Matthean community, or was it written for wide circulation among the Christian churches of the late first century? Are a Gospel's implied readers a specific Christian community (consisting of one or more specific local churches), or are they the members of any and every Christian community of the late first century to which that Gospel might circulate? Whereas the first of our two questions has sometimes been discussed, with some substantial arguments deployed in its discussion, this second question is remarkable for having never, so far as I can tell, been discussed in print.

The point is not, of course, that this question is not relevant to the concerns of current or recent Gospels scholarship. Quite the opposite. One of the two possible answers to this question — the option that each Gospel was written for a specific Christian community — has been taken entirely for granted in most Gospels scholarship for some decades now.[3] As an assumption on which arguments about the Gospels are based, it has come to play a more and more dominant role in Gospels scholarship, which since the late 1960s has become increasingly interested in reconstructing the circumstances and character of

2. This is consistent with the second-century evidence that the Gospels did find some non-Christian readers: Gamble, *Books and Readers*, 103.

3. Of course, some important works on the Gospels that show no interest at all in the question of their audience also continue to be published, e.g., H. Koester, *Ancient Christian Gospels* (London: SCM Press; Philadelphia: Trinity Press International, 1990).

the community for which, it is assumed, each Gospel was written. Almost all contemporary writing about the Gospels shares the unargued assumption that each evangelist, himself[4] no doubt a teacher in a particular church, wrote his Gospel for that particular church, with its particular situation, character, and needs at the forefront of his mind. The so-called Matthean, Markan, Lukan, or Johannine (or for that matter, Thomasine[5]) community may be understood as, not just one church, but a small group of churches, but in that case it is treated as axiomatic that this group of churches was homogeneous in composition and circumstances. The unargued assumption in every case is that each Gospel addresses a localized community in its own, quite specific context and character.

Nearly all the literature of the last few decades that makes this assumption and increasingly builds large and highly sophisticated arguments upon it seems to regard this assumption as completely self-evident, as though no alternative could ever have occurred to anyone. There is, of course, a perfectly obvious alternative possibility: that an evangelist writing a Gospel expected his work to circulate widely among the churches, had no particular Christian audience in view, but envisaged as his audience any church (or any church in which Greek was understood) to which his work might find its way. This is the possibility that the present chapter argues deserves to be given very serious consideration. The purpose of the chapter is not simply to challenge the established consensus but to open up a discussion that has never so far taken place. Not only has no one apparently ever, so far as I have been able to discover, argued for the consensus view in more than a few sentences; it is also the case that no one has ever argued for the

---

4. I refer to evangelists as male, not because the possibility of a female author of a Gospel can be excluded, but because what we know about authorship in the ancient world makes it relatively improbable.

5. For various reconstructions of the Thomasine community, see B. Lincoln, "Thomas-Gospel and Thomas-Community: A New Approach to a Familiar Text," *Novum Testamentum* 19 (1977): 65-76; K. King, "Kingdom in the Gospel of Thomas," *Foundations and Facets Forum* 3, no. 1 (1987): 48-97; S. J. Patterson, *The Gospel of Thomas and Jesus* (Sonoma, Calif.: Polebridge, 1993), especially chapters 5-7.

alternative view, which I shall propose as more plausible. There has never been any debate.

To challenge a scholarly consensus is inevitably and understandably to encounter resistance from readers immersed in the consensus. Such readers are naturally disposed to think that a consensus which not only is so universally accepted but which also has proved so fruitful in generating exciting and interesting work on the Gospels must be right. Any argument against this kind of consensus has an uphill struggle merely to gain an unprejudiced hearing, if there were such a thing. Therefore I begin with a preliminary argument whose function is merely to sow an initial seed of possibility that there might perhaps be something to be said for the view I shall propose.

I put this argument in a form that presupposes the most widely accepted view of Synoptic relationships, but it could easily be restated to accommodate any theory of Synoptic relationship. (None of the argument of this chapter depends on any particular theory of Synoptic relationships.) Since the present argument has to be stated in one form or another, I assume Markan priority. On the assumption of Markan priority, how is it that Matthew and Luke both had Mark's Gospel available to them? No one imagines all three evangelists belonged to the same local Christian community. So the view that is generally taken for granted is that by the time Matthew and Luke wrote, Mark's Gospel had already circulated quite widely around the churches and was being read in the churches to which Matthew and Luke respectively belonged. This is a very reasonable view, since we know quite certainly that at a slightly later date Mark's Gospel was known in churches other than Mark's own, wherever that was. Matthew and Luke, in other words, knew Mark as a Gospel that had in fact circulated quite widely among the churches and was proving to be useful and valued in many Christian churches. Whatever Mark had meant his Gospel to be, his work, when Matthew and Luke knew it, had already in fact come to be used and valued, not as a work focused on highly particular circumstances in Mark's own community, but as a work generally useful to various different churches. Matthew's and Luke's model for what a Gospel was must have been Mark as it was actually circulated and used in the churches. They must have expected their Gospels to circulate at least as widely as Mark's had already done. They must have envisaged an audience at least as broad as Mark's Gospel had already achieved. Most likely Matthew and Luke each expected his own Gospel to replace Mark's. To suppose that Matthew and Luke, knowing that Mark's Gospel had in fact circulated to many churches, nevertheless each addressed his own Gospel to the much more restricted audience of his own community, seems *prima facie* very improbable. Such a view would need rather careful argument and certainly should not be treated as a self-evident axiom.

II

The way the current consensus on this issue has come about, without anyone ever having seriously argued the case for it, would make a significant topic for study in the history of New Testament scholarship. It could also provoke reflections, perhaps rather disturbing reflections, about the sociology and psychology of New Testament studies as a discipline. In this section of the present chapter, I can only indicate some broad features of the history of scholarship that provide background for engagement with the current consensus.

The view that each evangelist wrote for his own community is an old view in British scholarship, going back at least to the end of the nineteenth century, though it was not the only view in older British scholarship. The earliest example of it I know is in H. B. Swete's commentary on Mark (first edition, 1898), a major commentary in its time. Swete claims, in fact, that it was "the prevalent belief of the ancient Church" that "St. Mark wrote his Gospel in Rome and for the Roman Church."[6] The idea here rests on patristic evidence, which Swete, like most of his contemporaries, accepts with little discussion. That Mark was written not only in Rome but also for the Roman church seems in fact to be based only on the account of Clement of Alexandria (*ap.* Eusebius, *Hist. Eccl.* 6.14.6-7), which need not strictly require this

---

6. H. B. Swete, *The Gospel According to St. Mark*, 3d ed. (London: Macmillan, 1909), xxxix; cf. xl.

conclusion.[7] However, it is important to notice that for Swete Mark's intended readership is merely an aspect of the usual introductory questions about the Gospel; it has no significant consequences for exegesis. It does not occur to him that Mark adapted his thoroughly historical record of Jesus to address specific needs or issues in the Roman church. We are dealing with an idea that has at this date a very limited function in Gospels scholarship but which would come into its own when Mark was read as something other than a straightforwardly historical record.

At the same time as Swete, Alfred Plummer in his International Critical Commentary on Luke (first edition, 1898) takes a different view — at least of Luke's audience. Dismissing the idea that Luke wrote only for Theophilus, he claims: "It is evident that he writes for the instruction and encouragement of all Gentile converts."[8] That Luke might have written for a specific church does not occur to him. But the view that each Gospel had a specific community in view must have been given considerable impetus in British scholarship by B. H. Streeter's book *The Four Gospels: A Study of Origins* (1924), which was a landmark in English-speaking Gospels scholarship, establishing the dominance of the four-document hypothesis for a long time to come. Integral to Streeter's argument was the view that each of the four Gospels must have originated in a major center of Christianity (in fact, respectively Antioch, Rome, Caesarea, and Ephesus). Only this, in his view, accounts for the prestige of all four and their eventual canonization. They acquired this prestige not simply by having originated from these important churches but from having been originally used in these churches: "each of the Gospels must have attained local recognition as

---

7. According to Clement, Mark wrote his Gospel, a record of Peter's preaching, at the request of those who heard Peter's preaching in Rome and distributed copies of it to those who had asked him. This is quite consistent with the view that Mark would have expected further copies to be passed on to other churches, in the normal way in which literature circulated in the early Christian movement. It is very doubtful whether Clement had any source for his account other than Papias's account of the origin of Mark's Gospel, but nevertheless the way in which he envisaged a Gospel beginning to circulate is of interest.

8. A. Plummer, *A Critical and Exegetical Commentary on the Gospel According to S. Luke,* 4th ed. (Edinburgh: T. & T. Clark, 1901), xxxiv.

a religious classic, if not yet an inspired scripture, before the four were combined into a collection recognized by the whole Church."[9] Mark in particular survived the competition from Matthew and Luke because of the prestige it had acquired locally as the Roman church's Gospel. In my view there are serious flaws in this argument,[10] which need not detain us because the argument is rarely found today, but we should note that, if it is true that the idea of the Gospels as local Gospels (Streeter's term) became popular as a result of Streeter's work, then it did so on the basis of a single argument that has long since been forgotten by most who exploit the idea for purposes unknown to Streeter. In any case, Streeter would seem to be one of the first scholars to stress the local origins of all four Gospels in such a way as to fuse the two questions of the local context *in which* a Gospel was written and the audience *for which* it was written.[11] As he puts it, "The Gospels were written in and for different churches"[12] — a statement that encapsulates the axiom of the current consensus which I wish to question.

A most interesting representative (still within British scholarship) of the process by which the consensus has come about is G. D. Kilpatrick's *The Origins of the Gospel According to St. Matthew* (1946). Some readers may be surprised to find at this date so strong an emphasis on the specific *Sitz im Leben* in which the Gospel was written and its formative influence on the making of the Gospel. Kilpatrick is already discussing the major issues that those who write about the kind of

9. B. H. Streeter, *The Four Gospels: A Study of Origins* (London: Macmillan, 1924), 12.

10. Even if the four Gospels originally had the prestige of being the local Gospels of particular major churches, there is no evidence at all that this factor was operative in the second century, when the survival of all four to form the four-Gospel canon was at stake. The association of Mark's Gospel with Peter is far more likely to have been a major factor in the survival of Mark alongside Matthew and Luke.

11. B. W. Bacon, *Is Mark a Roman Gospel?* Harvard Theological Studies 7 (Cambridge, Mass.: Harvard University Press, 1919) also fuses these questions, in relation to Mark. Though his argument is almost entirely concerned with the location in which Mark was written, occasionally he reveals that for him this is the same question as that about the implied readership of Mark (66, 85).

12. Streeter, *The Four Gospels,* 12.

context in which Matthew originated still discuss. A chapter on "The Gospel and Judaism" covers the now very familiar ground of relating Matthew to late-first-century developments in Judaism and in Jewish-Christian relations. In a chapter on "The Community of the Gospel" he speaks of "the Matthean church" and uses the clues provided by the Gospel to argue that the church in which Matthew wrote was well-to-do, had a ministry of prophets and teachers, was suffering persecution, was imperiled by false teaching, and so on. Crucially, he takes it for granted — without argument — that the church in which Matthew wrote was the church for which Matthew wrote.[13] His reconstruction of the Matthean community and its context in fact depends on this assumption, since it presupposes that everything Matthew implies about his readers is specifically true of his own church.

Kilpatrick's book is the direct ancestor of the way recent major commentaries on the Gospels — for example, Davies and Allison on Matthew,[14] Fitzmyer on Luke[15] — discuss the introductory questions about the Gospels, simply assuming that the question about the context in which a Gospel was written and the question about the audience for which a Gospel was written are the same question. Such discussions therefore regularly and systematically confuse the evidence for these two different questions. Precisely in the context where one might expect to find *arguments* for the view that has become the consensus — in discussions of the conventional set of introductory questions about Gospels — one finds only the assumption of precisely what needs to be proved and a consequent confusion of issues.

Latent in Kilpatrick's method of reconstructing the Matthean community's character and situation from the Gospel was the potential for

13. G. D. Kilpatrick, *The Origins of the Gospel According to St. Matthew* (Oxford: Clarendon, 1946), 130.

14. W. D. Davies and D. C. Allison, *A Critical and Exegetical Commentary on the Gospel According to Saint Matthew,* vol. 1, International Critical Commentary (Edinburgh: T. & T. Clark, 1988), 138-47.

15. J. A. Fitzmyer, *The Gospel According to Luke I–IX,* Anchor Bible 28 (New York: Doubleday, 1981), 57-59. Other recent examples are D. A. Hagner, *Matthew 1–13,* Word Biblical Commentary 33A (Dallas: Word, 1993), lxv-lxxi; U. Luz, *Matthew 1–7,* trans. W. C. Linss (Edinburgh: T. & T. Clark, 1989), 82-90.

reading the Gospel as addressing the particular needs and concerns of the community. Though this potential is mostly undeveloped in Kilpatrick's book, the book does show how well the ground was already prepared, in English-speaking scholarship, for the approach that developed within redaction-critical studies, especially of Mark, in the 1960s and 70s. Not all redaction critics were especially concerned with the evangelist's community; some used redaction criticism primarily as a means of highlighting the particular theology of each evangelist, without relating this theology to a specific community and its situation. But in the late 1960s and 70s a series of books developed an approach that aimed to reconstruct the distinctive features of the Markan community and to explain the Gospel as addressing specific issues within the community. Best known of the pioneering books along these lines is Theodore Weeden's *Mark: Traditions in Conflict* (1968), which also marks the rise of American Gospels scholarship to leadership in this field, but the approach is also found, for example, in the German work of K. G. Reploh, *Markus, Lehrer der Gemeinde* (1969). It is characteristic of these works that they take it entirely for granted that a Gospel was written for a particular church. They do not even treat this as a working hypothesis that their work may show to be plausible. They treat it as self-evident fact, on which their work can build. This is the point, crucial in the history of Gospels scholarship, at which an unargued assumption, previously confined to discussions of introductory questions, became the basis for interpretative strategies that found the specific circumstances and needs of a particular community addressed in a Gospel.[16]

---

16. An illustration of the axiomatic status so widely attributed to this assumption can be found in J. R. Donahue, "The Quest for the Community of Mark's Gospel," in *The Four Gospels 1992*, ed. F. Van Segbroeck, C. M. Tuckett, G. Van Belle, and J. Verheyden, Festschrift for F. Neirynck; Bibliotheca Ephemeridum Theologicarum Lovaniensium 100 (Leuven: Leuven University Press/Peeters, 1992), 2:817-38. He surveys attempts to locate the origin of Mark's Gospel and to identify the "Markan community" as the Gospel's implied readership (treating, as usual, the two issues as the same), refers to the "interesting questions about the whole enterprise of the quest for the communities behind the gospels" raised by M. A. Tolbert (835), who argues that Mark was not written for a specific local community but for a wide readership, and continues: "Even if this total

The redaction critics often complained that form criticism, despite its professed emphasis on the Christian community as the *Sitz im Leben* of the Gospel traditions, always considered the community in highly general terms. The only distinctions between communities that mattered to form criticism were the much-used categories of Palestinian Jewish Christianity, Hellenistic Jewish Christianity, and Gentile Christianity. Moreover, when the great form critics, Dibelius and Bultmann, did discuss the written Gospels as the end products of the oral tradition, the community dimension seemed to disappear entirely. The redaction critics were intent on much more specificity. For example, Howard Kee in his *Community of the New Age* writes:

> What was the *Sitz im Leben* from which and for which Mark's gospel was written? To answer that question responsibly it is not sufficient to attach a general label to Mark — such as Hellenistic-Jewish-Christian, or Palestinian-Jewish-Christian. By analysis of the text itself, but with the aid of paradigms for the study of eschatological communities as well as historical analogies with apocalyptic communities close in space and time to primitive Christianity in the first century, it should be possible to trace the contours of the Markan community.[17]

Study of Mark along these lines led the way; that of Matthew and Luke for the most part followed rather belatedly. But it is important to notice that developments in Johannine scholarship kept close pace with Markan scholarship. Since form criticism and redaction criticism as applied to the Synoptics were not usually thought appropriate to the

---

skepticism may be unwarranted . . ." (836). While this sounds as though some skepticism might be warranted, Donahue proceeds merely to throw doubt on the use of some kinds of evidence for reconstructing Mark's community (836-37). That Mark's implied readership was his own community, which improved methods will be able to reconstruct, he never for a moment doubts. That the "interesting questions" raised by Tolbert require this unargued assumption to be examined seems to be a thought Donahue is so incapable of taking seriously that he fails to recognize it even while stating it.

17. H. C. Kee, *Community of the New Age* (Philadelphia: Westminster, 1977), 77.

special case of the Fourth Gospel, Johannine scholarship pursued its own peculiar path, increasingly a highly introverted field of scholarship. Books on the Fourth Gospel rarely refer to Synoptic scholarship, or books on the Synoptic Gospels to Johannine scholarship. But the appearance of the first edition of J. L. Martyn's vastly influential *History and Theology in the Fourth Gospel* in 1968 can hardly be unrelated to the work of Weeden and others on Mark at precisely that time (and also in America), though Martyn makes no reference to them. Martyn's book does for John what Weeden and others did for Mark. John Ashton calls it, "for all its brevity . . . probably the most important single work on the Gospel since Bultmann's commentary,"[18] since it was the source of that obsession with the Johannine community that has dominated most subsequent Johannine scholarship.[19] That the Johannine community is the implied audience of the Fourth Gospel and that this community can therefore be reconstructed from the Gospel are assumptions that began to affect Johannine scholarship largely from the publication of Martyn's book onwards. No more than the Synoptic scholars does Martyn offer any argument for the assumption that John addresses his own community.

The sustained attempt since the late 1960s to take seriously the claim that each Gospel addresses the specific situation of a particular Christian community has had two main characteristics. One is the development of more or less allegorical readings of the Gospels in the service of reconstructing not only the character but the history of the

18. J. Ashton, *Understanding the Fourth Gospel* (Oxford: Clarendon, 1991), 107. Cf. D. Moody Smith, "The Contribution of J. Louis Martyn to the Understanding of the Gospel of John," in *The Conversation Continues: Studies in Paul and John,* ed. R. T. Fortna and B. R. Gaventa, J. L. Martyn Festschrift (Nashville: Abingdon, 1990), 293 n. 30: "Martyn's thesis has become a paradigm, to borrow from Thomas Kuhn. It is a part of what students imbibe from standard works, such as commentaries and textbooks, as knowledge generally received and held to be valid."

19. The "Johannine community" as the implied readership of the Fourth Gospel first enters — unobtrusively but momentously — Ashton's survey of the history of Johannine scholarship at the point where he discusses Martyn's work (Ashton, *Understanding,* 108).

community behind the Gospel. Characters and events in the Gospel story are taken to represent groups within the community and experiences of the community. The disciples in Mark stand for proponents of a *theios-aner* Christology that Mark is fighting within his community, the relatives of Jesus represent the Jerusalem Jewish Christian leaders, Nicodemus stands for Christians whose inadequate Christology prevents them from making a complete break with the synagogue, and so on. The successful mission of Jesus and the disciples to Samaritans in John 4 is supposed to reflect a stage in the history of the Johannine community when it engaged in successful mission to Samaritans. Weeden pioneered this way of reading Mark, and Martyn this way of reading John. There have been many subsequent reconstructions of the history of the Markan and Johannine communities. The many different reconstructions throw some doubt on the method, which to a skeptic looks like a kind of historical fantasy.[20] It is difficult to avoid supposing that those who no longer think it possible to use the Gospels to reconstruct the historical Jesus compensate for this loss by using them to reconstruct the communities that produced the Gospels. All the historical specificity for which historical critics long is transferred from the historical Jesus to the evangelist's community. The principle that the Gospels inform us not about Jesus but about the church is taken so literally that the narrative, ostensibly about Jesus, has to be understood as an allegory in which the community actually tells its own story.

The second characteristic of work in this tradition is the increasingly sophisticated use of social-scientific methods for reconstructing the community behind each Gospel. For Mark this began with Kee's *The Community of the New Age* and for John probably with Wayne Meeks's enormously influential 1972 article on Johannine sectarianism.[21] Philip Esler pioneered such work on Luke

---

20. For a survey of the very varied attempts to reconstruct the Johannine community and its history, drawing an appropriately skeptical conclusion, see T. L. Brodie, *The Quest for the Origin of John's Gospel* (New York: Oxford University Press, 1993), 15-21.

21. W. A. Meeks, "The Man from Heaven in Johannine Sectarianism," *Journal of Biblical Literature* 91 (1972): 44-72; reprinted in *The Interpretation of John,* ed. J. Ashton (London: SPCK, 1968), 141-73.

(1987),[22] while Matthew has recently become a major focus, with Andrew Overman's *Matthew's Gospel and Formative Judaism* (1990),[23] and several essays in the multi-authored volume *Social History of the Matthean Community* (1991).[24] Once again it has to be said that virtually all this work takes the usual unargued assumption for granted. Unexceptionable arguments for the use of social-scientific methods to study the relation between a literary work and its social context are simply applied to the unexamined premise that this relation means, in the case of a Gospel, its dual relationship to a single context in which it was written and for which it was written. It is this assumption, built into the use of the social-scientific methods from the start, that produces reconstructions of communities each

22. P. F. Esler, *Community and Gospel in Luke-Acts,* Society for New Testament Studies Monograph Series 57 (Cambridge: Cambridge University Press, 1987). Esler is a rare case of a writer who sees some need to argue for the view that a Gospel, in this case Luke, was addressed to a specific Christian community or at least group of communities. But his argument (24-25) is premised on the validity of the common view that each of the other three canonical Gospels was addressed to its own community and is merely concerned to rebut the views of those who see Luke-Acts as an exception to this otherwise general rule. Thereby he gives the impression that little argument is actually needed. The evidence he offers is the use of the image of the flock for Jesus' disciples in the Gospel (Luke 12:32) and for the church at Ephesus in Acts (20:17-35); the way this image is used evokes the circumstances of "a small Christian community beset by difficulties from within and without" (25). The implication is that, since the whole church was not such a community, Luke-Acts does not address the whole church, but one such community. However, if Luke wrote for a general Christian audience, this means he wrote for any and every specific community to which he could expect his work to circulate. At the end of the first century, any such community would be a small community beset by difficulties from within and without. Luke could easily expect any Christian community to find such imagery appropriate to itself. What is actually striking about Paul's address to the Ephesian elders is how generalized the language is. The reference to false teaching could refer to any kind of false teaching.

23. J. A. Overman, *Matthew's Gospel and Formative Judaism: The Social World of the Matthean Community* (Minneapolis: Fortress, 1990).

24. D. L. Balch, ed., *Social History of the Matthean Community: Cross-Disciplinary Approaches* (Minneapolis: Fortress, 1991).

apparently unrelated to the rest of the Christian movement, each apparently treating itself self-sufficiently as *the* Christian social world. In this respect recent social-scientific studies of the Gospels are directly continuous with redaction criticism. Though asking different questions about the relationship between a Gospel and its original audience, they have taken over without question the same unargued assumption about the definition of the implied audience.

III

At this point I need to address this question: Even if I am right that the assumption that each Gospel was written for the evangelist's own community has come to be widely accepted largely without having been argued, might one not suppose that this assumption has been *confirmed by the results* that Gospels scholarship has built upon it? A large body of literature has been devoted to reconstructing each Gospel's own community and illuminating each Gospel by reading it as addressed to that reconstructed community, with its particular theological views and debates (the main concern of earlier redaction criticism), its particular social composition and social context (the concern of more recent study with social-scientific ingredients), even its own history (elaborately reconstructed in Johannine scholarship especially). A properly argued case for the view I am disputing would certainly have to draw on this work, but the work itself does not constitute such a case. With only occasional exceptions in detail, this body of scholarship does not proceed by arguing that certain features of a Gospel text are explicable only if understood as addressed to a specific Christian audience rather than to a general Christian audience. Its results are the results of applying to the text a particular reading strategy, not of showing that this reading strategy does better justice to the text than another reading strategy.

The point can be illustrated by observing what goes on in typical instances of this reading strategy. One form of it consists in applying to a specific Christian community textual implications that would readily apply to a very large number of Christian communities. Take, for example, J. Louis Martyn's classic argument that chapter 9 of the Fourth Gospel should be read, on one level, as a narrative of the Johannine community's expulsion from its local synagogue.[25] Does this constitute evidence that the Gospel addresses the specific situation of the evangelist's own community? Not at all, not even if one wholly accepts Martyn's account of when and how the expulsion of Jewish Christians from synagogues occurred. Precisely Martyn's own argument, that the introduction of the *Birkat ha-Minim* into synagogue liturgy late in the first century had the effect of forcing Jewish Christians out of synagogues,[26] is an argument for a general process that, if he is correct, must have been going on in many diaspora cities where Jewish Christians had previously attended synagogue. If John 9 addresses that situation, it addresses, not a circumstance peculiar to the Johannine community, but a circumstance that would have been common in the churches of the late first century. Only because Martyn starts with the presupposition that the Fourth Gospel was written for the Johannine community, and because he has no intention of trying to prove this

25. J. L. Martyn, *History and Theology in the Fourth Gospel,* rev. ed. (Nashville: Abingdon, 1979), part I.

26. I accept Martyn's case here for the sake of argument, but it needs radical reassessment in the light of more recent discussion of the *Birkat ha-Minim:* see P. Schäfer, "Die sogenannte Synod von Jabne: Zur Trennung von Juden und Christen im ersten/zweiten Jh. n. Chr.," *Judaica* 31 (1975): 54-64; R. Kimelman, "*Birkat Ha-Minim* and the Lack of Evidence for an Anti-Christian Jewish Prayer in Late Antiquity," in *Jewish and Christian Self-Definition,* ed. E. P. Sanders and A. I. Baumgarten, vol. 2: *Aspects of Judaism in the Graeco-Roman Period* (London: SCM, 1981), 226-44; W. Horbury, "The Benediction of the Minim and the Early Jewish-Christian Controversy," *Journal of Theological Studies* 33 (1982): 19-61; S. T. Katz, "Issues in the Separation of Judaism and Christianity After 70 C.E.: A Reconsideration," *Journal of Biblical Literature* 103 (1984): 43-76; R. A. Pritz, *Nazarene Jewish Christianity,* Studia Post-Biblica 37 (Jerusalem: Magnes; Leiden: Brill, 1988), 102-7; P. S. Alexander, "'The Parting of the Ways' from the Perspective of Rabbinic Judaism," in *Jews and Christians: The Parting of the Ways A.D. 70 to 135,* ed. J. D. G. Dunn, Wissenschaftliche Untersuchungen zum Neuen Testament 66 (Tübingen: Mohr [Siebeck], 1993), 1-25; R. Bauckham, "The *Apocalypse of Peter:* A Jewish Christian Apocalypse from the Time of Bar Kokhba," *Apocrypha* 5 (1994): 87-90.

point, can his argument function for him to characterize only the Johannine community's relationship to the synagogue.

The same consideration applies to many such arguments. Probably most Christian communities in the period when the canonical Gospels were being written were located in cities, contained both Jewish and Gentile members, including Gentiles who had been attached to the synagogue, and included some people, even if not many, from both ends of the socio-economic spectrum.

If it is objected that such features, while not confined to one specific community, would still not have been true of every Christian community, then it is time to introduce the second aspect of the reading strategy that I observe in such arguments. This consists in supposing that all textual indications of the character and circumstances of the audience must all apply to the whole of the implied audience. Then one need only compile all such indications in order to produce an identikit description of the evangelist's community. However, supposing the Gospels were written for general circulation and therefore envisage the range of audiences their authors might expect them to acquire in the churches of the late first century, then there is no reason at all why every aspect of a Gospel should be equally relevant to all readers or hearers. An evangelist might well address features of Christian life and social circumstances he knew to be fairly widespread in his time, without supposing his Gospel would therefore have no appeal or use in churches lacking some of these features. If so, he was right: the four canonical Gospels survived precisely because within a fairly short space of time they did prove relevant enough to most churches to come to be used very widely.

The argument that not everything in a Gospel need be there for all readers applies also to other types of material. When John finds it necessary to explain what the words *Rabbi* and *Messiah* mean (explanations which it is hard to believe even diaspora Jews would require), this need only imply that some of his readers would need such explanations, not that all or even a majority would need them. When Mark tells us that Simon of Cyrene was the father of Alexander and Rufus (15:21), he need only be supposing that these persons would have been known in a significant number of churches, which is entirely possible,[27] not that every church to which his Gospel might circulate would have heard of them. Knowing these names already would give added significance to Mark's narrative for those who did know them, but not knowing them would be no impediment to other readers.

A third aspect of the reading strategy adopted by the current consensus is that the strong commitment of interpreters of the Gospels to the project of reconstructing each Gospel's community from the text leads them to understand as indications of the nature of a Gospel's implied audience features of the text that need not be so understood at all. For example, it is not obvious what the study of the social status of characters in Mark's Gospel can tell us about the social status of Mark's

27. E. Best, "Mark's Readers: A Profile," in *The Four Gospels 1992*, ed. Van Segbroeck, Tuckett, Van Belle and Verheyden, 2:857, rejects the identification of this Rufus with the Rufus of Romans 16:13, which has often been used to locate Mark's Gospel in Rome, on the grounds that "Rufus was not an uncommon name" (he might have added that Jews used it as the Latin equivalent of Reuben), and continues: "There is no reason to suppose that Mark's Rufus and Alexander were widely known; if they were not this implies that Mark was writing to a very limited group of people, probably all living in the same place. However widely the Gospel may be known today the original audience was very limited and probably confined to one small area." But this is highly tendentious argument. If there is no reason to suppose that Mark's Rufus and Alexander were widely known, neither is there any reason to suppose that they were not widely known. Where lies the burden of proof? That only Mark mentions them is no reason to suppose they were not widely known, since our evidence about individual Christians in the period is extremely limited. For example, it is clear from Romans 16:7 that the apostles Andronicus and Junia were widely traveled and widely known, but they are nowhere else mentioned in the surviving literature. That Matthew (27:32) and Luke (23:26) omit reference to the sons of Simon of Cyrene might be due simply to their habitual practice of abbreviating Mark. It might indicate that they were less confident than Mark that readers of their Gospels would know of Alexander and Rufus, which would be consistent with the hypothesis that Alexander and Rufus were well known in some, but not all, of the churches to which Mark could expect his Gospel to circulate. Finally, the difference between the Synoptic evangelists here might indicate that Alexander and Rufus were alive when Mark wrote, dead when Matthew and Luke wrote. In the light of these various possibilities, Mark 15:21 is an extremely insecure basis for supposing that Mark's implied audience is a limited circle of Christians.

implied audience.[28] To suppose that one must correspond closely to the other presupposes far too crude a notion of the way readers find stories relevant to themselves. It also begs questions about the scope Mark allowed himself to manipulate his traditions. Should we really suppose that, had Mark been writing for a church composed largely of very wealthy people, he would have omitted all the stories of destitute beggars that occurred in the traditions about Jesus he knew and created numerous stories about wealthy people welcoming and following Jesus? In this, as in other aspects of our topic, a highly debatable method is employed without debate because the overall interpretative aim seems to require it. A Gospel text has to be treated as transparently revelatory of the community for which it was written because the interpretative aim of reconstructing this community would be defeated by any other kind of text.

In conclusion, therefore, the relative success of a reading strategy based on the assumption that a Gospel addresses a specific community is no proof at all that a reading strategy based on the contrary assumption would not be equally or even more successful.

IV

The rest of my argument in this chapter aims to establish the antecedent probability that someone writing a Gospel in the late first century would have envisaged the kind of general Christian audience which the Gospels in fact very soon achieved through circulation around the churches.

The first stage of the argument consists in contrasting Gospels and Pauline epistles.[29] This stage is important because what the consensus I

28. An example of this approach is R. Rohrbaugh, "The Social Location of the Markan Audience," *Interpretation* 47 (1993): 380-95.

29. Cf. G. N. Stanton, *A Gospel for a New People: Studies in Matthew* (Edinburgh: T. & T. Clark, 1992), 45 ("Matthew is writing a gospel, not a letter"), 50-51. Here Stanton queries the hypothesis of a Matthean community as the Gospel's implied audience and thinks it "more likely that Matthew, like Luke, envisaged that his gospel would circulate widely" (51). Elsewhere in the same collection of essays he still speaks freely of "the Matthean community." In the introduction (adopting a compromise?) he speaks of "the communities to whom

am attacking has in effect done is to attempt to treat Gospels hermeneutically as though they were Pauline epistles. In other words, scholars have sought to see the audience and therefore also the message of the Gospels in just as local and particularized terms as those of the major Pauline letters, which certainly are addressed to specific Christian communities and envisage the specific needs and problems of those communities. The fact that our reading of 1 Corinthians, for example, is therefore illuminated by our attempts to reconstruct the specifically Corinthian situation Paul addressed has led Gospels scholars to seek the same kind of illumination of Gospel texts by reconstructing the specific church context in which they originated. However, Gospels are not letters, and to appreciate the crucial difference we need to put together two considerations.

The first is the question of genre. It is a special quality of the letter genre that it enables a writer to address specified addressees in all the particularity of their circumstances.[30] Even if other people read 1 Corinthians (as they fairly soon did), the genre encourages them to read

---

[Matthew] wrote" as "a cluster of Christian churches which are defining themselves over against local synagogues" (2), "minority groups living in the shadow of thriving local Jewish communities" (3). Even if the latter description of the implied audience is justifiable, it is not clear to me why it requires Stanton still to think of the implied readership as a defined rather than an open category. The description could apply to Christian communities in many cities of the Roman Empire, and Matthew could easily have supposed that many churches of which he knew little or nothing, to which his Gospel might well find its way, would be in such a situation. Stanton's argument is restated in "Revisiting Matthew's Communities," *Society of Biblical Literature Seminar Papers* (Atlanta: Scholars, 1994), 9-23, with more emphasis on the issue of genre (11: "Matthew's *gospel* should not be read as if it were a Pauline *letter*," cf. 22), more strictures against the attempt to derive "*detailed* information about the social setting of the first recipients" (11), rejection of the view that Matthew would have written so carefully crafted a *bios* for a single house church which could have composed no more than fifty people (11-12), and reassertion of the view that the implied audience must be "a loosely linked set of communities over a wide geographical area" (12).

30. Of course, the letter genre *can* be used to address a very wide audience in very general terms. It is a mistake to regard a circular letter such as 1 Peter as less genuinely a letter than Philemon. But the letter genre does enable particularity of address to specific readers to an extent that no other ancient literary genre does.

it *as* a letter addressed to the Corinthians. To some extent every attentive reader of 1 Corinthians has always felt obliged to imagine what the specifically Corinthian situation Paul addressed was. This is not the case with the Gospels. From the second century to the mid-twentieth century no one ever supposed that the specific situation of the Matthean community was relevant to reading the Gospel of Matthew.

Of course, the genre of the Gospels is debated, but recent discussion[31] has very much strengthened the case — in fact has all but conclusively established the case — that contemporaries would have recognized them as a special category of the Greco-Roman *bios* (which we can translate "biography" provided we understand the term in the sense of ancient, not modern biography). Although the implied readership of the ancient biography is a topic which might repay investigation, it seems unlikely that anyone would expect a *bios* to address the very specific circumstances of a small community of people. A *bios* certainly aimed at relevance to its readers. Its subject could be depicted as a moral or religious inspiration to its readers. It could be highly propagandist literature, recommending a political, philosophical, or religious point of view. But its relevance would be pitched in relatively broad terms for any competent reader.

However, the full force of the difference of genre will come home to us only if we add a second consideration. We need to ask, about both an apostolic letter and a Gospel, the question: Why should anyone *write* it? — by which I mean: Why should anyone put this down *in writing?* In the case of 1 Corinthians, for example, the answer is clear: Paul could not or preferred not to visit Corinth. Paul seems only to have written anything when distance required him to communicate in writing what he would otherwise have spoken orally to one of his churches. It was distance that required writing, whereas orality sufficed for presence. So the more Gospels scholarship envisages the Gospels in terms approximating to a Pauline letter, addressing the specific situation of one community, the more odd it seems that the evangelist is supposed

31. See especially R. A. Burridge, *What Are the Gospels? A Comparison with Graeco-Roman Biography,* Society of New Testament Studies Monograph Series 70 (Cambridge: Cambridge University Press, 1992).

to be writing for *the community in which he lives.* An evangelist writing his Gospel is like Paul writing 1 Corinthians while permanently resident in Corinth. Paul did not do this, so why should Matthew or the other evangelists have done so? Anyone who wrote a Gospel must have had the opportunity of teaching his community orally. Indeed, most Gospels scholars assume that he frequently did so. He could retell and interpret the community's Gospel traditions so as to address his community's situation by means of them in this oral context. Why should he go to the considerable trouble of writing a Gospel for a community to which he was regularly preaching? Indeed, why should he go to such trouble to *freeze* in writing his response to a specific local situation which was liable to change and to which he could respond much more flexibly and therefore appropriately in oral preaching?

The obvious function of writing was its capacity to communicate widely with readers unable to be present at its author's oral teaching.[32] Oral teaching could be passed on, but much less effectively than a book. Books, like letters, were designed to cross distances orality could not so effectively cross. But whereas letters usually (though not invariably) stopped at their first recipients, anyone in the first century who wrote a book such as a *bios* expected it to circulate to readers unknown to its author. That small circle to which the author might initially read it or those friends to whom he might initially give copies were merely the first step to wider circulation. Once there was a copy outside the author's possession, he would expect others to make copies for their own use and his book to have embarked on a journey into the world beyond his control. This was true even of the religious literature of a minority culture such as the Jews, probably the most obvious model for the

---

32. The evidence suggests that in early Christianity this function of writing (communication across space) was more important than the ability of writing to give permanence (communication over time). Few early Christian teachers seem to have felt the need to give their teaching permanence by writing it. Even where we suspect this must have been an important factor, as in the case of the book of Revelation, communication across space remains at least the ostensible occasion (Revelation was written from Patmos as a circular letter to the seven churches of Asia). It seems that the oral Gospel tradition continued vigorously and enjoyed respect long after the production of written Gospels.

Christian author who wrote the first Gospel. Jewish religious literature in Greek, wherever it might have been written, circulated among the communities of the western diaspora, presumably by the normal channels of personal contacts and traveling, that account for the circulation of most literature in the period.[33] Why should Mark, if Mark was the first evangelist, have written merely for the few hundred people, at most, who composed the Christian community in his own city,[34] when the very act of writing a book would naturally suggest the possibility of communicating with Greek-speaking Christians everywhere?

V

For the major stage of my argument for the likelihood that Gospels would have been written for general circulation we must turn to a crucial feature of the general character of the early Christian movement. The early Christian movement was not a scattering of isolated, self-sufficient communities with little or no communication between them, but quite the opposite: a network of communities with constant, close communication among themselves. In other words, the social character of early Christianity was such that the idea of writing a Gospel purely for one's own community is unlikely to have occurred to anyone.

The consensus I am challenging seems to depend on a view of an

33. For communication between the diaspora communities, see now J. M. G. Barclay, *Jews in the Mediterranean Diaspora from Alexander to Trajan (323 BCE–117 CE)* (Edinburgh: T. & T. Clark, 1996), 418-24.

34. Stanton, "Revisiting," 12, calculates (from the size of rooms in large houses) that a single house church could have comprised no more than fifty people; similarly, J. Murphy-O'Connor, *St Paul's Corinth* (Collegeville, Minn.: Liturgical, 1983), 166-67. But B. Blue, "Acts and the House Church," in *The Book of Acts in Its Graeco-Roman Setting* ed. D. W. J. Gill and C. Gempf (Grand Rapids: Eerdmans; Carlisle: Paternoster, 1994), 142-43 (cf. 175), argues for rather larger numbers (75 in a large reception hall, with the possibility of accommodating more in adjoining rooms). Since the whole church in Corinth could (presumably only occasionally) meet in the house of Gaius (Rom. 16:23), it is unlikely to have numbered more than about one hundred at that time. But in some cities there could have been several house churches, which would not have been able to meet all together in a single house.

early Christian community as a self-contained, self-sufficient, intro-verted group, having little contact with other Christian communities and little sense of participation in a worldwide Christian movement. Identity, issues, and concerns, it seems to be presupposed, are thoroughly local. Andrew Overman's recent book on Matthew, for example, contains no reference at all to a Christian world beyond Matthew's own community (which consists of a small group of churches). That Matthew even knew about other Christian communi-ties, still less that his community had any kinds of relationships with them, is never suggested, despite the notably universal thrust of the Gospel itself, with its strong indications of a worldwide Christian mission.[35] Overman discusses the Matthean community's theological and social self-understanding as though the Matthean community were the only Christian community in existence. Even the role of Peter is discussed as though it related solely to the Matthean community,[36] despite the fact that the key Petrine passage (Matt. 16:17-19) is notable for using the word ἐκκλησία in the singular to refer to the universal church, rather than with its more common reference to a local Christian community. Such a picture of isolated and inward-looking parochialism is both generated by and then serves to reinforce the notion that a Gospel has only a particular community in view. But it is in serious conflict with all the real evidence we have about the early Christian movement. Therefore, in this section of the chapter, I shall indicate, by sampling only, the large amount of relevant evidence we have in the sources — information that deserves precedence over tenuous infer-

35. It is difficult to be sure what the brief discussion of Matthew 28:18-20 in Overman, *Matthew's Gospel,* 121-22, is meant precisely to imply. Apparently, the Matthean community as a whole understands itself to be engaged in mission to the Gentile world, but whether missionaries travel from the Matthean com-munity to evangelize Gentiles in other places is left unclear. But, in any case, it is taken entirely for granted that this passage describes the mission of the Matthean community alone, not a mission in which the early Christian movement throughout the world is engaged. Matthew's implied readers are supposed to think only of themselves and the world, not of other Christian communities, nor of themselves as part of a worldwide Christian movement.

36. Overman, *Matthew's Gospel,* 136-40.

31

ences drawn from the Gospel texts on the basis of an already assumed model.

The first thing this information tells us is that mobility and communication in the first-century Roman world were exceptionally high.[37] Unprecedentedly good roads and unprecedentedly safe travel by both land and sea made the Mediterranean world of this time more closely interconnected than any large area of the ancient world had ever been. People traveled on business as merchants, traders, and bankers, on pilgrimage to religious festivals, in search of health and healing at the healing shrines and spas, to consult the oracles which flourished in this period, to attend the pan-Hellenic games and the various lesser versions of these all over the empire, as soldiers in the legions, as government personnel of many kinds, and even on vacation and as sightseers. In the forum of Rome, many cities maintained their own offices to assist their citizens who were doing business there or visiting the metropolis.[38] It was certainly not only the wealthy who traveled. Quite ordinary people traveled to healing shrines, religious festivals, and games. Slaves and servants frequently accompanied their masters on journeys. Runaway slaves, freed slaves returning home, people in search of work, soldiers and sailors and brigands all traveled. Travel was usually by foot and so was cheap. Therefore people quite typical of the members of the early Christian churches regularly traveled. Those who did not, if they lived in the cities, would constantly be meeting people passing through or arriving from elsewhere.

So the context in which the early Christian movement developed was not conducive to parochialism; quite the opposite. Frequent contact between the churches scattered across the empire was natural in such a society, but in addition to Christian participation in the ordinary mobility of this society,[39] much communication was deliberately fostered between the churches, as we shall see shortly.

37. For this paragraph, see especially L. Casson, *Travel in the Ancient World* (London: Allen & Unwin, 1974).

38. Casson, *Travel,* 129.

39. For example, Phoebe (Rom. 16:1-2) was presumably traveling to Rome from her home in Cenchrea on business of her own and therefore undertook to convey Paul's letter to the Roman Christians; Onesimus, a runaway slave from Colossae, met Paul in Rome or Ephesus (Philemon).

For, second, the evidence of early Christian literature (not least the Gospels) is that the early Christian movement had a strong sense of itself as a worldwide movement. For Jewish Christians who made up most of the early Christian leadership, this must have come naturally, since the communities of the Jewish diaspora were used to understanding themselves in terms of their common membership of a people scattered across the world. But Gentile converts were inculturated as Christians into a new social identity that was certainly not purely local. Paul's letters, for example, are constantly relating the churches he addresses to other churches and to the Christian movement as a whole (e.g. 1 Cor. 1:2), even to the churches of Judea (1 Thess. 2:14; 1 Cor. 16:3) and other non-Pauline churches (cf. 1 Cor. 9:5). The language of fictive kinship encouraged converts to replace their natural ties of family loyalty with new Christian ties that encompassed brothers and sisters throughout the world. Such ties could be important. A small minority group experiencing alienation and opposition in its immediate social context could compensate for its precarious minority position locally by a sense of solidarity with fellow-believers elsewhere and a sense of being part of a worldwide movement destined to become the worldwide kingdom of God. 1 Peter, for example, encourages its readers by reminding them that "your brothers and sisters in all the world are undergoing the same kinds of suffering" (5:9), while the book of Revelation enables potential martyrs to see themselves as belonging to an innumerable company drawn from every nation on earth (7:9-14). One wonders why it is that social-scientific study of the New Testament has not given an account of the functions that belonging to a worldwide movement performed for early Christians, instead of constructing such artificially isolated communities as Overman's Matthean community.

Third, we should note that most of the Christian leaders of whom we know in the New Testament period *moved around*.[40] Of course, Paul and those missionary colleagues who traveled with him or in close connection with his own travels (Timothy, Titus, Tychicus, and others) were constantly on the move, normally staying only weeks or months

---

40. On mobility in early Christianity and, in relation to it, the importance of hospitality, see A. J. Malherbe, *Social Aspects of Early Christianity* (Baton Rouge and London: Lousiana State University Press, 1977), 64-68.

at a time in one place. Others may not have been so constantly mobile, but most are to be found in several different locations at different times in their careers. This is true of Peter,[41] Barnabas,[42] Mark,[43] Silas/Silvanus,[44] Apollos,[45] Philip the evangelist[46] and his prophet daughters,[47] Aquila and Priscilla,[48] Andronicus and Junia,[49] Agabus,[50] and the brothers of the Lord.[51] Even the unknown author to the Hebrews,

41. Jerusalem (Acts 1–8; 11–12; 15; Gal. 1:18; 2:9); Samaria (Acts 8:14-25); Lydda, Joppa, Caesarea (Acts 8:32–10:48); Antioch (Gal. 2:11); Corinth? (1 Cor. 1:12); Rome (1 Pet. 5:13); and cf. 1 Cor. 9:5.

42. Jerusalem (Acts 4:36-37; 9:27; 11:22); Antioch (Acts 11:22-26); Jerusalem (Gal. 2:1-10; Acts 11:30; 12:25); Antioch (Acts 12:25–13:2); with Paul on the "first missionary journey" (Acts 13–14; cf. 1 Cor. 9:6); Antioch (Gal. 2:13; Acts 14:26–15:2); Jerusalem (Acts 15:4-22); Antioch (Acts 15:22, 30-39); Cyprus (Acts 15:39).

43. Jerusalem (Acts 12:12); Antioch (Acts 12:25); Cyprus (Acts 13:5); Pamphylia (Acts 13:13); Jerusalem (Acts 13:13); Antioch (Acts 15:37-38); Cyprus (Acts 15:39); Rome (1 Pet. 5:13; ? Philem. 24; ? Col. 4:10); Colossae? (Col. 4:10).

44. Jerusalem (Acts 15:22, 33); Antioch (Acts 15:30-32, 40); traveling with Paul from Antioch to Berea (Acts 15:40–17:15; 1 Thess. 2:2); Corinth (Acts 18:5; 2 Cor. 1:19; 1 Thess. 1:1; 2 Thess. 1:1); Rome (1 Pet. 5:12).

45. Alexandria (Acts 18:24); Ephesus (Acts 18:24-26); Corinth (1 Cor. 1:12; 3:4-6, 22; 4:6; Acts 18:27–19:1); Ephesus? (1 Cor. 16:12).

46. Jerusalem (Acts 6:5); Samaria (Acts 8:5-13); coastal plain of Palestine (Acts 8:26-40); Caesarea (Acts 8:40; 21:8); Hierapolis (Polycrates *ap.* Eusebius *Hist. eccl.* 5.24.2; Gaius *ap.* Eusebius *Hist. eccl.* 3.31.4).

47. Caesarea (Acts 21:9); Hierapolis (Papias *ap.* Eusebius *Hist. eccl.* 3.39.9; Polycrates *ap.* Eusebius *Hist. eccl.* 5.24.2; Gaius *ap.* Eusebius *Hist. eccl.* 3.31.4) and Ephesus (Polycrates *ap.* Eusebius *Hist. eccl.* 5.24.2).

48. Rome (Acts 18:2); Corinth (Acts 18:2-3); Ephesus (1 Cor. 16:19; Acts 18:18-19, 26; cf. Rom 16:4; 2 Tim. 4:19); Rome (Rom. 16:3-5).

49. Romans 16:7: Since they were "in Christ" before Paul they were Palestinian Jewish Christians, probably members of the Jerusalem church; somewhere (Antioch?) they were in prison together with Paul; and were then in Rome.

50. Jerusalem (Acts 11:27; 21:10); Antioch (Acts 11:27-28); Caesarea (Acts 21:10-11).

51. 1 Corinthians 9:5 shows that the brothers of the Lord were traveling missionaries. On the relatives of Jesus as traveling missionaries, see further R. Bauckham, *Jude and the Relatives of Jesus in the Early Church* (Edinburgh: T. & T. Clark, 1990), 57-70.

writing from one location, expects to be visiting his addressees in another (13:23). The prophet John, author of Revelation, must have been personally acquainted with the seven churches to which he writes. A considerable number of the prominent members of the church of Rome whom Paul greeted by name in Romans 16[52] were people he had come to know in the course of his missionary travels in the eastern Mediterranean who had subsequently moved to Rome.[53]

Further details of a few of these named persons will reinforce the point. John Mark, a member of a Cypriot Jewish family settled in Jerusalem and a member of the early Jerusalem church, was then in Antioch, accompanied his cousin Barnabas and Paul on their missionary journey as far as Pamphylia, later accompanied Barnabas to Cyprus, and is finally heard of in Rome, if Philemon was written from Rome, where 1 Peter also places him. Philip the evangelist, a member of the Jerusalem church, then a traveling missionary in Palestine, settled in Caesarea Maritima with his prophet daughters, and finally (according to reliable second-century tradition) in Hierapolis in Asia Minor with two of the daughters, while a third ended her days in Ephesus. Aquila and Priscilla, Jews who lived in Rome (though Aquila was originally from Pontus) until Jews were expelled from Rome under Claudius, were apparently already Christians when Paul first met them in Corinth, whence they moved to Ephesus, where the church met in their house, but later returned to Rome. There is no reason to suppose that such movements were untypical of the Christian leaders of the first generation.

52. Although D. Trobisch, *Paul's Letter Collection* (Minneapolis: Fortress, 1994), 69-73, still maintains the suggestion that Romans 16 was originally addressed to Ephesus (in his version of this suggestion, Romans 16 is a cover note added by Paul when he sent a copy of his letter to the Romans to Ephesus), most recent scholarship accepts that the church in Rome is addressed in this chapter: cf. J. D. G. Dunn, *Romans 9–16*, Word Biblical Commentary 38 (Dallas: Word, 1988), 884-85.

53. Not all of those named need have been personally known to Paul; some could have been known to him by reputation. But, in addition to Aquila and Priscilla, Andronicus and Junia, the following must fall into the category of people Paul had known before they moved to Rome: Epaenetus, Ampliatus, Urbanus, Stachys, Persis, and Rufus and his mother.

The importance of this point is that these are the people we should take as models for the kind of person who might have written a Gospel. Why do scholars so readily assume that the author of a Gospel would be someone who had spent all his Christian life attached to the same Christian community, when the real evidence we have about early Christian leaders suggests that he would more likely be someone who had spent much time traveling around various churches or someone who had spent some time established as a teacher in more than one church? In that case, his own experience of the Christian movement could well be far from parochial. And since the writing of a Gospel could well have taken several years, why should it be assumed that even the writing of a Gospel took place in the context only of one Christian community? Matthew, for example, may have lived in several very different and geographically distant Christian communities over the course of the years in which he compiled his Gospel. There is nothing to warrant us ignoring this possibility and much to suggest that theories about the Gospels need to allow for it.

Admittedly, the leaders just mentioned all belonged to the first Christian generation, and specific information about named Christian leaders from the later part of the first century is much more scarce. But there is no reason at all to suppose that Christian leaders became more static as the century grew old. Itinerant teachers traveling from one church to another were still common up to the end of the century: we find them in Revelation (2:2), the Johannine letters (2 John 10-11; 3 John 3-8) and the Didache (11:1-6). Moreover, in order to complete this picture of early Christian leaders as people whose experience and therefore vision of the church was far from confined to their own parochial patch, it is worth glancing into the second century, because, if we can establish an overall pattern of mobility in Christian leaders which is continuous from our earliest evidence in the time of Paul through to the late second century, thus encompassing the period in which the Gospels were written, the case will be the stronger. From the end of the first century onwards the leadership of traveling missionaries, teachers, and prophets probably gave way gradually to the leadership of local bishops. But it should be noticed that these bishops themselves, despite their attachment to local churches, maintained the habit of traveling and visiting other communities. For example, Polycarp, bishop of Smyrna, visited Rome,[54] and in his letter to the Philippians (13:1) envisages traveling to Syrian Antioch, should he be able to get away. Abercius, bishop of Hierapolis, who narrated his travels on his tombstone, traveled both west to Rome and east to Syria and across the Euphrates to Nisibis, finding a welcome everywhere, he says, from Christians (lines 7-12).[55] Melito, bishop of Sardis traveled to Palestine.[56] Another much-traveled second-century Christian was Hegesippus, probably a native of Palestine, who in the middle of the century recorded Palestinian Jewish Christian traditions, and who enjoyed the hospitality of the church of Corinth during what must have been a detour on his way to Rome, where he compiled a list of the bishops.[57] Other prominent second-century teachers seem, almost as a rule, to have taught for a time in more than one major Christian center: Justin Martyr, a native of Samaria, lived in both Ephesus and Rome; Tatian, who came from east Syria beyond the Euphrates, taught in Rome and then in Antioch before returning to his birthplace; the Gnostic teacher Valentinus taught in Alexandria, then in Rome; Basilides came to Alexandria from Antioch; Marcion came to Rome from his native Pontus.[58]

It seems that leaders who moved from church to church, to a greater or lesser extent, are a constant feature of the early Christian movement in the first century and a half of its existence. We must therefore reckon very seriously with the chances that some, if not all, of the evangelists were people whose own experience was far from limited to a single Christian community or even to the churches of a particular geographical region. Such a person would not naturally confine his attention, when composing a Gospel, to the local needs and problems of a single, homogeneous community but could well have in

---

54. Irenaeus *Adv. haer.* 3.3.4.

55. J. Quasten, *Patrology* (Utrecht and Brussels: Spectrum, 1950), 1:172.

56. Eusebius *Hist. eccl.* 4.26.13-14.

57. Eusebius *Hist. eccl.* 4.22.2-3.

58. Other examples of the mobility of bishops and teachers in the second century and later are in A. Harnack, *The Expansion of Christianity in the First Three Centuries,* trans. J. Moffatt (London: Williams & Norgate, 1904), 1:463-66.

view the variety of different contexts he had experienced in several churches he knew well. His own experience could give him the means of writing relevantly for a wide variety of churches in which his Gospel might be read, were it to circulate generally around the churches of the late-first-century Roman world.

Fourth, another feature of the early Christian movement that we can establish as a continuous practice from the time of Paul to the mid-second century is the sending of letters from one church to another.[59] We find, for example, the leadership of the Roman church writing a letter of pastoral concern to churches scattered over a wide area of Asia Minor (1 Peter) and another to the church of Corinth to deal with the problems and disputes in that church (1 Clement). From the early second century we have the letter of Polycarp of Smyrna to the church at Philippi, and the letters of Ignatius of Antioch to six different churches. Dionysius, bishop of Corinth, in the middle of the second century wrote at least seven letters to various churches, which Eusebius knew as a collection[60] but which are no longer extant. The work known as the *Martyrdom of Polycarp* is actually a letter from the church of Smyrna to, in the first instance, the church of Philomelium in Phrygia, which had asked for it, though it was intended also to circulate to other churches. These letters which have survived or which at least survived until Eusebius's time are only the tip of an iceberg. They are the ones that proved of lasting value; many more ephemeral letters must have perished, as we know that even some of Paul's did.

Letters establish more than literary connections between churches. Letters imply messengers. The messenger would either be a member of the sending church who was in any case traveling through or near the church addressed, or a member of the sending church who traveled specifically to carry the letter. Messengers stayed in the homes of members of the church, met with the whole church for worship, conveyed orally news not included in the letter, received news to take back home,

59. For later examples of the exchange of letters between churches, see Harnack, *Expansion*, 466-67.

60. *Hist. eccl.* 4.23.1-13. The collection Eusebius knew also included a letter to an individual: Chrysophora.

and surely forged warm personal contacts with their hosts. Because of the role of messengers, a letter is merely the formal, surviving element in a two-way communication with wider oral and personal dimensions.[61] Messengers were one way in which personal links between churches were created, which must have given even the most untraveled Christian a strong sense of participation in something much broader than his or her local church. But messengers carrying letters are only one example of the kind of informal contact that must have been constantly created by members of one church, traveling for all kinds of reasons, passing through and enjoying the hospitality and fellowship of other churches. (Of course, they also clashed and quarreled, as we shall notice shortly.)

Fifth, we have concrete evidence for close contacts between churches in the period around or soon after the writing of the Gospels. I will cite just three examples.

(1) The famous fragment of Papias's prologue to his lost work[62] affords us one glimpse of what happened. Though writing in the early second century, Papias was recalling a time in the late first century (precisely the time when Matthew, Luke, and John were being written). As a young man in Hierapolis, he had been an avid collector of oral traditions. He collected them not by traveling himself but by quizzing anyone who happened to pass through Hierapolis who had heard the teaching of personal disciples of Jesus either firsthand or secondhand.[63] Hierapolis is a little off the much-traveled route that ran east from Ephesus through Laodicea, and so we must suppose that Christians traveling that route sometimes turned aside specifically to visit the church at Hierapolis. (Perhaps the famous prophet daughters of Philip

---

61. On the role of messengers, see G. R. Llewelyn and R. A. Kearsley, "Letter-Carriers in the Early Church," in *New Documents Illustrating Early Christianity* (Sydney: Ancient History Documentary Research Centre, Macquarie University, 1994), 7:50-57. Messengers also sometimes conveyed information without letters: examples in Llewelyn and Kearsley, "Letter-Carriers," 55.

62. *Ap.* Eusebius *Hist. eccl.* 3.39.3-4.

63. On the relevant point of interpretation of Papias here, see R. Bauckham, "Papias and Polycrates on the Origin of the Fourth Gospel," *Journal of Theological Studies* 44 (1993): 60.

the evangelist, then living at Hierapolis, were the attraction.[64]) Papias's evidence therefore shows how far even a Christian community not on a major communication route would be visited regularly by Christians from other churches and kept in close touch with the wider Christian movement. A more strategically located church would be correspondingly more frequently in touch with a wider circle of other churches. Ephesus, for example, was a city so much traveled through that it is no surprise that Polycrates, bishop of Ephesus in the late second century, could claim to have conversed with Christian brethren from all parts of the world.[65] The claim is wholly credible and could equally have been made by a Christian leader in any of several major churches in the right locations at any time in the first two centuries of early Christian history.

(2) The letters of Ignatius, written only two or three decades after Matthew, Luke, and John, give us a remarkably detailed picture of an active communication network among the churches of the area from Syrian Antioch to Philippi, as well as between these churches and Rome. They record how, in the period when Ignatius was traveling from Syrian Antioch to Italy, letters, delegates, and even bishops traveled back and forth between these various churches for a variety of purposes. The movements can be reconstructed as follows. Ignatius, bishop of Antioch, was being taken to Rome, a prisoner under guard, expecting martyrdom there. The route took him and his guards across Asia Minor. At Smyrna he was visited by emissaries from the churches at Ephesus, Magnesia, and Tralles, each led by its bishop, and he wrote a letter for each delegation to take back to their own community (*Eph.* 1:3; 2:1; 21:1; *Magn.* 2:1; 15:1; *Trall.* 1:1; 13:1). From Smyrna Ignatius also wrote to the church in Rome, apparently responding to news he had already received from the Roman church, and also referring to Syrian Christians who had traveled to Rome ahead of him (*Rom.* 10:2), presumably to prepare the Roman church for his arrival.

At Troas, waiting to embark on the sea journey to Neapolis,

64. At least two of them were then living in Hierapolis: Polycrates *ap.* Eusebius *Hist. eccl.* 5.24.2.

65. Polycrates *ap.* Eusebius *Hist. eccl.* 5.24.7.

Ignatius wrote to the church at Smyrna, which he had just visited, and to the church at Philadelphia, which two of his companions had recently visited (*Philad.* 11:1). He also wrote a personal letter to Polycarp, the bishop of Smyrna. These letters were conveyed by Burrus, who had been delegated by the churches of Smyrna and Ephesus to accompany Ignatius (*Philad.* 11:2; *Smyrn.* 12:1). While at Troas Ignatius had received news from Antioch, to the effect that the church there, which had been troubled either by persecution or by internal disputes (it is not clear which), was now at peace (*Philad.* 10:1; *Pol.* 7:1). Ignatius was therefore anxious that all the churches of the area should send messengers with letters to Antioch to congratulate the Antiochene Christians. His letter to the Philadelphian Christians tells them to send a deacon, pointing out that churches nearer to Antioch had already sent bishops or presbyters or deacons (*Philad.* 10:1-2). His letter to the Smyrnean Christians tells them to send someone to Antioch with a letter (*Smyrn.* 11:2-3). In his letter to Polycarp, he not only asks him to convene a meeting of the church to appoint someone really suitable for this task (*Pol.* 7:2), he also explains that he is having to leave Troas before he has had time to write to the other churches this side of Antioch (meaning, probably, those in Asia Minor). So Polycarp is deputed to do this, telling them all to send, if possible, messengers to Antioch, or at least a letter by the hand of the messengers from Smyrna (*Pol.* 8:1).

Finally, when Ignatius passed through Philippi, he asked the church there also to communicate with Antioch. Since Philippi was a considerable journey from Antioch, the Philippians decided to send their messenger only as far as Smyrna and to entrust their letter to the Smyrnean messenger. Polycarp of Smyrna, writing back to the Philippians, assures them this will be done, and expects himself to be going to Antioch, if only he can get away (Polycarp *Phil.* 13:1).

Thus, in the period it took Ignatius and his guards to travel from Antioch to Italy, two delegations of Christians had left for Rome (one from Antioch, one from Troas or Ephesus), major delegations had traveled from Ephesus, Magnesia, and Tralles to Smyrna, some Ephesian Christians had traveled on to Troas, messengers had gone from Troas to Philadelphia and to Smyrna, and from Philippi to Smyrna and back, and many of these churches had sent delegations, some including their bishops, to Antioch. Probably delegations and letters would also have reached Antioch for the same purpose from churches to the south and east of Antioch. The communication network is even more vigorous and complex than it had been when Paul and his missionary colleagues traveled the area.

An indication of the way this network made the circulation of literature easy and natural is also provided by these events. When the Philippian Christians sent their messenger to Smyrna, they asked Polycarp to send them copies of any letters of Ignatius that the church at Smyrna had received from him, together with copies of any other letters of Ignatius the church at Smyrna had. Polycarp did this (Polycarp *Phil.* 13:2). In other words, already the church at Smyrna had copies of letters of Ignatius to other churches, as well as to themselves, and already they were making copies of all these letters to send to another, rather more distant church. If letters of Ignatius circulated so quickly, we must surely conclude that the Gospels written in the preceding few decades would have circulated around the churches just as rapidly.

(3) Another insight into the way that Christian literature circulated comes from the *Shepherd of Hermas.* The Roman Christian prophet Hermas in his apocalyptic visions tells how the visionary figure, an elderly woman, who disclosed the revelations to him told him to write them in a book, which he and the elders were to read to the Roman church. But he was also to make two copies. One was for Grapte, who would use it to instruct the widows and orphans. Evidently Grapte was in charge of the church's charitable work. The other copy was for Clement, who "will send it to the cities abroad, because this is his job" (*Vis.* 2:4:3).[66] Clement was the Roman church's secretary responsible for communications with other churches. This apparently included having multiple copies made of Christian literature produced in Rome and sending the copies out by messengers to other churches. (If he sent to churches in major centers, they would presumably take care of further, more local distribution.) Clement also sent out letters to particular churches, as we know from the fact that so-called 1 Clement, the letter from the church in Rome to the church

---

66. πέμψει οὖν Κλήμης εἰς τὰς ἔξω πόλεις, ἐκείνῳ γὰρ ἐπιτέτραπται.

in Corinth, is attributed to him. Evidently Clement's job of sending out literature to churches abroad was already his job in the late first century when 1 Clement was written. Quite probably therefore Hermas's *Visions* were also written at that time. So Hermas provides us with concrete information, from the very period in which Matthew, Luke, and John were being written, about the way newly written Christian literature was widely and very deliberately circulated around the churches.

Sixth, and finally, the evidence for conflict and diversity in early Christianity supports my picture of the early Christian movement as a network of communities in constant communication. This picture should not be misunderstood as though it portrayed the Christian movement as entirely harmonious and homogeneous. It does not require the evidence for conflict and diversity to be played down. On the contrary, it is clear that this network of communication among the early Christian churches was a vehicle for conflict and disagreement, as well as for fellowship and support. All the evidence we have for rivalry between Christian teachers or conflict between different versions of the Christian message, from Paul's letters through to Revelation and the letters of Ignatius, shows us that conflict operating across the network of communication I have depicted. Teachers of one version of Christianity do not keep to a small patch of like-minded churches. On the contrary, itinerant teachers of any persuasion are always liable to turn up in any church. Congregations divide. Leaders from elsewhere write to support one faction or another. Much as some leaders strove to get teachers of whom they disapproved excluded from churches where they had influence, clearly they constantly failed. None of this evidence for conflict and disagreement suggests that any version of Christianity formed a homogeneous little enclave of churches, out of communication with other churches and renouncing any interest or involvement with the wider Christian movement. Quite the opposite: all such evidence confirms my picture. Churches take an intense interest in conflicts happening elsewhere. Leaders and teachers actively promote their versions of the Gospel anywhere and everywhere in the Christian world. These are not the introverted communities and teachers who would produce written Gospels purely for home consumption.

In view of all this evidence that the early Christian movement was a network of communities in constant communication with each other, by messengers, letters, and movements of leaders and teachers — moreover, a network around which Christian literature circulated easily, quickly, and widely — surely the idea of writing a Gospel purely for the members of the writer's own church or even for a few neighboring churches is unlikely to have occurred to anyone. The burden of proof must lie with those who claim it did.

VI

I conclude with a number of hermeneutical observations:

First, the attempt by the current consensus in Gospels scholarship to give the so-called Matthean, Markan, Lukan, and Johannine communities a key hermeneutical role in the interpretation of the Gospels is wholly mistaken. If the Gospels do not address those communities in particular, those communities have no hermeneutical relevance. As a matter of fact, it seems very doubtful whether we can know anything worth knowing about them. If the Gospels were not written for specific communities, then the situation is quite different from that which enables us to know quite a lot about Paul's Corinthian church. Certainly it may be argued that the community in which a Gospel was written is likely to have influenced the writing of the Gospel even though it is not addressed by the Gospel. But it does not follow that we have any chance of reconstructing that community. As I have already indicated, we certainly cannot take it for granted that a Gospel was written in only one community. It is entirely possible that a Gospel was written over a period during which its author was resident for a time in each of two or more very different communities. Even apart from this possibility, we cannot take it for granted that the author of a Gospel would have been influenced by only one community context. Even if his Gospel was written within a specific Christian community, it is quite probable that he himself would have previously lived and taught in other communities. The influences on him and therefore on his Gospel would be various. In view of the extent and intensity of communication throughout the early Christian movement, even a writer of a Gospel who had lived all his life in one Christian community would be very well aware of the Christian movement as a more-than-local phenomenon and would have all kinds of contacts, personal and literary, with many churches other than his own. Finally, the way in which a creative writer is influenced by and responds to his or her context is simply not calculable. The chances of being able to deduce from an author's work what the influences on the author were, if we have only the work to inform us, are minimal. Hence the enterprise of reconstructing an evangelist's community is, for a series of cogent reasons, doomed to failure. But, much more importantly, it is in any case of no *hermeneutical* value, since the Gospels were not addressed to or intended to be understood solely by such a community. Whatever the influences on an evangelist's work may have been, its *implied readership* is not a specific audience, large or small, but an indefinite readership: any or every church of the late first century to which his Gospel might circulate. This, not what we may or may not be able to guess about the evangelist's community, is the hermeneutically relevant fact. Thus any reader who finds the argument of this chapter convincing should cease using the terms Matthean community, Markan community, Lukan community, and Johannine community. They no longer have a useful meaning.

Second, the implication of the argument of this chapter is not just that the implied audience of the Gospels is broader than the current consensus allows. A few recent writers on the Gospels have diverged from the dominant trend in Gospels scholarship to the extent of envisaging a larger rather than a smaller implied audience.[67] The evangelist may have had in mind quite a range of churches located over a specific geographical area, or a scattered network of churches he knew. Such an argument introduces more diversity into the implied audience and rejects the kind of detailed reconstructions of very specific circumstances that have been common in discussion of the evangelists' communities. However, to modify the consensus merely to the extent of widening the audience for which an evangelist allegedly wrote is not at all the paradigm shift proposed in this chapter. In such a move it is still presupposed that an evangelist had in mind specific churches for which he wrote. In principle he could have listed the major churches

---

67. See especially G. N. Stanton's work, discussed in n. 29 above.

to which he expected his Gospel to circulate and which constituted his intended readership. The audience, though relatively large, is still specific. This chapter has proposed, not merely that the implied audience of a Gospel is larger than the current consensus allows, but that it is *indefinite rather than specific*. This is a difference of kind, not just of degree, from the current consensus. The evangelists, I have argued, did not write for specific churches they knew or knew about, not even for a very large number of such churches. Rather, drawing on their experience and knowledge of several or many specific churches, they wrote *for any and every church* to which their Gospels might circulate. No more than almost any other author, at their time or at most other periods, could they know which specific readers and hearers their work would reach. Thus, to ask, for example, if Luke knew whether there were any Christian churches in Gaul at the time when he wrote, and, supposing he knew there were, if he intended to address them in his Gospel, is to ask altogether the wrong sort of question. His intended audience was an *open category* — any and every church to which his Gospel might circulate — not a specified audience in which he had consciously either to include churches in Gaul or not.

Third, from what has been said so far in these hermeneutical conclusions, some readers immersed in the consensus may suppose that the effect of the argument of this chapter is to decontextualize the Gospels and to render historical context hermeneutically irrelevant. But this is not the case. The argument does not represent the Gospels as autonomous literary works floating free of any historical context. The Gospels have a historical context, but that context is not the evangelist's community. It is the early Christian movement in the late first century. We can bring to the interpretation of the Gospels everything we know about that movement and its political, social, economic, religious, and ideological contexts. This context is much less specific than the current consensus in Gospels scholarship desires, but it is no more general than the context that most literature of that period addresses, or the context that most literature of any society in any period addresses. Literature addressing a specific community in a specific locality is very rare, but to claim that most authors address wider contexts than this does not decontextualize their work.

However, fourth, it is certainly true that the argument of this chapter smooths the hermeneutical path from the way the Gospels addressed their first readers — an open category of readers/hearers in any late-first-century Christian church to which the Gospels might circulate — to the way the Gospels have been read ever since. This was not the intention with which the argument was developed, but it is the consequence of the argument. As I remarked earlier in the chapter, no attentive reader can miss the hermeneutical relevance of the church at Corinth to the interpretation of 1 Corinthians. But all readers without exception before the mid-twentieth century missed the (alleged) hermeneutical relevance of the Matthean community to the interpretation of Matthew. Historical scholarship does not, after all, require us to suppose that they were all mistaken.

Fifth, the argument of this chapter does not require us to underestimate the diversity of the Gospels. It simply denies what the consensus assumes: that this diversity requires a diversity of readers. The highly distinctive nature of the Fourth Gospel, for example, does not imply that its intended readers were a highly distinctive branch of early Christianity, different from the readership of other Gospels. It implies only that its author (or authors) wished to propagate his own distinctive theological rendering of the Gospel story among whatever readers it might reach. The argument of this chapter leaves open many questions about the diversity of the Gospels. That the evangelists had different understandings of Jesus and his story, and made different judgments about the problems and priorities of being Christians in the late-first-century world, is clear. Whether a later evangelist who knew that his Gospel would be read by readers who already knew an earlier Gospel expected his Gospel to supplement or to supplant the earlier is left by my argument entirely open. Whether the relationships between the Gospels as they first circulated around the churches were understood as irenical or polemical, complementary or competitive, is again left entirely open. How far their divergent approaches are indeed complementary or contradictory is also left entirely open by the argument of this chapter and remains a key hermeneutical issue in the interpretation of the Gospels. The argument of this chapter merely excludes, as a factor in accounting for or understanding the diversity of the Gospels, the hypothesis that each was written for a different community. Many other ways of accounting for and understanding the diversity of the Gospels remain.

Sixth, it is appropriate to conclude by pointing out that the mistake made by the consensus view which this chapter has attacked derives from a misplaced desire for historical specificity. It has behind it that tremendous drive towards historical specificity which has fueled a considerable part of the whole enterprise of modern biblical scholarship. The desire is to define the historical meaning of the text as specifically as possible by defining its historical context as closely as possible. Just as we know that we have understood 1 Corinthians 8–10 better when we have studied pagan sacrificial meals in Corinth, so we think we shall know more precisely what Luke's teaching on wealth and poverty means if only we can define just where the dozen rich people in Luke's community belonged in the social hierarchy and exactly how they were actually treating the poor.

This is a hermeneutical mistake, but the mistake does not consist in thinking historical context relevant. It lies in failing to see that texts vary in the extent to which they are context-specific. Some texts, which Umberto Eco calls "closed texts," define their implied reader very closely and also have a determinate meaning that depends on knowing what the implied reader is supposed to know. If one does not know this, one can misunderstand badly. If we knew nothing at all about idol-meat in Corinth, we might well mistake Paul's meaning quite seriously. But other texts, which Eco calls "open texts," leave their implied readership more open and consequently leave their meaning more open to their real readers' participation in producing meaning.[68] The Gospels are relatively open texts, though not as open as some kinds of text (a lyric poem, for example). For various late-first-century churches hearing Matthew's Gospel in differing situations Jesus' command to love one's enemies would have meant rather different things. I do not think Matthew would have minded at all. To think we do not know what Matthew meant unless we can pin down what sort of enemies his community had is trying to read an open text as a closed one.

68. U. Eco, *The Role of the Reader* (London: Hutchinson, 1981), 8-10.

The Holy Internet:
Communication Between Churches
in the First Christian Generation[1]

MICHAEL B. THOMPSON

This essay seeks to explore aspects of communication within the network of the first Christians that existed between 30 and 70 A.D. Scholars have already analyzed the local networks reflected in the New Testament in some respects, either in general studies of Christian community, or with regard to particular aspects, such as Paul's co-workers. Some have concentrated on the social rank and status of early Christians,[2] and others are now starting to apply the sociological discipline of "network analysis" to the New Testament to explore the range and nature of *relations* between believers.[3] I will focus on the subject

1. A revised and adapted version of the Tyndale New Testament Lecture, given at Tyndale House, Cambridge, on July 2, 1996. I wish to thank one of my students, Jeremy Brooks, whose assistance in helping me calculate travel times was invaluable.

2. E.g. W. Meeks, *The First Urban Christians* (New Haven: Yale University Press, 1983); A. J. Malherbe, *Social Aspects of Early Christianity* (Baton Rouge and London: Louisiana State University Press, 1977).

3. L. M. White, ed., *Semeia 56: Social Networks in the Early Christian Environment: Issues and Methods for Social History* (Atlanta: Scholars Press, 1992). Although there are different schemes for analyzing social networks, R. F. Hock cites (1) four morphological characteristics of networks: anchorage (identification

of communication between churches, looking particularly at their motivation, means, and frequency of contact. This is important, because the more specialized our studies become on the individual New Testament writings, the greater the temptation to see them as products of communities in isolation from other churches.

1. Paths for Communication

In the ancient world, the closest thing to an information superhighway was the grid of Roman roads and clear shipping lanes that made travel far safer and easier than it had ever been before.[4] On the ground, the Appian Way connected Rome and Italy's crucial eastern port of Brundisium. Just across the Adriatic lay the Egnatian Way, the backbone of the Imperial Roman post. Extending from Dyrrachium and Apollonia to Thessalonica, Philippi, and eventually to Byzantium, this major land artery linked Rome and its eastern provinces.[5] Other Roman roads

---

of the primary and secondary circles of influence in the network), reachability, density, range; and (2) five interactional characteristics: content, directedness (the extent to which communication flows in one particular direction), durability (how long do the links last), intensity, and frequency (" 'By the Gods, It's My One Desire to See an Actual Stoic': Epictetus' Relations with Students and Visitors in His Personal Network," *Social Networks,* 126).

4. L. Casson, *Travel in the Ancient World* (London: George Allen & Unwin, 1974) offers the most accessible discussion of travel in early times. For more recent work, cf. e.g. B. M. Rapske, "Acts, Travel and Shipwreck," in *The Book of Acts in Its Graeco-Roman Setting,* ed. D. W. J. Gill and C. Gempf (Grand Rapids: Eerdmans, 1994), 1-47; J. Murphy-O'Connor's more popular, "On the Road and on the Sea with St. Paul," *Bible Review* 1 (1985): 38-47; and further bibliography in R. Riesner, *Studien zur Chronologie, Missionsstrategie und Theologie* (Tübingen: J. C. B. Mohr [Paul Siebeck], 1994), 273f nn. 1, 3. C. A. J. Skeel's *Travel in the First Century After Christ, with Special Reference to Asia Minor* (Cambridge: At the University Press, 1901), and W. M. Ramsay's article, "Roads and Travel (In NT)," in the supplementary volume of *A Dictionary of the Bible,* ed. J. Hastings (Edinburgh: T. & T. Clark, 1904), 375-402, remain mines of information.

5. Cf. F. O'Sullivan, *The Egnatian Way* (Newton Abbot, U.K.: David & Charles; Harrisburg, Penn.: Stackpole Books, 1972); N. H. H. Sitwell, *Roman Roads of Europe* (London: Cassell, 1981).

crisscrossed Asia Minor,[6] and the fine web of highways in Palestine has recently been documented in detail.[7]

There was no official postal system for private citizens, and it is doubtful that the *cursus publicus* (the imperial transport system) carried Christian letters,[8] at least in the earliest days. But the preservation of order in the empire depended on a regular, secure system for communication. Its success required the presence of staging posts or rest stops along the roads when towns were further than a day's journey.[9] These served private travelers, as well as the official couriers. Roman milestones placed every five thousand feet along the way offered a sense of progress and told how far it was to the next stop.[10] Some travelers carried with them *itineraria* (handlists of stops and distances) and maps. We have a medieval copy of one ancient map of Roman roads, the Peutinger Table, a twenty-two-foot long parchment complete with little symbols indicating the nature of the services available — a sort of *Michelin Guide* in its day.[11] Bad weather closed many roads in winter, but not the Egnatian Way.[12] Despite its

6. D. H. French, "The Roman Road-System of Asia Minor," in *Aufstieg und Niedergang der römischen Welt* II.7.2, ed. H. Temporini and W. Hasse (Berlin and New York: Walter de Gruyter, 1980), 698-729.

7. D. A. Dorsey, *The Roads and Highways of Ancient Israel,* American Schools of Oriental Research Library of Biblical and Near Eastern Archaeology (Baltimore and London: Johns Hopkins University Press, 1991).

8. Contra C. J. Hemer, *The Book of Acts in the Setting of Hellenistic History* (Tübingen: J. C. B. Mohr, 1989), 273-75, 393; cf. S. R. Llewelyn, "Sending Letters in the Ancient World: Paul and the Philippians," *Tyndale Bulletin* 46 (1995): 337-56, and F. F. Bruce, "Travel and Communication (The New Testament World)," in *The Anchor Bible Dictionary,* ed. D. N. Freedman (New York: Doubleday, 1992), 6:649. For a recent discussion of the postal system see S. R. Llewelyn, *New Documents Illustrating Early Christianity* (Sydney: Ancient History Documentary Research Centre, Macquarie University, 1994), 7:13-25.

9. T. Cornell and J. Matthew, *Atlas of the Roman World* (Oxford: Phaidon, 1982), 114. Some have questioned whether the network of relay stations was fully developed in the Roman provinces by the first century A.D., but there is good evidence that its basic structure was in place (Llewelyn, *Documents,* 14-22; "Letters," 341).

10. Casson, *Travel,* 173.

11. Casson, *Travel,* 186f.; see K. Miller, *Itineraria Romana. Römische Reisewege an der Hand der Tabula Peutingeriana* (Stuttgart: Strecker und Schröder, 1916).

12. Ramsay, "Roads," 384.

perils of demanding geography and possible encounters with the occasional wild animal or bandit, land travel had the benefit of an infrastructure designed to promote communication.

During the first two centuries after Christ, the sea lanes were crossed by the mightiest merchant marine the world had ever seen or would see for another thousand years.[13] Juvenal described how crowded the Mediterranean became during the season of navigation: "Look at our ports, our seas, crowded with big ships! The men at sea now outnumber those on shore" (xiv.275; Loeb). Journey by sea could be perilous because of the weather (Paul was shipwrecked at least four times; 2 Cor. 11:25; Acts 27), but Pompeii had cleared the shipping lanes of danger from Cilician pirates in 67 B.C.[14] Although people had to wait for a ship going in the right direction and for favorable winds (Acts 27:4-24),[15] a constant stream of merchant vessels enabled travel. There was no such thing as a passenger vessel in the ancient world, but trading ships commonly carried travelers.[16]

Particularly important was the Roman grain fleet that plied the Mediterranean between Italy and Alexandria in Egypt via Rhodes and the Lycian ports.[17] The grain vessels were large; Josephus crossed to Rome on a ship carrying six hundred persons (Vita 15). Port authorities required an exit pass (at least from some places), costing from 5 drachmae for a sailor to 108 for a prostitute. As a skilled laborer Paul would probably have paid 8, had he ever sailed from Egypt.[18] The ship's charge for passage was more affordable: a trip from Alexandria to Athens cost a family only two drachmae.[19]

13. L. Casson, *The Ancient Mariners: Seafarers and Sea Fighters of the Mediterranean in Ancient Times,* 2d ed. (Princeton: Princeton University Press, 1991), 191. For discussion of sea travel see also Rapske, "Acts," 22-47; Murphy-O'Connor, "Road."

14. Casson, *Mariners,* 180-83.

15. See R. Jewett, *Dating Paul's Life* (London: SCM, 1979), 56f., on optimal times to travel.

16. Casson, *Travel,* 152f.

17. Bruce, "Travel and Communication," 6:649.

18. Casson, *Travel,* 154.

19. E. Ferguson, *Backgrounds of Early Christianity* (Grand Rapids: Eerdmans, 1987), 65.

People got what they paid for. Accommodation was primitive —
passengers normally stayed on deck, sleeping out in the open or under
tentlike shelters put up in the evening and taken down in the morning.
They brought their own food, which they could prepare in the ship's
galley after the crew had eaten; water was provided.[20] Sailing between
mid-November and mid-March was very dangerous and rarely undertaken, but Rome's insatiable demand for grain led some owners of
free-merchant vessels to risk it for lucrative reward.[21] If people had a
will to get somewhere, they could find a way.

2. Archives of Information

The network "servers"[22] of the holy internet were the churches, where
Christian traditions were collected, created, remembered, shaped, and
dispersed. Like their modern counterparts, the ancient "servers" also
differed in size, power, and content, some being more open to new
input than others. They effectively functioned as the junction or meeting point through which messages passed to and from individuals and
other congregations.

We can scarcely overemphasize Jerusalem's significance as the
prime information "hub" in early Christian communication.[23] Aside
from the church's obvious importance, we should not forget the role
of annual Jewish festivals in giving a steady pulse to the holy internet.
Acts tells us of the first Christian converts who came for Pentecost from
all over the Diaspora (Acts 2:9-11). Did these people visit Jerusalem
only that year? If they had a good Jewish reason for making the journey,
they now had an additional incentive to share news of their fellowships,
to hear more about Jesus, and to learn new songs. Acts tells us about

20. Casson, *Mariners*, 193.
21. Rapske, "Acts," 22-29.
22. "Servers" are the computers that store and disseminate information on
modern networks.
23. On the influence of the Jerusalem church and its early leadership, see,
e.g., R. Bauckham, "James and the Jerusalem Church," in *The Book of Acts in Its
Palestinian Setting*, ed. R. Bauckham (Grand Rapids: Eerdmans, 1995), 415-80.

Pentecost, but every year, even more Christian Jews gathered for Passover and the other major feasts, where friendships were created and renewed. We may question what percentage of these followers of Jesus would feel at home in Pauline churches, but certainly they would have played a crucial role in the dissemination of Jewish-oriented traditions (such as the letter of James) and news throughout the empire.

Other major cities formed hubs in the holy internet. Rome quickly became a critical server because of its political, financial, and social significance.[24] The first Christian Pentecost included both Hebrew and Gentile proselyte Roman believers (Acts 2:10), who, returning to the capital, formed the nuclei of networks there. On his missionary journeys, Paul carried with him traditions from the server in Syrian Antioch, one of the three or four largest cities in the ancient world. Philippi became another hub of communication, with its location on the Egnatian Way and its proximity to the major sea ports of Neapolis and Thessalonica.[25] Like Jerusalem with its religious festivals, Corinth, "the half-way house between Italy and Asia,"[26] swarmed with traders and regularly swelled with visitors coming from all directions for the biennial Isthmian games — another repeating pulse in the net. The great city of Ephesus was effectively the capital of Asia.[27] Secondary servers in Asia Minor were the hubs along the way from Palestine to Ephesus, including Caesarea, Tarsus, Iconium, and Laodicea, each of which was a center where the roads of a whole district converged.[28]

---

24. Casson states that the events that drew the greatest throngs of tourists were the grandiose spectacles put on by the emperors. "By the second century A.D., 130 days out of the year were holidays, given over to lavish public entertainments that featured chariot racing, boxing, theatrical performances, and the like" (*Travel,* 137).

25. Llewelyn, "Letters," 349.

26. Ramsay, "Roads," 389.

27. D. P. Cole, "Corinth & Ephesus: Why Did Paul Spend Half His Journeys in These Cities?" *Bible Review* 4 (1988): 20-30.

28. Ramsay, "Roads," 388.

3. Access to the Internet

Access to the holy internet started with the "gateway" of faith and baptism, which was free, but not cheap. Belonging to the body of Christ meant immediate access to the network of Christian believers, but communication also depended on the "protocol software" of hospitality, without which no church could meet and no message could travel. In Paul's churches, the households of the well-to-do such as Gaius (Rom. 16:23) and Lydia (Acts 16:14-15, 40) provided more than a place for meeting; as centers, they increased the likelihood of communication between places, because people of means had the resources either to go themselves, to send messengers, or they had the social contacts to find someone who could carry the message.

Hospitality was so important to the early Christians that it became a *paraenetic topos* (Rom. 12:13, 1 Pet. 4:9; Heb. 13:2; etc.), and a requirement of *episkopoi* (Titus 1:7-8).[29] It was essential both for local worship (when believers met in a person's home; Rom. 16:23)[30] and for Christian travelers who would hope to avoid the conditions and temptations of the boarding houses and wayside inns along the Roman roads. Travelers staying at those one-star establishments could sometimes face the prospect of primitive and unclean facilities, leaky ceilings, multiple bedbugs, bad food, adulterated wine, dubious hosts, shady clientele, and a general atmosphere of loose morals.[31] An inability to

29. D. W. Riddle, "Early Christian Hospitality, a Factor in the Gospel Transmission," *Journal of Biblical Literature* 57 (1938): 143. See also 1 Tim. 5:10; *1 Clement* 1:2; 10:7; 11:1; 12:1; Herm. *Mand.* 8.10; *Sim.* 9.27.2; Justin *Apologia* 14. For discussion of its importance cf. also J. H. Elliott, *A Home for the Homeless: A Sociological Exegesis of 1 Peter, Its Situation and Strategy* (Philadelphia: Fortress, 1981), 145-50; Malherbe, *Aspects,* 65-70; and J. Koenig, *New Testament Hospitality: Partnership with Strangers as Promise and Mission,* Overtures to Biblical Theology 17 (Philadelphia: Fortress, 1985).

30. Cf. R. Banks, *Paul's Idea of Community,* rev. ed. (Peabody, Mass.: Hendrickson, 1994). On the physical conditions of house churches, see B. Blue, "Acts and the House Church," in *The Book of Acts in Its Graeco-Roman Setting,* ed. D. W. J. Gill and C. Gempf (Grand Rapids: Eerdmans, 1994), 119-222.

31. Rapske, "Acts," 15; see Murphy-O'Connor, "Road," 42, and Casson, *Travel,* 197-218, for vivid descriptions of travelers' experiences.

find suitable accommodation best explains Paul's description of his experiences: "through many a sleepless night, hungry and thirsty, often without food, cold and naked" (2 Cor. 11:27).

Paul says the Thessalonians were known to "love all the brothers and sisters throughout Macedonia" (1 Thess. 4:10). As a commercial center and seaport, Thessalonica would see many travelers passing through, and the apostle's words almost certainly include the practice of hospitality here.[32] From Christians he expected lodging (a guest room, Philem. 22; spending a winter, 1 Cor. 16:6-7) and provisions for further travel (Rom. 15:23-24; 1 Cor. 16:6). He claimed the same for his coworkers like Phoebe (Rom. 16:1-2) and Timothy (1 Cor. 16:11; cf. 2 Cor. 7:15).

Provision of hospitality was more than a practical need. In Luke's writings we can see most clearly that it was also a theological necessity, inherited from Judaism and reflecting the primacy of grace and Christian mission, particularly through the sharing of meals and care for the outsider.[33] It ensured social cohesion and solidarity for each smaller network within the larger Christian web, as the first generation of believers worked out the meaning of love.[34]

4. Motivations and Uses

The holy internet hummed with traffic for many reasons. Travel was a necessity for a wide variety of people, including merchants (buying, selling, and shipping), freedmen in pursuit of new jobs, letter carriers, artisans, actors, athletes, runaway slaves, teachers, students, the sick seeking mineral springs and places for healing,[35] government officials, soldiers, and tourists out to see the sights.[36] The tomb inscription in

32. E. Best, *A Commentary on the First and Second Epistles to the Thessalonians,* Black's New Testament Commentary (London: A. and C. Black, 1972), 173f.

33. Koenig, *Hospitality;* Malherbe, *Aspects,* 66f.

34. Elliott, *Home,* 145, 148.

35. Casson, *Travel,* 130-36; he notes that doctors sometimes prescribed long sea voyages for recovery from specific illnesses (130).

36. See Casson, *Travel,* 253-61, regarding the prime tourist sites. In addition

Hierapolis for a man named Flavius Zeuxis records that he had sailed as a tradesman round Malea (the southern tip of Greece) into Italy seventy-two times (*CIG* 3920). In addition to the annual festivals already mentioned, we know of Jewish precedents for communication through the pastoral correspondence between Jewish authorities and diaspora Jews.[37] The collection of temple revenues in provincial centers brought people together from various parts of the region.[38] Paul himself traveled for a number of reasons: as an official (Acts 9:1), a craftsman, a preacher, a pilgrim to a festival (Acts 20:16), and a prisoner (Acts 27:1–28:14).[39]

One particular motivation for contact between the earliest congregations stands out. The presence of so many denominations and forms of belief today should not cause us to forget that humanly speaking, the early churches' very existence lay perpetually in peril. As someone has observed, Christianity is always one generation away from extinction. This was never more evident than for the first believers. Their culture offered little reason to keep the faith; to paraphrase Paul,

---

to the Isthmian games, other festivals that regularly drew visitors included the Panathenea (celebrated annually at Athens), the Olympian games (held every four years in Elis), the Nemean (biennial in Argolis in honor of Zeus), and the Pythian (every fourth year at Delphi in honor of Apollos); see S. V. McCasland, "Travel and Communication in the NT," in *The Interpreters Dictionary of the Bible,* ed. G. A. Buttrick et al. (Nashville: Abingdon, 1952), 4:691f.

37. W. G. Doty, *Letters in Primitive Christianity,* Guides to Biblical Scholarship (Philadelphia: Fortress, 1973) 22f; cf. Acts 9:1; 28:21, and D. E. Aune, *The New Testament in Its Literary Environment* (Philadelphia: Westminster, 1987), 177-79. Although not many ancient Jewish letters survive, Stowers concludes that from Josephus, Philo, and 1 and 2 Maccabbees "we know of extensive Jewish letter-writing activity in the Hellenistic period and the early empire" (*Letter Writing in Greco-Roman Antiquity,* Library of Early Christianity [Philadelphia: Westminster, 1986], 41f.). For an extensive list of Jewish letters see Llewelyn, *Documents,* 22 fn. 80.

38. On the network of contacts in diaspora Judaism see J. M. G. Barclay, *Jews in the Mediterranean Diaspora from Alexander to Trajan (323 BCE–117 CE)* (Edinburgh: T. & T. Clark, 1996), 418-24.

39. Noted by E. D. Freed, *The New Testament: A Critical Introduction* (London: SCM, 1991).

belief in a crucified deliverer was a stumbling block to half the people in the world and idiocy to the rest (1 Cor. 1:23). Whenever congregations were founded, their future hung in the balance. Especially in the early days, survival of the local body of Christ depended on a network of support.

The holy internet *hungered for news.* Their shared commitment in love and their sense of community as God's family naturally led Christians to desire information about how brothers and sisters were faring. I doubt that Paul was the only one who became anxious and sometimes wondered if ministry was in vain (1 Cor. 11:28; 1 Thess. 3:5; Gal. 2:2; 4:11; Phil. 2:16, 28). Belief in the efficacy of prayer in support of others — to say nothing of natural curiosity — was a strong motivation for sharing.[40] News fueled prayer (Col. 1:9), and people wanted to know if their requests were answered. The latest update offered yet another reason to glorify God (Acts 14:27; Phil. 1:26).

Being a member of the body of Christ meant communicating not only to hear about others but also *to participate in their needs.* Paul went up to Jerusalem because of a revelation (Gal. 2:2), probably with money for famine relief (Acts 11:27-30). More than once, the Philippians sent money to him while he worked in Thessalonica (Phil. 4:16). Epaphroditus was apparently their gift to Paul in Rome (Phil. 2:25, 30). Whatever we may conclude about Paul's motives for the Jerusalem collection, that effort reinforced an existing web of relationships among his churches (1 Cor. 16:1-4; 2 Cor. 8–9; Rom. 15:25-27; cf. Acts 24:17).

Christians had *a goal of character-building* which gave incentive for teaching, exhorting, and reminding.[41] Paul and other leaders were keen to encourage the faith and obedience of fledgling congregations so that Christ could be formed in them (1 Thess. 3:6, 10; 2 Cor. 7:12; cf. Rom. 1:5; Gal. 4:19; cf. Heb. 10:25). That meant sending co-workers like Timothy (1 Thess. 3:2), Epaphras (Col. 1:7-8), and Epaphroditus (Phil. 2:25-30), whose missions strengthened the links con-

---

40. See 1 Thess. 5:25; 2 Thess. 3:1-2; Rom. 15:30-32; Philem. 22; 2 Cor. 1:11.

41. Stowers, *Writing,* 42.

necting subgroups in the holy internet.[42] With them they brought not only the Spirit, but also their traditions (1 Cor. 11:23; 15:3; 2 Thess. 2:15; 3:6).

Paul's emphasis on *imitation and example*[43] offers another insight into the importance of contacts between congregations: if a practice proved worthwhile, it was noted; if edifying, it was a pattern worth repeating elsewhere (e.g. 1 Thess. 1:6-10; 2:13-16; 2 Thess. 3:6-13; Phil. 4.8-9). The Macedonians' sacrificial giving became a prod for the Corinthians (2 Cor. 8:1-7). Paul boasted of the Thessalonians in the other churches because of their steadfastness and faith in the face of persecution and affliction (2 Thess. 1:4). The effect was twofold — a challenge and inspiration to the hearers and an incentive for the folk back home not to let Paul down (cf. 2 Cor. 7:4; 8:24; 9:2-5).

Eschatological fervor gave a further urgency to sharing news. Hunger for news of the Messiah's return made every morsel of information potentially significant. We hear the note of expectancy in 1 Thessalonians 4:13–5:11; 1 Corinthians 7:29-31; Romans 13:11-12, and Philippians 4:5; cf. James 5:8; 1 Peter 4:7; Hebrews 10:25. Mistaken reports in one form or another that the Day of the Lord had come troubled the Thessalonian congregation (2 Thess. 2:1-4); such news attracted just as much attention as the latest misunderstanding in our own congregations. Paul hoped that news of his ministry would provoke Jews to a jealousy that featured in God's ultimate plan (Rom. 11:13-16).

Not all motives for communication were good ones, at least as far as Paul was concerned. His opponents were just as keen to win a media war, and they too were part of the holy internet. Evidence for this ranges from the polemic in Galatia (Gal. 1:6-9; 2:4; 3:1; 4:17; 6:12-16), Corinth (2 Cor. 2:17; 11:4-5, 13-15; 12:11), and Philippi

---

42. Cf. F. F. Bruce, *The Pauline Circle* (Grand Rapids: Eerdmans, 1985); E. E. Ellis, "Paul and His Co-Workers," *New Testament Studies* 17 (1971): 437-52.

43. Cf. M. B. Thompson, *Clothed with Christ: The Example and Teaching of Jesus in Romans 12.1–15.13,* Journal for the Study of the New Testament Supplement Series 59 (Sheffield: Journal for the Study of the Old Testament Press, 1991); W. P. De Boer, *The Imitation of Paul: An Exegetical Study* (Kampen: Kok, 1962); D. M. Stanley, "Become Imitators of Me: The Pauline Conception of Apostolic Tradition," *Biblica* 40 (1958): 859-77.

(Phil. 3:2) to the slanderous distortions reflected in Romans 3:8 (cf. 6:1; Gal. 2:17) and probably James 2:14-26.[44]

Rather than causing congregations to withdraw from the holy internet into isolation, *conflict and differences* over theology and practice fueled further communication. Contact was vital to maintaining a measure of authority and control (cf. Acts 15:23-29).[45] Cephas and the men from James did not come to Antioch from Jerusalem just to make a social call (Gal. 2:11-13; cf. Acts 8:14). Paul wrote to anticipate errors (Col. 2:4), as well as to correct misunderstandings and misrepresentations of his Gospel (Gal. 1:7; 3:1; 5:10, 12; 2 Thess. 2). Obviously not all Christians shared Paul's enthusiasm and vision of mutual interdependence. The Corinthians' lack of interest in contributing to the needs of the saints in Jerusalem is a case in point.[46] That however did not lead to isolationism; if anything, their factionalism led them to pursue more contact with the leaders they followed (1 Cor. 1:11-12). This too resulted in a message — from Paul; a rebuke was in order for some (1 Cor. 3:1-4; 4:17; 2 Cor. 2:3-10; 7:8-12). In short, even if we leave aside the fundamental missionary impulse that drove Paul and others to range widely (and to seek bases for doing so; Rom. 16:24, 28), a constellation of other factors impelled interchurch travel.

5. Speed

Compared to traffic on the modern Internet, messages in the ancient world moved at a snail's pace, requiring someone to embark on a journey. As an example, news of Tiberius's death in A.D. 37 reached the legate of Syria in Jerusalem (the route is unknown) within five weeks.[47]

---

44. Llewelyn thinks the news of Epaphroditus's illness came to the Philippians via one of Paul's opponents or their messenger ("Letters," 356).

45. Stowers notes the Christians' "supralocal organizational impulse that made letter writing essential for the Roman imperial administration" (*Writing*, 42).

46. For this observation I am indebted to John Barclay.

47. Tacitus *Annales* 6.50; Josephus *Antiquities* 18.122-24; see Bruce, "Travel," 649.

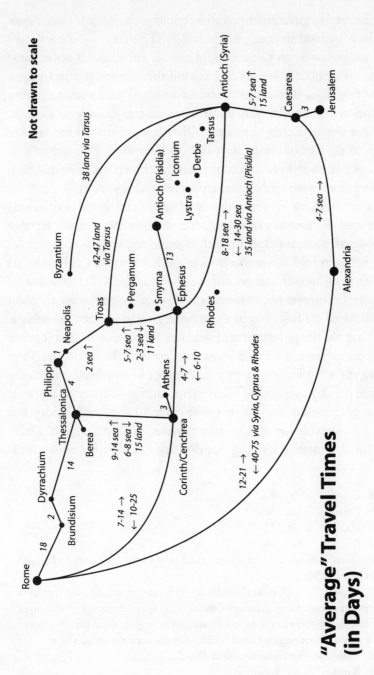

Not drawn to scale

Rome — 18 — Brundisium — 2 — Dyrrachium — 14 — Thessalonica — 4 — Philippi — 1 — Neapolis — 2 sea ↑ — Troas

Berea

7-14 → / ← 10-25

9-14 sea ↑ / 6-8 sea ↓ / 15 land

Thessalonica — Athens — 3 — Corinth/Cenchrea

5-7 sea ↑ / 2-3 sea ↓ / 11 land — Troas

Byzantium

42-47 land via Tarsus

38 land via Tarsus

Pergamum — 13 — Antioch (Pisidia)

Smyrna — Ephesus

Iconium

Lystra

Derbe

Tarsus

4-7 → / ← 6-10 — Athens / Corinth/Cenchrea

8-18 sea → / ← 14-30 sea / 35 land via Antioch (Pisidia) — Antioch (Syria)

5-7 sea ↑ / 15 land — Caesarea — 3 — Jerusalem

Rhodes

12-21 → / ← 40-75 via Syria, Cyprus & Rhodes

4-7 sea → — Alexandria

"Average" Travel Times (in Days)

Assumptions: (1) clear sailing routes and Roman roads, (2) good weather and a fair wind, (3) minimal stopovers, (4) ships, and (5) land travel by foot at a rate of 20 miles per day.

More commonly, government couriers could get a message from Rome to Antioch by land in about forty days.[48] Travelers from the empire's capital on their way to Greece could choose either an all-water route through the straits of Messina and around the Peloponnese to Corinth (at least five days, but usually between one and two weeks), or they could follow the Appian Way to Brindisium, the gateway to the east, and take a shorter sailing across the Adriatic and through the Gulf of Corinth to the harbor on the west side of the isthmus.[49] It was an easy sail from Corinth to Ephesus or Smyrna, the chief ports of Asia Minor; from here ships were ready to take people north or south.[50]

Computing travel times over land is difficult because of uncertainty about the location of routes, and variables such as the weather and mode of transport. Land travel in some areas was not a popular option between mid-November and mid-March, although Rapske argues that Paul himself was no fair-weather traveler.[51] Travel was slow but steady, unless one encountered a Roman army on the way.[52] Most people traveled on foot, except those belonging to wealthy households or working for the government. Estimates for a normal day's journey on foot range from 15 to 25 statute miles; Acts 10:23-24 has Peter traveling the 40 miles from Joppa to Caesarea in two days, confirming a 20-mile per day average.[53] Government couriers journeying by horse and changing mounts frequently could cover 40 to 60 miles a day, but we have little evidence of Christian travelers who rode (Acts 23:24; 21:15-16?).[54] Horseback riding was difficult and slow for most people

48. Casson, *Travel*, 188.

49. Casson, *Travel*, 150-52.

50. Casson, *Travel*, 151.

51. Rapske, "Acts," 3-6.

52. Casson observes that a legion could stop traffic for hours and an army for days (*Travel*, 130).

53. Rapske, "Acts," 6, and n. 20 for different views; Dorsey confirms a 20-mile per day average in Palestine (*Roads*, 12). Skeel estimates 40-50 miles a day or more for travelers in carriages (*Travel*, 70f), but Casson thinks 25-30 miles per day is more representative (*Travel*, 189). On the different modes of transport, see Skeel, *Travel*, 56-60; Casson, *Travel*, 179-81.

54. Rapske, "Acts," 9-12.

because of primitive saddles and the lack of horseshoes and stirrups.[55] In any case, animals could be requisitioned on the spot by imperial officials and others with the power to do so.[56] Most commercial traffic on the roads was local, whereas shipping provided a cheaper and quicker way to move goods long distances.[57]

The speed of sailing vessels depended upon their design, the course, and the weather. With a favorable wind, ancient ships averaged between 4 and 6 knots over open water, and from 3 to 4 knots when working through islands or along coasts; against the wind they managed from less than 2 to 2.5 knots — half the speed.[58] At the right time of the year, a journey from Rome to Alexandria lasted between ten days and three weeks, but the return voyage could take two months or more.[59] One letter from Syria took fifty days to reach Rome; another, double that time.[60]

Travelers covering long distances commonly combined land and sea travel. When he traveled of his own free will, Paul journeyed east by ship (despite his experiences of shipwreck; 2 Cor. 11:25), and west by land, avoiding the frustration of being delayed by adverse winds.[61] His one sailing west was as a prisoner (Acts 25:12).

Sometimes Paul apparently traveled alone (Acts 18:1), but normally he was accompanied by others (Acts 9:7; 13:13; 15:40; 18:18), and the groups could be large (Acts 20:4; 21:16). There was safety in numbers, something to be valued on a ship full of non-Christian Jewish

55. Casson, *Travel,* 181.

56. Rapske, "Acts," 14; Murphy-O'Connor, "Road," 40; Llewelyn, *Documents,* 59-87.

57. Cornell and Matthew, *Atlas,* 114.

58. L. Casson, "Speed Under Sail of Ancient Ships," *Transactions and Proceedings of the American Philological Association* 82 (1951): 142f. Fifty years earlier, Skeel had estimated the average speeds to be five nautical miles per hour for an ordinary vessel, and up to seven and a half for a fast sailing ship (*Travel,* 99).

59. Casson, *Travel,* 152.

60. Cicero *Epistulae ad familiares* 12.10.2 (50 days); *ad Att.* 14.9.3 (over 100); Casson, *Travel,* 222.

61. Murphy-O'Connor, "Road," 46.

pilgrims. Traveling in a group also allowed companionship and time together for sharing of stories and traditions,[62] helping to ensure that whatever happened, the message would continue.

Although travel on foot was slow, there is plenty of evidence in the New Testament that good (and bad) information spread quickly. The Galatians knew of Paul's earlier life in Judaism, apparently apart from what he told them (Gal. 1:13). The churches in Judea certainly heard and kept hearing (ἀκούοντες ἦσαν) of his preaching ministry (Gal. 1:23). Apart from his stays in Corinth and Ephesus, Paul appears to have spent only a few weeks or months with his new converts. Others traveled as well, including Priscilla and Aquila, and Lydia, originally from Asia Minor (Thyatira) but converted in Philippi. Writing to Rome, a city he had not yet visited, Paul knew by name at least twenty-six people there (Rom. 16:3-15).[63]

Paul knew the faith(fulness) of the Roman Christians to be proclaimed "throughout the world" (Rom. 1:8; 16:19). The Thessalonians became "an example to all the believers in Macedonia and Achaia" (1 Thess. 1:7-9). Paul the pastor exaggerates here, but the latter passage is striking, given that it was only a short period between his visit and the writing of 1 Thessalonians (2:17). Not only Paul, but people in Macedonia and Achaia reported to others what kind of reception he, Timothy, and Silas had had with the Thessalonians (1 Thess. 1:9); this they learned through hospitality given and received (1 Thess. 4:10). We see again the first generation's concern that good news travel fast.

Communiqués to a wider readership presupposed a measure of speed in spreading the message. Paul sought to remind his readers that they belonged to a larger entity (cf. 1 Cor. 1:2). It was imperative that the apostolic message be spread to *all* in the community (1 Thess. 5:27), even though its content might be *directly* addressed to an individual

62. R. F. Hock, *The Social Context of Paul's Ministry: Tentmaking and Apostleship* (Philadelphia: Fortress, 1980), 28f.
63. Although the textual problem is notorious, H. Gamble has argued decisively that chapter sixteen originally belonged in the letter (*The Textual History of the Letter to the Romans: A Study in Textual and Literary Criticism,* Studies and Documents [Grand Rapids: Eerdmans, 1977]).

(Philemon),[64] and despite the fact that all might not gladly receive it. He assumed and requested that at least some of his letters would be heard by more than one congregation (2 Cor. 1:1 [including probably Athens and Cenchrea]; Gal. 1:2; Col. 4:16; Rom. 1:7 [noting the absence of reference to "*the* church"]; and the circular letter Ephesians, if authentic).[65] Likewise 1 Peter assumes a wide distribution (1 Pet. 1:1). For that goal to be accomplished *swiftly* — and the urgency of at least some of these writings required that — an efficient network and an able messenger were essential.

6. Volume and Content

The arrival of epistles from Christians such as Paul brought more information than the text of the letters themselves. Strangers were sometimes used in the ancient world to carry letters,[66] and no doubt many messages between individual Christians passed through the hands of non-Christians.[67] But it is highly unlikely that the apostles committed their papyri for congregations to those who, in their eyes, were under the dominion of the god of this world. Any danger of political intrigue would necessitate the use of trusted messengers.[68]

64. L. Hartman writes, "I doubt that Paul widens the address in order to put pressure on Philemon; the apostle's personal support of Onesimus would be sufficient. Rather, Paul is of the opinion that the letter pleaded the case of Onesimus in such a way that it had something to say to the larger Christian community" ("On Reading Others' Letters," in *Christians Among Jews and Gentiles: Essays in Honor of Krister Stendahl on His Sixty-Fifth Birthday,* ed. G. W. E. Nickelsburg and G. W. MacRae [Philadelphia: Fortress, 1986], 144).

65. Hartman argues that Paul generally had a wider readership in mind when he wrote his letters ("Reading").

66. J. L. White, *Light from Ancient Letters* (Philadelphia: Fortress, 1986), 215f.; Llewelyn, *Documents,* 26-29.

67. For discussion of the availability of couriers and the giving of directions, see Llewelyn, *Documents,* 26-45.

68. Cf. Doty, who notes "the late-Hellenistic tendency to send the real message along with the trusted carrier rather than including it in the letter" (*Letters,* 45); cf. also Llewelyn, *Documents,* 26f.

Several of the letters we possess imply the people who carried them.[69] We do not know who composed the sermon we know as the letter to the Hebrews, but whoever delivered it to its first hearers had a face and a name. Anonymity was *not* a characteristic feature of the holy internet.

The performative aspect of a letter's delivery was crucial.[70] Calculations vary, but a recent major study estimates the percentage of literate people in the ancient Mediterranean world to have been no more than 10 percent, although the figure may have risen to 15 or 20 percent in certain cities.[71] Written messages to a Christian community were delivered with a power and immediacy that was far more gripping than text on a printed page or a computer monitor's screen. P. J. Botha reminds us of our different worlds:

> How we read Paul's letters is in fact a reflection of our self-conception. We strive our very best to present visual knowledge: a neatly

69. E.g. Phoebe (Rom. 16:1-2); Epaphroditus (Phil. 2:25-29); Epaphras, Tychicus, and Onesimus (Col. 1:7; 4:7-9); Titus and an unnamed brother (2 Cor. 8:16-24; 9:3-5); possibly Timothy (1 Cor. 4:17) and Onesimus (Philem. 12); cf. Tychicus (Eph. 6:21-22). Titus probably carried the "severe letter" to the Corinthians (2 Cor. 2:4; 7:6-13). Paul makes no mention of the bearer(s) of the Thessalonian letters and Galatians.

70. See for instance, R. F. Ward, "Pauline Voice and Presence as Strategic Communication," in *Semeia* 65: *Orality and Textuality in Early Christian Literature,* ed. J. Dewey (Atlanta: Scholars Press, 1995), 95-107; this is something to be remembered when Scripture is read today in services of worship.

71. W. V. Harris, *Ancient Literacy* (Cambridge, Mass., and London: Harvard University Press, 1989); H. Y. Gamble essentially agrees, arguing that literacy among Christians was probably even lower (*Books and Readers in the Early Church: A History of Early Christian Texts* [New Haven: Yale University Press, 1995], 1-41). Some put the figure as low as 2 to 4 percent (J. Dewey, "Textuality in an Oral Culture: A Survey of the Pauline Traditions," in *Orality and Textuality in Early Christian Literature,* 39). Dewey comments, "It is virtually impossible for modern academics to realize how unimportant writing and reading were for the conduct of daily life" (44). Literate Christians mentioned in the Pauline letters and Acts would have included Luke the physician (Philem. 24; cf. Col. 4:14), Erastus the city official (Rom. 16:23), and possibly Lydia of Philippi (Acts 16:14, 40) and Crispus (Acts 18:8; cf 1 Cor. 1:14).

printed text, with a clearly marked argument, well balanced paragraphs and properly supporting notes. The intention is to present the perfect visual communication. . . . But what *Paul* did was to engage in dictation. He sent a handwritten, corrected but not without errors, . . . ambiguous, damaged, travel-worn manuscript with someone he trusted, to have that one, or someone else, present his intentions and symbols verbally and bodily to others. What we are looking for is the "objective argument," the "line of thought," the "flow of the argument," which can be represented in spatial lines, diagrammatically, on paper. What we *should* be looking for is an emotional, subjective, playing-up-to-the-audience human being, making meaning present and evoking authority.[72]

When individuals brought letters, the oral report could be just as significant and more thorough than any text. White cites a non-Christian letter that states, "The rest please learn from the man who brings you the letter."[73] Cicero often trusted the remarks of the letter carrier more than the news in the letters he received.[74] Augustus changed the imperial postal system by replacing the relay of couriers with a relay of vehicles, so that the same messenger could make the entire journey, sacrificing speed for fuller information.[75] For a congregation, the first reading of an epistle was only the beginning of the story.[76] Paul assures the Colossians that Tychicus and Onesimus "will tell you about *everything* here" (πάντα ὑμῖν γνωρίσουσιν τὰ ὧδε — Col. 4:7-9; cf. Eph. 6:21); this was evidently a practice they learned from Paul, as Eutychus could testify (Acts 20:7-11). Communication was expanded further

72. P. J. Botha, "The Verbal Art of the Pauline Letters: Rhetoric, Performance and Presence," in *Rhetoric and the New Testament: Essays from the 1992 Heidelberg Conference,* ed. S. E. Porter and T. H. Olbricht (Sheffield: Journal for the Study of the Old Testament Press, 1993), 412f.; his italics.

73. White, *Light,* 216.

74. Botha, "Art," 417, citing *Epistulae ad familiares* 5.4.1; cf. 5.6.1.

75. Llewelyn, *Documents,* 15.

76. "Paul, who made such a point of indicating his trust in the carriers (co-workers), did not think of his written letters as exhausting what he wished to communicate. He thought of his associates, especially those commissioned to carry his letters, as able to extend his own teachings" (Doty, *Letters,* 45).

when Peter, the Lord's brothers, and others were accompanied by their wives who, no doubt, brought a different perspective from that of their husbands (1 Cor. 9:4).

Although he belonged to the next Christian generation, Papias asked all who could tell him what people who had been with Jesus used to say, "for I did not suppose that information from books would help me so much as the word of a living and surviving voice."[77] In the largely nonliterate culture shared by the earliest followers of Jesus, many would have agreed. Data transmission through the holy internet was certainly not as precise as what we get on a screen today, but flesh and blood carried a greater and more immediate content than any hard disk can contain.

7. Conclusion

I have attempted to show that the churches from A.D. 30 to 70 had the motivation and the means to communicate often and in depth with each other. If I am right, news and information could spread relatively quickly between the congregations in the great cities of the empire, and from there into the surrounding regions. As the accompanying chart indicates, many churches were less than a week's travel away from a main hub in the Christian network. News from Ephesus and Corinth, the twin poles of trade in the Aegean Sea and the two places where Paul extended his visits, could reach Rome and Jerusalem in a month or less, if conditions were favorable. Because of the winds, news from the west spread eastward more quickly than news from the east.

It would thus not take long for the word to spread eastward from Rome that Mark had produced a helpful account about Jesus, especially if it was based on Peter's preaching. If the composition of Mark predates the fall of Jerusalem, news of that Gospel would move even quicker once Roman Jewish-Christian pilgrims traveled to the Holy Land for a festival (whether they approved of Mark's theology or not). From there, the information would radiate back to other hubs in the network of Jesus' followers.

77. Eusebius, *Hist. eccl.* 3.39.4 (Loeb edition).

It is one thing to say that information *could* spread quickly, and quite another to prove that it *did.* That remains to be demonstrated in a larger study.[78] Nevertheless, we can say with confidence that Acts and the early epistles preserve good evidence that the early churches had strong reasons for staying in close touch with each other. The implications are wide-ranging and profound, but I will conclude with only three observations relating to the Gospels, the subjects of this book.

First, to my mind it becomes more likely that the Gospels were written not over a period of decades, but within only a few years of each other. Certainly the burden of proof lies on the shoulders of any who would claim that evangelists wrote *many* years apart *and* in ignorance of their predecessors. Recalling the point made earlier about Christians learning from and imitating useful practices, I wonder whether congregations and authors would not want to produce their own version of the Gospel story once they knew that believers in another place had theirs. Some would do so to supplement or complement the traditions they received from their neighbors with additional sayings, stories, and emphases; others might well write to correct or to supplant them. My quotation of Papias's preference for oral tradition may seem to shoot this in the foot, but as many have noted, Papias was comparing the relative significance of an eyewitness with a written witness, not commenting on the absolute value of a text.[79]

A second conclusion follows closely after the first. Unless a community wanted their gospel traditions to be kept secret in Gnostic fashion, we would expect a fairly wide and rapid dissemination of *at least* the knowledge of the existence of their written texts, if not the texts themselves. If our thesis about communication is correct, the

---

78. In addition to the evidence cited here, see also Bauckham's initial article in the present volume.

79. I am not persuaded by W. Kelber's sharp antithesis between oral and written traditions (*The Oral and Written Gospel: The Hermeneutics of Speaking and Writing in the Synoptic Tradition, Mark, Paul and Q* [Philadelphia: Fortress, 1983)]. Cf. e.g. L. Hurtado, "The Gospel of Mark: Evolutionary or Revolutionary Document?" *Journal for the Study of the New Testament* 40 (1990): 15-32; J. Halverson, "Oral and Written Gospel: A Critique of Werner Kelber," *New Testament Studies* 40 (1994): 180-95; and Gamble, *Books,* 28-32.

existence and use of a Gospel becomes harder to keep quiet, and Luke's knowledge of *many* (πολλοί) others' efforts, more understandable (Luke 1:1). It is thus less likely that the gospels were produced for a select few, and more likely that they were written with an eye to their dissemination.

Third and finally, we are again reminded that theories about the origins and relations of the Gospels must be rooted not only in the observed presence or (especially) in the absence of vocabulary and theology, but also in the concrete reality of the first-century world — a world in which communication along the holy internet had a high priority.

Ancient Book Production and the Circulation of the Gospels

LOVEDAY ALEXANDER

Richard Bauckham has put forward the proposition that the Gospels were not, as is commonly supposed, written for particular local congregations but that they were from the start intended for a wider audience. On a broader front, this proposal raises an essentially pragmatic question: How did early Christian books circulate? It is of course impossible to provide a definitive answer to such a question, given the paucity of our information about the practical details of early Christian life in the first century: "The specific motivations and mechanisms by which NT writings were transmitted in the early centuries are still obscure, though understandable enough in broad outline."[1] We can only attempt to proceed, as so often, by analogy and by the disciplined use of the historical imagination, the discipline being provided in this case by the few (often disconnected) pieces of hard information we do possess, like the stray fragments of a long-broken pot which it is the archeologist's job to try to put together again. Any such reconstruction is bound to contain a large amount that is frankly hypothetical: but

1. Eldon Jay Epp, "The Papyrus Manuscripts of the New Testament," in *The Text of the New Testament in Contemporary Research: Essays on the* Status Quaestionis, ed. Bart D. Ehrman and Michael W. Holmes, Studies and Documents 46 (Grand Rapids: Eerdmans, 1995), 10.

the best story, in these circumstances, is simply the one that makes the most convincing use of the largest number of fragments, while retaining an awareness of its essentially hypothetical nature.

What kinds of evidence can we use to construct a hypothetical model for the circulation of books in the early church? There are a number of areas that could fruitfully be explored in this connection: the question of literacy, for example, is a large and important topic that I shall not be able to investigate here. But there are two areas that seem immediately relevant. First, there is abundant material evidence for book production among the early Christians, though it dates not from the first century but from the second and beyond; and, second, there is a copious flow of ancient literary evidence on the production and distribution of non-Christian texts in the ancient world. In what follows I shall look at these two areas separately before asking whether in the end they provide sufficient data to allow us to construct a plausible model for the circulation of Christian texts (especially the Gospels) in the first century.

I. Material Evidence for Early Christian Book Production

There is an accumulation of data from paleography and papyrology that suggests that the early church showed an unusual interest in book production from the earliest centuries of its existence.[2] The sheer volume of early Christian papyri from the second century A.D. onwards (including the many Christian texts of the Greek Old Testament) is an impressive testimony to this fact in itself, as is the early development of a characteristic script ("reformed documentary") and of the distinctive verbal contractions of frequently used names, especially the *nomina*

---

2. The fullest and most recent survey of the evidence on early Christian book production is now Harry Y. Gamble, *Books and Readers in the Early Church: A History of Early Christian Texts* (New Haven and London: Yale University Press, 1995). Christian texts are also discussed at length in Frederick G. Kenyon, *Books and Readers in Ancient Greece and Rome*, 2d ed. (Oxford: Clarendon, 1951), and in E. G. Turner, *Greek Papyri: An Introduction* (Oxford: Clarendon, 1968).

sacra.[3] Equally impressive is the evidence of concerted attempts to stabilize the multiform textual tradition that resulted from this explosion of literary activity, and which suggests that some sections of the church at least could command the kinds of text-critical skills associated with the pagan scholars of Alexandria, perhaps as early as 100 A.D..[4] And above all there is the odd but clearly significant fact that Christian scribes and readers showed a remarkable preference for the new technology of the codex, which they seem to have used more extensively and more consistently than their pagan contemporaries from at least as early as the second century.[5]

This last point is worth spending a little more time on. The codex in Greco-Roman antiquity was effectively a notebook: "proper" books were written in roll form. The term originally denoted a block of wood *(caudex),* and reflects the popularity throughout antiquity of notebooks made of thin wooden boards, which could be joined together by strings or leather thongs to create a shape similar to that of the modern book. The classic format (visible in many paintings and mosaics) consisted of two waxed boards joined together to create a double tablet that could be used and reused at will to record the ephemera of everyday life (school exercises, accounts, notes, lists). Women and schoolboys are often depicted holding these tablets, together with a stylus, which was used both to write in the wax surface

---

3. The evidence is set out fully in C. H. Roberts, *Manuscript, Society and Belief in Early Christian Egypt,* Schweich Lectures 1977 (London: British Academy [Oxford University Press], 1979); Gamble, *Books and Readers,* chap. 2, 42-81. For second-century papyri, see Roberts, *Manuscript, Society and Belief,* 13-14; cf. also E. J. Epp, "Papyrus Manuscripts of the NT," 3-21, in Ehrman and Holmes, *New Testament in Contemporary Research.* For the "reformed documentary," see Roberts, *Manuscript, Society and Belief,* 14. For the *nomina sacra,* cf. Roberts, chap. 2, 26-48.

4. Cf. G. Zuntz, *The Text of the Epistles: A Disquisition upon the* Corpus Paulinum, Schweich Lectures 1946 (London: British Academy [Oxford University Press], 1953), 263-83, esp. 279.

5. The classic study of this phenomenon is C. H. Roberts, "The Codex," *Proceedings of the British Academy* 40 (1954): 168-204, followed by C. H. Roberts and T. C. Skeat, *The Birth of the Codex* (London: British Museum, 1987). Gamble, *Books and Readers,* 49-66, provides a useful survey of more recent discussion.

and to smooth it over for reuse.[6] Larger formats, using as many as ten tablets, were used for archives and ledgers.[7] Writing tablets could also be made from thin slivers of wood cut (like a veneer) from the inside of the timber, which were smooth and white enough to take writing direct. These tablets (which seem to have replaced papyrus as a cheap and readily available writing material in the northern provinces) were typically folded down the middle and sealed for delivery as letters: but they could also be stored (rather in the manner of the modern file card) in archives or jointed concertina-fashion to make a longer notebook. Like papyrus, they are used for letters, draft documents, military dockets and memoranda, and accounts.[8] By the end of the first century A.D., the Romans at least had begun to make small books in the codex format out of parchment, but for the most part these were still thought of as notebooks (Quintilian *Inst. Or.* 10.3.31-2). The fact that the Latin term *membranae* continues to be used as a Greek loanword for a parchment codex strongly suggests that this particular innovation originated in the Western Empire.[9]

6. Cf. the schoolboy in a Gallo-Roman mosaic now in the Landesmuseum, Trier (see fig. 1 below); the "Poetess" from Pompeii, now in the Naples Museum (Kenyon, *Books and Readers,* plate 1; Gamble, *Books and Readers,* plate 1); the "Baker's wife" from Pompeii, also in the Naples Museum (illustrated, e.g., in Peter Clayton, *Treasures of Ancient Rome* [London: Bison Books, 1986], 81). Tablets and styli also appear as decorative motifs in wall paintings: Gamble, *Books and Readers,* plate 5.

7. Cf. the Ostia relief illustrated in Turner, *Greek Papyri,* plate VI, and the tax-collecting scene on the Zirkusdenkmal in the Landesmuseum at Trier (see fig. 2 below). These must be the *polyptychi* described by Vegetius as receptacles for the copious recording of taxation details that was so essential to the bureaucracy of the empire: *Epitoma rei militaris* 2.19, cited in Bowman, *Life and Letters* (see next note), 35.

8. An important collection of these tablets dating from the beginning of the second century A.D. has been discovered at Vindolanda on Hadrian's Wall, and a full description is given in Alan K. Bowman, *Life and Letters on the Roman Frontier* (London: British Museum, 1994). The Vindolanda tablets are published in *The Vindolanda Writing-Tablets (Tabulae Vindolandenses II),* ed. Alan K. Bowman and J. David Thomas (London: British Museum, 1994).

9. Roberts, "The Codex," 174-76; Gamble, *Books and Readers,* 50-52. Gamble plausibly suggests (following Roberts, 190) that the *membranae* of 2 Timothy 4:13 refers to a codex or parchment notebook.

The first attested reference to the use of the codex for literary texts is again from Rome at the end of the first century A.D., in Martial's *Epigrams*. Martial encourages his reader to buy his poems in something that must be some kind of parchment notebook: *"quos artat brevibus membrana tabellis"* [which parchment compresses in small tablets] (*Epigr.* 1.2.3). Its advantages include the fact that it is easy to carry in one hand and offers "companionship on a long journey." Martial here is clearly speaking of a commercial venture and of something of a novelty. Other works were apparently available in the same format: Martial's list of gifts for the Saturnalia includes a number of books, of which some at least must be in the form of parchment codices: a Homer *"in pugillaribus membranis"* [in parchment writing tablets] and texts of Vergil, Cicero, Ovid, and Livy *"in membranis"* [in parchment] (*Epigr.* 14.184, 186, 188, 190, 192). Again, the novelty of this technology is stressed: Martial highlights the compact size of these volumes (186) and their usefulness for long journeys (188).[10] But this enterprising development seems to have been something of a cul-de-sac, at least for the commercial book trade, where the roll remained the dominant medium for literary texts until well into the third century. The codex represents a very small proportion of surviving texts among non-Christian literary papyri in the second century A.D. (around 2 percent of the total), and even in the third century the roll still accounts for 80 percent of non-Christian literary production. It is only in the fourth century that the codex begins to approach parity with the roll in pagan circles.[11]

Christian texts found in Egypt, on the other hand, are almost all in codex form from the early second century onwards.[12] These are not

10. The passages are listed and discussed in Kenyon, *Books and Readers,* 93-95, 130-34; further, Roberts, "The Codex," 177-78. Some at least of these volumes may have been miniatures or epitomes — it is hard to see any other way Livy could be fitted into *pellibus exiguis* (190). The Vergil apparently sports a picture of the author on the first *tabella* (186).

11. Gamble, *Books and Readers,* 49 (and n. 33) and 52 (and n. 41). Roberts, "The Codex," 184 n. 2, gives details of nine second-century pagan codices; cf. further Roberts & Skeat, *The Birth of the Codex,* 71.

12. Epp, "Papyrus Manuscripts of the NT," 5, lists four New Testament papyri (P[12], P[13], P[18], and P[22]) as exceptions to this pattern, but these are either

mere parchment notebooks: the majority are made of papyrus (a medium more difficult to sew together), and codex technology has developed sufficiently to be able to hold an entire Gospel, perhaps even (by the end of the second century) all four canonical Gospels.[13] Estimates vary as to the precise pace and extent of this technological change, but it is clear that, while the technology is not (and was never claimed to be) uniquely Christian, Christians show a "stronger and more effective preference for the codex at an earlier time than non-Christians," and seem to have adapted much faster and more creatively to the new technology than their pagan counterparts.[14]

A number of reasons have been put forward to account for the phenomenal success of the codex among Christian readers. One obvious advantage of the codex over the roll is (as Martial had spotted) its portability, and this certainly came to be appreciated in later centuries.[15] It is also (to our eyes, at least), more easily adaptable for checking references and for teaching purposes: and this may be a common factor which could explain the few non-Christian literary codices of the second

---

opisthographs (i.e., written on the verso of a papyrus roll being reused as scrap paper) or on both sides of the roll, and hence not typical of pagan literary practice. But note also the apparent reference to rolls (described as *libri* and stored in a *capsa*) in the *Acts of the Scillitan Martyrs:* Kenyon, *Books and Readers,* 65 n. 1.

13. T. C. Skeat, "The Oldest Manuscript of the Four Gospels?" *New Testament Studies* 43, no. 1 (1997): 1-34; G. N. Stanton, "The Fourfold Gospel," *New Testament Studies* 43, no. 3 (1997): 317-46.

14. Gamble, *Books and Readers,* 54.

15. Gamble, *Books and Readers,* 275 n. 106, cites the example of a fifth-century Coptic codex of Acts with a cover of wooden boards which could be held tightly shut for safe transport by the attached leather straps. Similar bindings from the sixth century are preserved among the Chester-Beatty papyri in Dublin, illustrated in W. Lockwood, *The Word of God* (Dublin: Chester Beatty Library, 1987), 40-41. These reconstructed bindings, found in a pot buried near the pyramids at Gizeh (probably buried at the time of the Persian occupation, A.D. 616-626) consist of heavy wooden boards with leather spines, tightly closed by long wrapping-bands of leather with bone slip, designed to protect and preserve the book in transit. The traveling missionaries of the Irish church seem to have used leather book-satchels for a similar purpose: cf. the tenth-century Anglo-Saxon cross at Stonegrave Minster, near Helmsley, North Yorkshire (fig. 3 below).

century, which "contain a high proportion of technical or professional texts."[16] But it is hard to see why either of these factors should have been more decisive among Christians than among similar contemporary groups, and a number of scholars have proposed that the crucial factor may have been the success of an authoritative text circulating in the church which happened to use the codex format. C. H. Roberts suggested that the Gospel of Mark (given the connection with Rome) might have been such a text.[17] More recently Harry Gamble has put forward the interesting suggestion that it was the Pauline corpus (taking advantage of the enhanced comprehensiveness of the codex) that provided the impetus.[18] This hypothesis has much to recommend it and should perhaps be linked with the potential role of ancient archival practice in the preservation and collection of Paul's letters: the widespread use of the codex both for private notebooks and for the keeping of accounts would make it an easy development.[19]

16. Roberts, "The Codex," 185. Cf. L. C. A. Alexander, *The Preface to Luke's Gospel,* Society for New Testament Studies Monograph Series 78 (Cambridge: Cambridge University Press, 1993), 172 n. 5; Roberts and Skeat's list of second-century pagan codices (*The Birth of the Codex,* 71) "includes two grammatical manuals and two medical treatises, plus a commentary on Demosthenes, a lexicon to Homer and a *Homeromanteion.* The remainder are copies of classical authors, ranging from Homer to Demosthenes," which may well be school texts. Strikingly, the list also includes two novels (a very high porportion given the paucity of novel texts among the papyri), one of them an Achilles Tatius that must have been hot off the press if the assigned date is correct.

17. Roberts, "The Codex," 187-90.

18. Gamble, *Books and Readers,* 58-65.

19. We know that Paul used secretaries, and it is reasonable to assume that they would have kept copies of the letters he sent out (so, rightly, Gamble, *Books and Readers,* 100-101). This would be in keeping with standard archival practice in the ancient world: cf. Turner, *Greek Papyri,* 47-48, 77-78, 127, 131, 136ff. Cf. Bowman, *Life and Letters,* chap. 4 (on archival practice in the army) and p. 88 (on draft letters). Cf. also J. L. White, *Light from Ancient Letters* (Philadelphia: Fortress, 1986), nos. 5-26, 27-28, 44-51, 63-65; the Theophanes archive (Rylands Papyri IV nos. 623-42) provides a later example from the fourth century A.D., containing household accounts, public documents, private letters and travel accounts. These "archives" are simply collections of loose documents written on single sheets or rolls of papyrus, the universal writing medium in Egypt, though

Whatever its origins, the pattern of Christian usage of the new technology is an observable phenomenon and throws interesting light on a social group which may always have been distinctive in its pattern of book use. We might perhaps compare the situation of the early Irish monastic communities, which combined an otherwise minimal material culture with a lavish and ecstatic devotion to the production of books. It is also important to remember the contemporary analogy of the Qumran sect, which shows a similar surprising fecundity of literary production for a (relatively) small community: note the pragmatic use of locally sourced materials (rolls of sheepskin), with no restriction to uniform sizes for literary texts, and using a range of fast-evolving scripts which are clear, professional, and scholarly but which also show a remarkable diversity and capacity for development over a relatively short period of time.[20] Clearly one common factor shared by these groups is

---

we have cases of draft letters written *seriatim* on the back of a single roll (cf., e.g., White no. 6 = P. Cair. Zen. I 59015 verso). Elsewhere, however, there is evidence for the use of large codices for official accounts and records (cf. n. 7 above), and it is tempting to suggest that such a book might have been used for keeping copies of Paul's letters (and other documents) — cf. 2 Timothy 4:13 (n. 9 above). This seems at least as likely as the suggestion that the letters started life as small codices — Gamble, *Books and Readers,* 64 and n. 94. On Paul's secretaries, see E. R. Richards, *The Secretary in the Letters of Paul,* Wissenschaftliche Untersuchungen zum Neuen Testament 42 (Tübingen: Mohr, 1991).

20. It is unlikely that all the texts found at Qumran were actually produced there, but it is clear at least that multiple copies were produced of sectarian documents like the Community Rule: cf. the 4QS fragments from Cave IV (*Discoveries in the Judaean Desert XXVI, Qumran Cave 4 XIX: Serek ha-Yahad,* ed. P. S. Alexander and G. Vermes [Oxford: Clarendon, 1977]). On the paleography of the Dead Sea Scrolls, see the fundamental studies of N. Avigad, "The Palaeography of the Dead Sea Scrolls and Related Documents," in *Aspects of the Dead Sea Scrolls,* Scripta Hierosolymitana 4 (Jerusalem: Magnes, 1958), 56-87; and F. M. Cross, "The Development of the Jewish Scripts," in *The Bible and the Ancient Near East: Essays in Honour of William Foxwell Albright* (Garden City, N.Y.: Doubleday, 1965), 170-264. On broader aspects of scribal practice, cf. Emmanuel Tov, "Scribal Practices Reflected in the Documents from the Judean Desert and in the Rabbinic Literature: A Comparative Study," in *Texts, Temples, and Traditions: A Tribute to Menahem Haran,* ed. Michael V. Fox et al. (Winona Lake: Eisenbrauns, 1966), 383-403.

the intensive and central importance attached in all of them to the "Word," both written and oral — something not characteristic of ancient religion, nor of the household groups and dining clubs that the churches in other respects resemble: as Nock remarked long ago, to the pagan observer, the average Jewish or Christian group would have looked more like a school than a religion.[21]

But the analogy with medieval Ireland would be misleading if it encouraged us to think of the early Christian book along the lines of the Book of Kells or the Lindisfarne Gospels. The grand illuminated vellum codex of the Carolingian period has been described as "a book capable of the greatest magnificence and beauty that books have ever reached."[22] The papyrus books of antiquity were generally on a far more utilitarian level: even among the bibliolatrous grandees of Republican Rome, "books were not the extravagantly illuminated, almost magical objects they often became in the Middle Ages."[23] But what is true of ancient books in general is even more true of the codex, which seems (apart from the short-lived commercial experiment recorded by Martial) to have occupied a distinctly inferior status to the roll, both in iconography and in terms of its practical use.

Codices and *tabellae* appear not infrequently in the monumental and decorative art of the Roman world, especially in portraits and in the vivid grave-reliefs that commemorate the trades and professions of

21. I have pursued this analogy at greater depth in L. C. A. Alexander, "Schools, Hellenistic," in *The Anchor Bible Dictionary* (New York: Doubleday, 1992), 5:1005-11, and in "Paul and the Hellenistic Schools: The Evidence of Galen," in *Paul in His Hellenistic Context,* ed. Troels Engberg-Pedersen (Minneapolis: Augsburg Fortress, 1995), 60-83.

22. Kenyon, *Books and Readers,* 120. For an illuminating account of the great Irish and Carolingian manuscripts, see C. de Hamel, *A History of Illuminated Manuscripts,* 2d ed. (London: Phaidon, 1994), esp. chap. 1 ("Books for Missionaries") and chap. 2 ("Books for Emperors"). Further, Bernard Meehan, *The Book of Kells* (London: Thames & Hudson, 1994); Janet Backhouse, *The Lindisfarne Gospels* (London: Phaidon, 1981), both with further bibliography.

23. Elizabeth Rawson, *Intellectual Life in the Late Roman Republic* (London: Duckworth, 1985), 45. On the luxury book trade in antiquity, cf. Lucian, *The Ignorant Book-collector (Pros ton apaideuton kai polla biblia onoumenon):* LCL, vol. III.

the middle classes. But in the iconography of these monuments, it is noticeable that the codex seems to hold a rather ambiguous status, often associated with dependent figures: wives, schoolchildren, clerks. In the well-known portrait pair of "The baker and his wife" (probably a minor official) from Pompeii, he carries a roll and she holds writing tablets, most obviously symbolizing her virtues as a careful housewife.[24] The tablets of the famous "Poetess"[25] may have an equally prosaic symbolic value — although (as we shall see) tablets were also used for the first drafts of poems, and it would be a mistake to assume that women were never depicted as anything other than housewives.[26] The differentiation of status between roll and codex is illustrated even more graphically on an early–third-century funerary relief from Roman Gaul: here the householder is commemorated full-size on the front of a large and handsome monument (see fig. 4 below), standing next to his wife and holding a roll (perhaps symbolizing his will), while he sits with his estate clerks in a half-size scene on the side of the monument (see fig. 5 below), busily recording rents (or some other goods received from the peasants whose breeches are dimly discernible in the background) in large *tabellae*. The codex-form belongs to the world of work and commerce on which the householder's wealth is based, not to the leisured, aristocratic lifestyle evoked by the front of the monument.

Similar large *tabellae* appear in other reliefs in the same collection, in scenes connected with the receipt of taxes or harbor dues (see fig. 6 below), and smaller ones in the hands of schoolboys.[27] The scribes who appear writing in large tablet-books in a relief from Ostia, while a bearded figure lectures from a podium center stage, are too old to be schoolboys (one has a beard), but they are clearly in some kind of subordinate position, either taking dictation or recording the speeches

24. Cf. n. 6 above. W. V. Harris, *Ancient Literacy* (Cambridge, Mass.: Harvard University Press, 1989), 107 n. 183 gives further references to illustrations of women holding rolls and tablets.

25. For the "Poetess" cf. n. 6 above. But cf. also n. 26 below.

26. Cf. the Romano-Egyptian mummy-case that commemorates "Hermione grammatike": Turner *Greek Papyri*, pl. III and p. 77.

27. Landesmuseum, Trier. For school scene, cf. Kenyon, *Books and Readers*, opp. p. 56.

and debates going on in the background.[28] These scenes are a salutary reminder that literacy skills are not necessarily an index of elite social status in Greco-Roman society. Many of those who performed writing (and reading) tasks for the elite were in a socially dependent position, like the largely anonymous *servi litterati* who played such a vital role in the intellectual life of Cicero and his circle;[29] and professional scribes and copyists, even when free, were not accorded high social prestige.[30] In these circumstances it may be more appropriate to see literacy as a craft that could be owned and controlled by the wealthy elite, but was not necessarily practiced by them in person; the codex, on this reading, is on a par with other "tools of the trade" that figure in monumental art depicting the skills of craftsmen.[31]

The iconographic status value accorded to the codex in these pictures is of course purely symbolic (*tabellae* were used by writers of

28. Turner, *Greek Papyri*, pl. VI. (Perhaps a law-court scene? Turner suggests a rhetorician or a teacher: p. 189.)

29. Rawson, *Intellectual Life*, 45. The long-suffering slaves of Pliny the Elder would be another example (Plin. *Epp.* III.5). But anyone in the ancient world (including Paul) who dictated a letter illustrates the same principle: those who could not afford a secretary of their own simply used the services of a professional letter-writer.

30. Cf. P. E. Easterling and B. M. W. Knox, "Books and Readers in the Greek World," in *The Cambridge History of Classical Literature*, vol. 1, part 4: *The Hellenistic Period and the Empire*, ed. P. E. Easterling and B. M. W. Knox (Cambridge: Cambridge University Press, 1989), 173: "The copyists were professional craftsmen whose living depended on writing book hands. Many of them must have been slaves; and the profession as a whole never achieved social prestige, except perhaps at the village level, where a scribe might be the only literate member of the community." The ambivalent status of literacy is illustrated neatly by a story told by Josephus in *Ant.* XVI.203: Herod's expensively educated sons are threatened with being reduced to the position of "village clerks," on the grounds that "their present concern with the education which had carefully been given them fitted them for such a position" (tr. LCL; I am indebted to Brook Pearson for this reference).

31. On the importance of craftsmen's tools and implements in Gallo-Roman funerary reliefs, cf. M. Reddé, "Les scènes de métier dans la sculpture funéraire Gallo-romaine," *Gallia* 36, no. 1 (1978): 43-63. Stephen Mitchell, *Anatolia* (Oxford: Clarendon, 1993), 2:61, plate 18, shows a writing tablet appearing in a more schematic form on a gravestone as a symbol of literacy.

all status levels for writing notes or first drafts: see below); but such symbols are not without significance in the status-conscious world of the Greco-Roman city. This particular symbolism may help us to explain why the codex caught on so fast among the early Christians — or rather, perhaps, why it failed to catch on with equal speed among pagan *litterati*. Urban Christians tended to belong precisely to the socially ambiguous groups associated with the codex in iconography: prosperous artisans, small businesspeople and clerks, clients and dependents of the educated elite, but not, for the most part, fully participant in the restricted social world of the dominant literary elite.[32] They may, quite simply (as C. H. Roberts[33] suggested long ago) have had fewer inhibitions about using something that looked like an account book for writing down a serious and substantial religious text. With a smaller stake in the *status quo,* they may also have been more adaptable to innovation, less hidebound by bibliographic convention. We may compare the earlier story of the Athenian cobbler, Simon the Shoemaker, who was immortalized in philosophical tradition for his inventiveness in using leather scraps to jot down notes *(hyposemeioseis)* of the philosophical conversations Socrates held in his workshop.[34]

But the codex also has an intersecting "intermediate" status in

32. For a fuller defense of this reading of the evidence, cf. Alexander, *Preface to Luke's Gospel,* 178-79.

33. Roberts, "The Codex," 187-88; cf. 178, "It is likely enough that the fashionable author or discriminating bibliophile would not favor a format that suggested the lecture room or the counting house."

34. DL II.122-24. These leather notes could be seen as an undeveloped prototype for the use of the parchment notebook for lecture notes. By the time of Diogenes (or his Hellenistic source), however, the dialogues had been recopied and were circulating in the more standard format of the roll: they must have been quite short, given that Diogenes tells us that there are fifteen in one *biblion.* Simon's experiment does not seem to have caught on. Donfried has suggested that Paul the tentmaker (or perhaps Priscilla and Aquila) might have made a similar inspired innovative leap: K. P. Donfried, "Paul as Σκηνοποιός and the Use of the Codex in Early Christianity," in *Christus Bezeugen (für Wolfgang Trilling),* ed. K. Kertelge, T. Holtz, and C.-P. März, Erfurter Theologischer Studien 59 (Freiburg: Herder, 1988), 249-56.

terms of the practical processes of book production: it was "used above all for first drafts, and therefore the *deltos* [tablet] is often put as his symbol by the poet."[35] This primarily practical function is reflected in the many passages that refer to the use of tablets for writing first drafts of poems or speeches.[36] Quintilian recommends wax for first drafts precisely because of the ease of deletion and correction, but he admits that for those with poor sight a parchment notebook may be preferable (X.3.31). If these notes were to be published in book form, however, they would be transferred to rolls (*in libros digesti* X.7.30).[37] The elder Pliny was accompanied everywhere by a "shorthand writer, with book and tablets" ready to take dictation, but the voluminous results of his labors came down to his nephew in the form of 160 opisthograph rolls.[38] Tablets were also used by students (and others) to make lecture notes: when young Marcus Cicero, studying in Athens in 44 B.C., requests the use of a Greek copyist, this is presumably to transfer his notes from tablets to papyrus rolls.[39] The distinctive page layout of the notebook is clearly still thought of as an oddity by Suetonius at the end of the first century A.D. when he describes Julius Caesar's letters to the Senate as "written in a manner never practiced by any before him; for they are distinguished into pages in the form of a memorandum book *(ad paginas et formam memorialis libelli convertisse);* whereas the consuls and commanders till then, used constantly in their letters to continue the line quite across the sheet, without any folding or distinc-

35. Or poetess, of course: cf. n. 21 above. The quotation is from Turner, *Greek Papyri*, 6-7.

36. Cf., e.g., Quintilian XI.2.32: *iisdem quibus scripserit ceris;* X.3.28 *(codices);* X.3.30 *(ceris).*

37. Even Cicero's notes, written as *commentarii* and never intended for publication, underwent some kind of editing at the hands of the faithful Tiro, which may imply that they were transferred to rolls: Quint. X.7.31.

38. Plin. *Epp.* III.5. The implication seems to be that they were recopied onto rolls: Rawson, *Intellectual Life*, 45 n. 29.

39. Cic. *Ad fam.* 16.21.8: *"Sed peto a te, ut quam celerrime mihi librarius mittatur, maxime quidem Graecus; multum enim eripitur operae in exscribendis hypomnematis.* [But I beg of you to see that a secretary is sent me as quickly as possible — best of all a Greek; for that will relieve me of a lot of trouble in writing out lecture notes.]" Cf. Rawson, *Intellectual Life*, 45, and n. 29.

tion of pages."[40] Whatever the meaning of this rather obscure sentence, it seems clear that the characteristic codex format, with one column to a page, made these letters stand out among Caesar's books. This association with notes and first drafts could well add up to a persistent feeling that texts written in codex form were in some way in a more provisional, more transient state than those transferred to a roll.[41] More broadly, the essentially pragmatic origins of the codex may well have colored its subsequent use and may in part account for its slow acceptance as a proper medium for finished books. As Gamble points out, "We should not imagine that the codex moved directly and immediately from the status of a notebook to that of a book. Rather, what began as a utilitarian notebook came to serve as a utilitarian book, which eventually gained regard as a book proper and a genuine peer of the roll."[42] Once again, the early Christians show themselves slightly at odds with the literary establishment, more pragmatic in their attitude to books and less bound by convention. Despite their prodigious interest in book production, this is a group worlds away from the antiquarian snobbery of Lucian's "Ignorant Book-Collector."

All of this material evidence should be kept in mind when considering the question of the circulation of the Gospels in the first

40. Suetonius *Vit. Caes.* 56, trans. Thomson/Forrester; cf. Lewis & Short, sv *libellus*. Kenyon (*Books and Readers,* 57 n. 1) takes this (with some hesitation) to mean "with columns of the narrow width usual in works of prose literature," but this does not seem quite to fit: a *memorialis libellus* must be a notebook or memorandum book, and the easier sense surely is that Caesar's innovation was actually to fold the papyrus sheets on which his letters were written to make a diptych or quire, as opposed to the normal practice of turning the roll ninety degrees and writing across the top end *(transversa charta)* for whatever length the letter demanded. Writing in narrow columns of the kind normally used for a literary text would surely not call for this kind of comment.

41. Gamble, *Books and Readers,* 70 n. 108, cites Turner's suggestion that "scribes who copied on a codex of papyrus in a single column were aware that they were writing a second-class book."

42. Gamble, *Books and Readers,* 65-66. Roberts, "The Codex," 180-81, cites a series of legal rulings from the third century on the definition of "books" for testamentary purposes which illustrate "how easy it was for a parchment notebook to acquire almost imperceptibly the status of a book."

century. It is clear that we are dealing with a group that used books intensively and professionally from very early on in its existence. The evidence of the papyri from the second century onwards suggests the early development (or at least the disproportionately early exploitation) of a technically sophisticated and distinctive book technology. The random but impressive distribution of Christian papyri also suggests that this was a group which had developed its own efficient networks of communication by the mid-second century.[43] And the particular book styles chosen suggest a pragmatic attitude to books that may also be relevant to the question of circulation. Christian books adopted the "utilitarian" format of the codex "not because they enjoyed a special status as aesthetic or cult objects, but because they were practical books for everyday use: the handbooks, as it were, of the Christian community." These are in-house productions, showing few signs of the professional book trade, and this practical attitude is also reflected in the "reformed documentary" script of the earliest Christian texts, "a script that is practical and legible, that by no means approaches a calligraphic bookhand and yet resists the tendencies toward documentary scrawl."[44] Other features shared with documentary rather than literary texts are the marking of paragraphs by larger initial letters, and the use of abbreviations (cf. the distinctively Christian development of contractions for certain frequently used divine titles, the *nomina sacra*); as Alan Millard has pointed out, both features may also be influenced by scribal practice from Syria-Palestine.[45] If this is correct, it is itself a reminder that early Christian book technology presupposes robust and vigorous intercommunity connections across the eastern Mediterranean area. And whatever their origins, these features help to create an effect of a distinctive book style which, "though not an esoteric code, stands out as an in-group convention

43. Gamble, *Books and Readers,* 82.

44. Gamble, *Books and Readers,* 66, 71.

45. Alan Millard, "Ancient Abbreviations and the *Nomina Sacra,*" in *The Unbroken Reed: Studies in the Culture and Heritage of Ancient Egypt, in Honour of A. F. Shore,* ed. C. Eyre, A. & L. M. Leahy (London: Egypt Exploration Society, 1994), 221-26.

that expressed a community consciousness and presumed a particular readership."[46]

II. The Circulation of Texts in the Greco-Roman World

It is easy to make anachronistic assumptions about ancient book production based on our experience of "print culture." The ancient book trade bears little resemblance to its modern counterpart — though the advent of new technologies, in the era of the photocopier, the pirate video, and the Internet, may paradoxically mean a return to conditions much more like those in which ancient authors worked.[47]

The primary means of publication in Greco-Roman antiquity was *oral performance*. This was as true in the Greek city-states of the Hellenistic and imperial periods as it had been in the archaic Greek world of Homer and Pindar, and Rome adopted the practice. It was not only the primary oral genres, like drama or rhetoric, that were performed in this way: Lucian, in the second century A.D., speaks of an audience "hearing" the latest histories read, and Tacitus paints a melancholy (if ironical) picture of the poet who has to hire a room and arrange the chairs himself in a vain pursuit of fame and fortune.[48] Rawson (1985, 51-53) paints a vivid picture of the variety of ways in which residents of Rome in the last century of the Republic might hear literary works performed: readings at dinner parties; public lectures or courses given by teachers of *grammatice* or medicine; theatrical performances; public recitations given by poets or orators in the Forum or the baths. The wealthy employed not only secretaries to do their writing but *anagnostae* to read to them and their friends, whether slaves or freedmen like the ones employed by Atticus and Cicero, or the tame household scholar who was "expected to be a walking dictionary, indeed a walking encyclopedia, for quotations and informa-

46. Gamble, *Books and Readers,* 78.

47. On publication in general see Gamble, *Books and Readers,* chap. 3; B. van Groningen, "ΕΚΔΟΣΙΣ," *Mnemonsyne* 16 (1963): 1-17; Raymond J. Starr, "The Circulation of Literary Texts in the Roman World," *Classical Quarterly* 37 (1987): 213-23; Easterling and Knox, "Books and Readers in the Greek World," 154-97.

tion of all sorts were, as is well known, difficult to check in rolls, even if the right works were available."[49] In the more developed performance culture of the cities of the Greek East, we might add the regular lectures put on by the gymnasium and the public speeches of visiting sophists.[50]

Alongside this lively tradition of oral performance there was also a *commercial booktrade,* though it bears little resemblance to the modern publishing business. The fundamental fact that there was no author's copyright in the ancient world meant that there was no authorial control over copying, and no means for reimbursing authors for multiple sales. A writer's prime motive for wanting sales for his books would be fame and publicity, not money.[51] There were profits to be made from books, but only by booksellers and copyists, not by authors or publishers. The older view of ancient "publishing houses," with trained scribes producing up to a thousand copies of a manuscript simultaneously from dictation, is widely recognized to be a fantasy.[52] Atticus's household of

48. Lucian *How to Write History* §5; Tacitus *Dialogue* §9.

49. Rawson, *Intellectual Life,* 51-53. On the ambiguous role of the dependent scholar, see further Lucian *On Salaried Posts in Great Houses,* and Rawson, "Roman Rulers and the Philosophic Adviser," in *Philosophia Togata,* ed. Miriam Griffin and Jonathan Barnes (Oxford: Clarendon, 1989), 233-57.

50. H. I. Marrou, *History of Education in Antiquity,* English trans. of 3d ed. (New York: Sheed & Ward, 1956), part 2, chap. 9. F. G. Downing, "A bas les aristos: The Relevance of Higher Literature for the Understanding of the Earliest Christian Writings," *Novum Testamentum* 30 (1988): 210-30, rightly stresses the importance of oral performance in the cultural life of the Greek city.

51. It is easy to assume that Martial had some financial interest in the sales of his books, given that he persistently refers friends who ask to be given copies of his books to the booksellers: Martial I.117.8-17; IV.72.1-4; XIII.3. But Starr ("Circulation of Literary Texts," 215) has a simpler explanation: Martial simply wants to avoid the trouble and expense of making the copy himself. It seems likely that an author in Martial's position might receive a flat fee from the bookseller for an authorized copy of a new manuscript (Gamble, *Books and Readers,* 87): but no further fees or royalties would be due to the author after the initial purchase, and there was nothing to stop the author continuing to distribute privately made copies at will.

52. R. Sommer, "T. Pomponius Atticus und die Verbreitung von Ciceros Werken," *Hermes* LXI (1926): 389-422; Starr, "Circulation of Literary Texts"; Easterling and Knox, "Books and Readers in the Greek World," 172-74; Gamble, *Books and Readers,* 88.

pueri litteratissimi, anagnostae optimi et plurimi librarii should almost certainly be seen as a rather lavish extension of the normal practice of private copying, not as a commercial enterprise.[53]

Nevertheless, there was a book trade, and booksellers and copyists must all have been able to make a living out of it, if only a modest one. The evidence goes as far back as the end of the fifth century B.C., and Xenophon's *Anabasis* at the beginning of the fourth century reports finding cases of books washed up on the Black Sea coast, clear testimony to a healthy export trade in books.[54] The founding of the great Hellenistic libraries in Alexandria and Pergamum must have provided further stimulus to the book trade.[55] But our best evidence comes from Rome, which seems to have seen an explosion of commercial book production in the first century A.D.: although Cicero complains of the scarcity of good copyists in the commercial book market, Galen in the second century A.D. implies that there are a large number of booksellers in the Sandalarium — though their reliability does not seem to have improved.[56] Roman writers like Horace and Martial make it clear that it was not difficult for the budding author in the first century of the principate to find booksellers who would be glad to copy and sell their wares, though there are many complaints about the carelessness of the professional copyists. The papyri demonstrate that there were professional scribes with professional standards producing large quantities of literary texts (especially the classics) for the cultured elite and their libraries. Certain standards were expected for "literary" works, at least in appearance, though the accuracy of the text itself could leave a lot to be desired.[57]

But the commonest method used to ensure the circulation of a literary text was "private" (as opposed to commercial) copying, whether

53. "Highly educated slaves, the best readers, and many copyists": Nepos *Vit. Att.* 13.3. Cf. Gamble, *Books and Readers,* 86, and n. 15.

54. Xenophon *Anabasis* VII.5.14: Easterling and Knox, "Books and Readers in the Greek World," 161-63.

55. Easterling and Knox, "Books and Readers in the Greek World," 189-90.

56. Cicero: cf. Rawson, *Intellectual Life,* 42-43. For Galen, see further below.

57. Carelessness: Rawson, *Intellectual Life,* pp. 42-43; Turner, *Greek Papyri,* 92-93, 107-109; Easterling and Knox, "Books and Readers in the Greek World," 173-74.

of an authorized text made available by the author or in the various pirated versions which could be circulated by auditors. The simplest way to obtain a copy of a book was to find a friend (or a library) who had an exemplar and would let you make your own copy from it: if you were wealthy enough to own a literate slave, you could get him (or her[58]) to do it for you. There is ample evidence to show that making one's own copy was normal practice in scholarly and intellectual circles in Rome and across the empire. Cicero's letters are full of passing references to his own libraries and those of his friends and acquaintances, where books new and old can be consulted or copied; one of the most famous cases is that of the newly discovered Aristotelian texts which came into Rome when Sulla captured the library of Apellicon.[59] Galen, encouraging a wealthy young man to spend his money on books rather than on gourmet meals, advises not only the purchase and preparation of books but the training of scribes and readers.[60] Students normally spent a great deal of their time (then as now) copying out notes, either of their lectures or of books in libraries: we have already mentioned the complaints of Marcus Cicero the younger on this score. In expert hands, such notes could in their turn form the basis of a digest or commentary, with the reader's glosses alongside excerpts from the original text. Ironically these privately made copies are often the "best" texts in scholarly terms: they are scholars' own working copies, written for private use and carefully corrected, but not necessarily the best-*looking* texts either in script or in material.[61] Lecture notes form another well-known category of "private" copies, this time derived more

58. In an interesting paper at the 1996 Society of Biblical Literature Annual Meeting, Kim Haines-Eitzen cited a number of epigraphic commemorations of female scribes.

59. For the Ciceronian evidence cf. Rawson, *Intellectual Life*, 39-44; Starr, "Circulation of Literary Texts," passim. The fate of Apellicon's library is well described by Luciano Canfora, *The Vanished Library* (London: Vintage, 1991), pp. 56-58, 173-82.

60. Galen, *The Diagnosis and Cure of the Soul's Passions*, ch. ix (Marquardt, *Galenus Scripta Minora* [Leipzig: Teubner, 1884], vol. I, 37.12-16).

61. Turner, *Greek Papyri*, 112-24; cf. 92-96: "There are of course beautiful handwritings among them; but in general the handwritings we shall find will be of a workaday kind."

or less directly from oral presentation. Teachers complained frequently of the inaccurate and garbled accounts of their classes which circulated in the form of students' notes (cf. the examples from Quintilian and Galen, cited below); but the fact is that many of our surviving texts from the ancient world originated as lecture notes, sometimes surviving in more than one version, and our knowledge of ancient philosophy and medicine (and other technical subjects) would be all the poorer without them.[62]

It is evident from all this that the lines of demarcation between oral performance and written text (or between author and reader) are much more complex and less clear-cut than our experience of "print culture" might lead us to expect. In recent scholarship much attention has been focused on the moment of transition from oral performance to written text.[63] Here we need not go into the heated debate about the hermeneutics of the process but simply pick up the point made by Richard Bauckham above, that when we talk about the composition of written Gospels we are already talking about texts that have in some degree made the transition from their primary oral situation. And the crossing of the oral/written boundary is often connected in the ancient world with an extension of the audience beyond the limits of the primary oral situation: in fact this is precisely the objection raised to the promulgation of written *technai* in Plato's *Phaedrus:*

62. For an example, cf. Arrian, *Discourses of Epictetus,* preface. Further discussion in W. W. Jaeger, Aristotle: *Fundamentals of the History of His Development,* 2d ed. (Oxford: Clarendon, 1948), esp. chap. IX; L. C. A. Alexander, *The Preface to Luke's Gospel,* chap. 4. Cf. David Sedley, "Philosophical Allegiance in the Greco-Roman World" (Griffin and Barnes, *Philosophia Togata,* 1989), 103f.: "Indeed, in Philodemus's philosophical texts the debt to his master is greater still, for some of them are really just his writing up of the lecture notes he took at Zeno's classes in Athens. His book *On Frankness . . .* is marked below the title as being ἐκ τῶν Ζήνωνος σχολῶν, that is, probably, based on notes 'from Zeno's classes,' as is at least one other work."

63. Notably, W. J. Ong, "Writing Is a Technology that Restructures Thought," in *The Written Word: Literacy in Transition,* ed. Gerd Baumann (Oxford: Clarendon, 1986), 23-50; Werner Kelber, *The Oral and the Written Gospel* (Philadelphia: Fortress, 1983). There are a number of interesting articles on this topic in Henry Wansborough, ed., *Jesus and the Oral Gospel Tradition* (Sheffield: Sheffield Academic Press, 1991), especially Andersen, "Oral Tradition," 17-58.

Once a thing is put in writing, the composition, whatever it may be, drifts all over the place, getting into the hands not only of those who understand it, but equally of those who have no business with it; it doesn't know how to address the right people, and not address the wrong. And when it is ill-treated and unfairly abused it always needs its parent to come to its help, being unable to defend or help itself.[64]

But the process is by no means a simple, one-step operation. A selection of concrete examples will illustrate the diversity of both motive and means involved in the circulation of texts in the ancient world.

1. The Corresponding Scholars Model

A papyrus letter from Oxyrhynchus towards the end of the second century A.D. gives us a vivid insight into "a circle of persons exchanging notes on how to procure and get copies made of works of scholarship, who are themselves professional scholars."[65] The letter (only the second column of which is legible) has two postscripts in different hands:

(1) Make and send me copies of Books 6 and 7 of Hypsicrates' *Komodoumenoi, Men Made Fun Of in Comedy.* For Harpocration says that they are among Polion's books. But it is likely that others, too, have got them. He also has his prose epitomes of Thersagoras's works *On the Myths of Tragedy.*

(2) According to Harpocration, Demetrius the bookseller has got them. I have instructed Apollonides to send me certain of my own books, which you will hear of in good time from Seleucus himself. Should you find any, apart from those which I possess, make copies and send them to me. Diodorus and his friends also have some which I haven't got.

64. Plato, *Phaedrus* 275e, trans. Hackforth.
65. P.Oxy. 2192, trans. Turner, *Greek Papyri,* 87. The scholars named in this text are known to have had a connection with the Museum.

What is interesting here is the way in which intersecting social circles of like-minded intellectuals are also vehicles for the transmission of texts via copying, a task that can be performed to order once the desired text has been located. The role of the bookseller in all this is almost incidental, though he is clearly useful as an extra potential source for scholarly books: what is central, and primary, is the expectation that books are for sharing, and that acquiring a particular book for oneself means having one's own copy made.[66]

But the pattern is a much older one, visible in Cicero (as we have seen), and in the letters that preface some of the mathematical treatises of Archimedes and Apollonius of Perga in the third century B.C.. These letters reflect the wide geographical extension of this particular social network: the Hellenistic mathematicians were never members of a geographically unified "school" but were always dependent on maintaining lines of communication by sending written texts to their peers across the Mediterranean.[67] Here the very existence of the letters testifies to an extension of personal and collegial communication across geographical space. Apollonius of Perga, for example, explains in a letter to Eudemus that the original impulse for writing the *Conics* was a visit from "Naucrates the geometer," to whom Apollonius entrusted an earlier, uncorrected draft; once this stage was reached, other visitors could be allowed to see drafts of the first two books. The letter is written to accompany a copy sent to Eudemus for correction. But the act of writing itself allows for and invites a further extension of the audience: Eudemus is invited to "share" the text with other mathematical friends if they pass through his home town, and after Eudemus's death, the habit of written communication is so well established that Apollonius continues to write letters and send books to another (and apparently less intimate) addressee.[68] Archimedes, similarly, maintains the habit of sending his mathematical theorems to colleagues across the Mediter-

---

66. Turner cites a contemporary note on the back of a prose farce: "From the library of Praxias. Heraclides copied it." Turner, *Greek Papyri*, 181 n. 37.

67. For a fuller description of these texts and their social context, cf. Alexander, *Preface to Luke's Gospel*, 47-52.

68. Apollonius of Perga *Conica:* prefaces to books I, II, and IV.

ranean even after the death of an earlier correspondent.[69] Committing one's ideas to writing is by no means an inevitable process: but once the Rubicon is crossed, it is almost as if the mere existence of a written text demands a wider audience.

2. The Rhetorical Performance Model

Rhetoric was essentially a performance art whose object was live, oral presentation of a carefully crafted speech appropriate to the occasion. A high premium was placed on the ability to extemporize, but it was widely accepted that in normal circumstances a speech would be prepared in advance on writing tablets. Quintilian insists, however, that the entire speech should be memorized for the performance itself: it was no more acceptable for an orator to read from a prepared script than for an actor to perform from a prompt copy. Only the briefest of notes — a bare reminder of the speech's headings — might be held in the hand to jog the memory.[70]

Written texts of speeches played an ambivalent role in this artificially maintained oral culture. In a famous scene of embarrassment, Philostratus tells of a professedly *ex tempore* declamation by the traveling sophist Philagrus that was rudely interrupted by ribald auditors, who, discovering that the speech had been given at the orator's previous location, obtained a written copy and started reading it aloud as an unwanted chorus, much to the speaker's discomfort and the amusement of the crowd.[71] Here the written text is used with mischievous intent to break the artificial constraints of the oral situation by circulating it in a way that is certainly contrary to the performer's intent. But a written text may also be used, quite legitimately, to preserve the gist (or even the whole script) of a speech long after the original oral situation is past. Quintilian tells of seeing Cicero's own notes for some of his speeches, which were still in circulation more than a century after

69. Cf., e.g., *de Lin. Spir.* pref., *Quadr.* pref.
70. Quintilian *Inst. Or.* XI.2.
71. Philostratus *Vitae Sophistarum* 579.

the author's death. These were genuine author's notes, Quintilian believed, collected and copied up by the faithful Tiro: *in libros digesti* presumably implies a process of translation from the wax tablets used for first drafts to the more permanent format of the roll (see above). The change could, of course, be an encouragement to give one's "notes" a rather more polished finish. Here again it is clear that the written text reaches a wider audience (both in space and in time) than the oral performance could have done: but the written text does not thereby lose the dramatic specificity of the original oral situation.

3. The Disappearing Lecture Notes Model

There was a similar ambivalence about the role of written texts in a teaching situation: others besides Papias maintained that learning from the "living voice" of the teacher was intrinsically superior to learning from books.[72] Nevertheless it is clear that written texts of (or based on) oral lectures circulated widely, both with and without their authors' consent. Quintilian prefaces his magnum opus on the training of the orator with a warning about an unauthorized edition, based on notes taken at his lectures, which is already in circulation (I. pref. 7-8, LCL):

> Two books on the art of rhetoric are at present circulating under my name, although never published by me nor composed for such a purpose *(neque editi a me neque in hoc comparati)*. One is a two-days' lecture which was taken down by the boys who were my audience. The other consists of such notes as my good pupils succeeded in taking down from a course of lectures on a somewhat more extensive scale: I appreciate their kindness, but they showed an excess of enthusiasm and a certain lack of discretion in doing my utterances the honor of publication *(temerario editionis honore)*. Consequently in the present work, although some passages remain the same, you

72. L. C. A. Alexander, "The Living Voice: Scepticism Towards the Written Word in Early Christian and in Greco-Roman Texts," in *The Bible in Three Dimensions*, ed. D. J. A. Clines, S. E. Fowl, and S. E. Porter (Sheffield: Sheffield Academic Press, 1990), 221-47.

will find many alterations and still more additions, while the whole theme will be treated with greater system and with as great perfection as lies within my power *(omnia vero compositiora et, quam nos poterimus, elaborata).*

As Quintilian tells it, the story is one of misguided student enterprise: but, as with Philagrus, the inevitable result is that the written text circulates more widely than the original audience of the lectures. Galen tells of many similar experiences, though in his case it was the author who initiated the process:

> Three other books . . . , when I was studying in Smyrna, I wrote to please a fellow-student who was about to travel to his homeland after being away, so that he could use them to practice making an anatomical demonstration. But in the meanwhile when the young man died the books were in the possession of certain people; it was suspected that they belonged to my practice, but somebody was caught adding a preface of some sort to them and then reading them as his own.[73]

Here the situation is exacerbated by the added factors of geographical distance and the death of the original recipient, which makes the determination of intellectual property rights even more difficult. In all these cases, the written text is essentially the same material as the oral performance but may be extended, fossilized, and finalized in different ways. And it is obvious that the written text that emerges from this situation is anything but fixed: texts like this positively invite additions, glosses, expansions, and rearrangements, as their authors frequently complain. Again, it is clear that the boundary between oral and written must be seen as fluid rather than fixed.

The results of this practice are graphically illustrated in the invaluable bibliographical monographs that Galen wrote to clarify the chaotic situation into which his books had fallen:

---

73. Galen *De libris propriis* II (Kühn XIX.17-21 = *Scripta Minora* II.97-101), author's translation.

The soundness of your advice, most excellent Bassus, about the writing of my books has been clearly demonstrated by events. Just there in the Sandalarium, where most of the booksellers in Rome are, we were watching some people arguing whether a particular book on sale was by me or by somebody else — for it was inscribed [*epigrapsetai*] "Galen the doctor." Someone had bought it on the assumption that it was mine when a certain learned man, arrested by the oddity of the inscription, decided to verify its claim. He read the two first lines and immediately threw the book away, saying only this by way of explanation: that this was not Galen's style and that the book was falsely inscribed. . . .[74]

Galen seems exasperated but not unduly distressed at this story: having one's name on the bookstalls, even if wrongly attributed, is presumably some index of a not entirely unwelcome notoriety. But it is clear that Galen's fame as a medical writer (which by this date is considerable) rests on two pillars quite independent of the commercial booktrade: his public lectures and demonstrations; and the circulation of his books among friends and students. Not that the latter is without its trials: friends and students seem to be quite as unscrupulous as the booksellers (though for different reasons) when it comes to accurate transmission and attribution:

So for this very reason, and because many people have mistreated my books in many different ways (for they have read them as their own among one nation or another, after taking things out, adding things and changing things), I think it best to demonstrate first the reason for this maltreatment, then to set out which were really written by me and what their contents are.

As for the reason why many read my books as their own, this you know yourself, most excellent Bassus; for they were given to friends or pupils without an inscription *(choris epigraphes)*, simply because they were not for publication but were done for those very people as they requested memoranda of what they had heard. Then when

74. Galen *De libris propriis* proem (Kühn XIX.8-11 = *Scripta Minora* II.91-93), author's translation.

some died, anyone who got hold of the books and liked them took to reading them as their own . . . [lacuna] . . . , [while others shared them with friends, who then] went home to their own country and after some delay, one in one place, one in another, started to perform their own demonstrations [or: lectures] from them. In time they were all detected and a number of people inscribed my name on the texts which had once again been recovered; but when they discovered that they were different from the texts held by others they brought them to me and begged me to correct them.

Now since, as I said, they had not been written for publication but according to the particular state and need of those who had requested them, it was only to be expected that some would have been expanded and others shortened, and that the explanation and the very teaching of the theorems would be complete in some cases and deficient in others. Particularly in the case of those that were written down from oral teaching, it was obvious that they would not have the instruction in a complete or accurate form, given that they neither wanted nor were able to learn everything accurately, before acquiring some practice in the essentials. Some of my predecessors called this type of book "outlines," just as some call them "sketches" or "introductions" or "synopses" or "guides." I just used to give them to my students without any inscription *(choris epigraphes),* and thus later as they came into the hands of others, one gave them one title, one another.

Galen appears to distinguish here between the notes he gave out himself to his auditors and the texts he prepared "for publication" *(pros ekdosin),* which are by implication more likely to carry a proper *epigraphe* giving the author's name and the title of the work.[75] What precisely Galen means by *ekdosis* is less clear: it may mean no more than the issuing of a revised, authorized edition from which copies could in turn be made,[76] but it is equally clear that copies of the earlier, "unauthorized" editions were freely available and in wide circulation.

75. See further Loveday Alexander, *Acts,* New Testament Readings, ed. John Court (London: Routledge, forthcoming 1998), chap. 2.
76. See the full discussion of the evidence in Starr, "Circulation of Literary Texts," and the literature cited there.

4. The Patronage Model

Dedicating a book to a patron may be seen as another means of extending a book's audience. "I have resolved," says one Hellenistic geographical writer to his royal patron, "to offer you this useful compilation so as to provide through you a common service for all those who wish to pursue learning."[77] This does not mean that the patron was expected to act as a "publisher" to the work, but it does imply that a patron might provide access to a wider audience.[78] This may be envisaged in a number of ways. Ps.-Scymnus, when he speaks (lines 61-63) of the king's "hearth," is invoking one of the simplest and oldest models of literary patronage, the court tradition of hospitality to a traveling poet or scholar involving the provision of not only board and lodging but also — and just as importantly — a social context for the public performance and discussion of the work. The great Hellenistic monarchies of Alexandria and Pergamum simply extended this ancient principle with their large-scale foundations of libraries and (at Alexandria) the Museum: but the idea that a wealthy patron could provide a social framework for scholarly communication is equally important within the great houses of republican and imperial Rome.[79] This system — with all its developments and ramifications — had the potential to offer an author an entree into a different social network of the patron's own peers, whether by oral performance within the patron's house, or by the deposition of a presentation copy of a book in the patron's private library. Once there, a book would implicitly be available to any of the patron's friends who wished to read or copy it.

It is important to remember, however, that this model provides a potential extension of a book's circulation, not a limitation. The evidence of the prefaces suggests that scientific and technical writers, at least, did not take the interests of their exalted patrons too seriously:

77. Ps.-Scymnus *Orbis descriptio*, lines 5-10, author's trans. (C. Müller, ed., *Geographi Graeci Minores* [Paris: Didot, 1855], I:196). Further on this dedication, Alexander, *Preface to Luke's Gospel*, 57.

78. Cf. the fuller discussion in Alexander, *Preface to Luke's Gospel*, 193-200.

79. Cf. especially Rawson, "Roman Rulers and the Philosophic Adviser."

Pliny, for example, makes it clear that he does not expect that Titus will actually *read* the *Natural History*.[80] In other words, as we have seen, technical authors had their own networks of communication and did not rely on the offices of a patron to distribute their works (this may be one reason why patronage — and access to the literary elite — was perhaps more important for poets.[81] Probably the relationship was most effective when there was some shared interest between patron and writer, for example, where the patron was a fellow-member of the same philosophical school, as in the case of Philodemus.

III. The Circulation of the Gospels

This summary can only scratch the surface of the immense pool of information, both literary and material, that we possess about the production and circulation of books in the ancient world. Much more remains to be considered — especially, perhaps, the Qumran scrolls, and the library at Herculaneum, both of which give us valuable information about book production outside Egypt.[82] However, certain points do begin to emerge more clearly and enable us to draw some tentative conclusions relevant to our question about the circulation of the Gospels.

One point that emerges clearly is the continuing importance of the "private" factor in the copying and production of texts, alongside the commercial copying of the booktrade (in fact neither booksellers nor authors could do anything to stop it). This factor in its turn underlines the extent to which the circulation of literature (any kind of literature) in the ancient world depended on the prior existence of social networks:

> Traditionally, then, publication took place in the context of social relations between persons interested in literature, and subsequent

80. Pliny *Nat. hist.* preface.

81. Starr, "The Circulation of Literary Texts," 222 n. 71.

82. Turner, *Greek Papyri,* 39) notes that quantities of wax tablets ("their number is legion") were found on the floor of the library at Herculaneum. See further Marcello Gigante, *Philodemus in Italy: The Books from Herculaneum,* trans. Dirk Obbink (Ann Arbor: University of Michigan Press, 1995), esp. chap. 2.

copies of the work circulated along paths of friendship or personal acquaintance. For the most part, these networks existed before and apart from literary interests, arising partly on the basis of those factors that defined the upper class, providing it the leisure to read, partly through the complex relations of patrons and clients, and partly through the natural affinity of persons of talent and cultivated interests.[83]

But the definition of these social networks should not be drawn too narrowly in terms of the literary interests of the "upper class." Technical and scientific interests created their own social networks, intersecting with but not identical with those of the leisured classes, and texts circulated fast along these circuits too. If the Christians had such networks, as Gamble points out (and clearly they did), they were simply exemplifying a variant of the normal patterns for the circulation of books in the ancient world.

Second, it is clear that there is support for Richard Bauckham's contention that the writing down of the Gospels itself implies the crossing of an invisible boundary between the implicitly limited audience of an oral performance and the wider audience that can be reached by a written text. Whatever the origins of Papias's and Clement's stories of the genesis of Mark's Gospel as a written version of Peter's oral preaching, there are good ancient parallels for the practice of circulating written texts based on authors' memoranda or auditors' notes of oral teaching.[84] But the messiness of the process suggests that we should be careful about painting the divide in too rigid terms. Galen's stories presuppose an element of continuity between oral performance and written text that should make us wary of seeing the process in terms of a simple dichotomy:

oral = specific audience
written = general audience

---

83. Gamble, *Books and Readers*, 85.

84. Papias *ap.* Euseb. *Hist. Eccl.* III.39; Clem. Alex. *Adumbrationes ad I Petr.* 5.13. Cf. Alexander, *Preface to Luke's Gospel*, 198-99.

Rather, we might reflect that the apparent ease with which the Gospels made the transition (despite the survival of a few apparent "fossils" like the "Alexander and Rufus" of Mark 15:21) suggests that the oral teaching that lies behind the written texts was itself perhaps more generally conceived "for all Christians" than we have been accustomed to think — or, to put it another way, that the communication networks between Christian congregations had an effect on the way teaching was structured and expressed even at the oral level. Teachers, after all, were mobile even before texts were: and though a written text could travel (as the letters do), it could equally be prized as something that could *stay* in a particular congregation when the teacher whose tradition it embodied moved on.

It may be relevant here to bring in the material evidence on early Christian book production. It is tempting to link the various kinds of lecture notes described by Galen and Quintilian with the traditional and well-attested use of the codex for these "intermediate" stages in book production, as discussed in part one above. The codex, as we have seen, was the normal vehicle both for authors' drafts and for students' notes of an oral performance or teaching. As long as the provisional format of the wax tablet is used, it may be possible to preserve the demarcation between draft/notes and *editio* without too much difficulty; the act of copying from tablets to roll must mark some kind of visible stage in the procedure, though it will not necessarily alter the nature and content of the text at all (Quintilian's students presumably copied their notes from tablets to rolls before circulating them: which may be what Quintilian means by *temerario editionis honore*). But once you start writing your notes in *membranae,* which do not have the same essentially transitory nature, there is no further need to transfer the text to rolls, and the distinction is effectively eliminated — provided your readers are prepared to overlook the book's unorthodox format. (It would be valuable to explore in this connection the *literary* evidence for the character of early Christian books: Tertullian, for example, calls the Gospels *commentarii,* i.e. *hypomnemata* or "notes."[85]) In this view,

---

85. Tertullian *De ieiunio* X.3. On the terminology, cf. F. Bömer, "Der *Commentarius,*" *Hermes* 81 (1953): 210-50.

the only unusual part of the process is the fact that Christian books retained and developed the codex format instead of being transferred to rolls: but there is some evidence, as we have seen, that textbooks and commentaries also retained this format.

Nevertheless it is clear, as we have already seen, that this kind of "private" copying involved as wide circulation as any other kind of "publication" in the ancient world. The process might be haphazard, but it could be remarkably effective:

> Copies were disseminated without regulation through an informal network composed of people who learned of the work, were interested enough to have a copy made, and knew someone who possessed the text and would permit it to be duplicated. Thus a text made its way into general circulation gradually and for the most part haphazardly, in a pattern of tangents radiating from the points, ever more numerous, where the text was available for copying.[86]

Moreover we can see from Galen that such lecture notes could be regarded as "intermediate" in another sense — that is, they represent a transitory stage between one oral performance (Galen's) and another ("they took to reading them as their own. . . . they started to perform their own demonstrations [or: lectures] from them"). The process in this case is represented as fraudulent: but there is no reason in principle why texts written as a summary of a body of material taught in one place should not be used as a basis for teaching in another.

It is relevant to bring in some of the literary features of our Gospel texts at this point. Luke's prefaces and dedications, as has often been observed, seem to indicate that the author is paying a certain degree of attention to the presentation of his work in book form. The use of a secondary preface to Acts (whether or not the two works were originally conceived as volumes of a unitary composition) suggests a certain consciousness of the dimensions of the work and of the need for readers

---

86. Gamble, *Books and Readers,* 85. In a review session on *Books and Readers in the Early Church* at the Society of Biblical Literature 1996 Annual Meeting, Harry Gamble underlined that one of the most important points to emerge from his study was the rapidity with which early Christian writings traveled.

to be aware of the connections between the two volumes: it has been estimated that the length of Luke and Acts corresponds very closely to the standard length for a book roll.[87] Moreover the dedication to Theophilus seems to indicate rather more ambitious literary aspirations than the kind of "notes" that we have been suggesting. Dedication, in fact, seems to be linked very often with a desire to "fix" a fluid tradition by depositing a definitive form of the text in the care (and probably in the library) of a patron. Such a text is more likely to represent the author's final thoughts than earlier versions based on first drafts or notes: Quintilian says that the complete and "authorized" version of his *Institutio oratoria,* which he is dedicating to Marcellus Victorius (I pref. 6) contains some things that are the same as the pirated versions, many changes and additions, and "everything more carefully composed and (so far as we are able) elaborated" (I pref. 8). We should not, however, assume that a dedicated text is necessarily radically different in nature or in content from a nondedicated one: in many cases where we can compare them, dedicated texts are not distinguishable in any other respect from the nondedicated works in the same corpus.[88]

It would also be a mistake to assume that dedication implies a limitation in the intended audience for a book. Where the patron is somehow seen as facilitating the "publication" of the book, this should be associated, as we have seen, with the ancient conventions whereby the aristocracy were expected to provide a "hearth" for the public performance of the poet's work, as well as a meeting place for wandering scholars and teachers. This performance aspect of patronage had by no means disappeared in the world of the New Testament, as we have seen: Atticus's literary dinner parties are in the direct line of this venerable tradition. But in the more bookish world of the first centuries B.C. and A.D., the patron could provide another, equally valuable kind of hospitality for an author's work in his library, where the text could be "deposited" (arguably the only form of "publication" in the ancient world) for consultation and copying by his friends. Such a role could well make sense for Theophilus, whom we could see as an equivalent

87. Kenyon, *Books and Readers,* 64.
88. See further Alexander, *Preface to Luke's Gospel,* 199-200.

to the patrons of house churches known from the Pauline letters: his library, in this case, could well have become the basis of the church's library.[89]

But even so, it does not follow that a text so deposited would be available only to the patron and his immediate circle: in fact the dedication may represent no more than an attempt to gain an extra, perhaps more elevated audience for the book in addition to its normal networks of communication. All the evidence suggests that dedicated books also retained their own preexisting social networks and circulated among the author's friends, students and their acquaintance, in exactly the same way as nondedicated books by the same author.[90] And this plurality of interweaving networks should further warn us against an oversimple dichotomy between "local" and "general" circulation of texts within the churches. The network model itself implies not a monolithic structure but a multiplicity of intersecting lines of communication. These will naturally generate sub-networks and individual patterns of attachment within the larger whole: even the Internet "highways," as a recent newspaper article lamented, are turning out to be a nexus of small communication groups rather than the "global" audiences envisioned in the propaganda. On this model, we would still allow for the circulation, say, of Johannine material primarily along a network of Johannine contacts within the wider community — though it remains true that the wider the circulation, the greater the potential for contact with adjacent networks.

Finally, a word should be said about the literary genre of the Gospels. I have suggested a possible link between the codex form used by the Christians from the second century onwards and the use of notebooks for "private" copies of texts or lecture notes that was widespread in antiquity (perhaps aided by the fact that Christians did not on the whole belong to the conservative literary elite, which preferred to stick to the roll). This may seem to conflict with current estimates of the literary character of the Gospels as carefully crafted compositions.

89. See further Alexander, *Preface to Luke's Gospel*, 197-99. For church libraries, see Gamble, *Books and Readers*, chap. 4.

90. Alexander, *Preface to Luke's Gospel*, 57-59, 196-97.

The conflict, however, is more apparent than real. First, any kind of text *could* be copied into a notebook, either as an author's draft or as a personal copy made by a scholar or student for his or her own use. In this sense the use of a notebook does not reflect any particular literary genre as such but tells us something about the practical stage in the process of book production which a particular copy represents. But it is clear, second, that certain kinds of text were more likely to retain the name *hypomnema* or *commentarius:* books which summarized the teaching tradition of a particular school or group, lecture notes, commentaries (scholars' glosses on classic texts), or "raw" narrative not considered to be sufficiently polished for publication as a finished history. Caesar's personal account of his campaigns falls into the last category, and it is clear from Suetonius's comments on them (Suet. *Caes.* 56) that contemporary critics were puzzled as to how to classify them. They were in fact, as Cicero observed, written with such classic ease and simplicity that it would be foolish to try to "improve" them: nevertheless the feeling persisted that they were hastily composed and intended to be revised for "a new and more correct edition." I have argued elsewhere that the Gospels, even (especially) Luke with his prefaces and dedications, may quite sensibly be classified as school handbooks, manuals of the teaching traditions of this pragmatically orientated group: and the *bios*-character of the traditions is no bar to such a classification. As narrative, we can be pretty sure, they fell far short of the literary standards of an elite that was dubious even about Caesar's elegant prose. Either way, the codex may well have seemed the appropriate vehicle for these texts, which clearly made their own way in the world along their own well-greased social pathways, blithely independent of the literary canon and its self-appointed guardians.

Schoolboy with tablets
Mosaic from Landesmuseum, Trier
Photo by Loveday Alexander

Large *tabellae* used for archives and ledgers
From the Zirkusdenkmal, Landesmuseum, Trier
Photo by Loveday Alexander

Book-satchel, Anglo-Saxon cross,
Stonegrave Minster, near Helmsley, Yorkshire
Photo by Keith Mears

Householder with roll
Landesmuseum, Trier
Photo by Loveday Alexander

Estate clerks with codex
Landesmuseum, Trier
Photo by Loveday Alexander

Receipt of taxes

Landesmuseum, Trier; photo by Loveday Alexander

About People, by People, for People: Gospel Genre and Audiences

RICHARD A. BURRIDGE

1. Introduction

Three basic questions about any literary communication, book, or work concern its subject, its author, and its reader or audience: What is it about? Who is it from? Who is it for? A quick consultation of the introduction to most Gospel commentaries will reveal that consideration of these questions takes up most of the space. A section on "source criticism" will consider the author(s) and theories of how the Gospel came to be written; "redaction criticism" will cover the particular interest of each Gospel and develop hypotheses about the intended recipients; and a section on the Gospel's theology will cover its content. However, behind these three questions is another prior issue, that of genre: What is it?

Genre is crucial for the interpretation of any text, including the question of its intended audience or readership.[1] All communication

---

1. See Richard A. Burridge, *What Are the Gospels? A Comparison with Graeco-Roman Biography,* Society for New Testament Studies Monograph Series 70 (Cambridge: Cambridge University Press, 1992), 26-54; also H. Dubrow, *Genre,* The Critical Idiom Series 42 (London: Methuen, 1982) and A. Fowler, *Kinds of Literature: An Introduction to the Theory of Genres and Modes* (Oxford: Oxford University Press, 1982).

involves a transmitter, a message, and a receiver, or in our terms, the author(s), the Gospel, and the reader/audience. If the sender is transmitting Morse code, but the receiver can only understand semaphore, there will be problems! Both must use the same language. Thus genre is crucial to any interpretation. One does not listen to a fairy story in exactly the same way as to a news broadcast — and the intended audiences are different. Correct interpretation of both text and audience depends on a correct identification of the kind of communication or genre. We differentiate between the visual and the verbal, between the spoken word and the written word, between fiction and nonfiction, poetry or prose, tragedy or comedy, legend or history, and so on — and each genre provides expectations about its audience.

Genre is thus one of the key conventions guiding both the composition and the interpretation of writings. Genre forms a kind of "contract" or agreement, often unspoken or unwritten, or even unconscious, between an author and a reader, by which the author sets out to write according to a whole set of expectations and conventions and we agree to read or to interpret the work using the same conventions, giving us an initial idea of what we might expect to find.[2] Thus, TV situational-comedies or soap operas are written with certain typical conventions and potential audiences in mind; the viewer recognizes what kind of program it is and interprets it accordingly. If, however, the viewer is expecting a documentary and interprets it according to those conventions, confusion and mistakes are likely to arise! To avoid such mistakes, we learn to identify genre through a wide range of "generic features." These may be known in advance through a review in the paper, a publisher's "blurb" on the dust jacket, or an advertisement; but generic features are also embedded in a work's formal and structural composition and content. We learn these features through practice, having read similar types of book or watched similar programs in the past, and so we pick up the clues, the generic features, as we receive the communication or read the book — and correct our interpretation accordingly as we go.

2. See E. D. Hirsch Jr., *Validity in Interpretation* (New Haven: Yale University Press, 1967), 83, and Dubrow, *Genre*, 31.

Thus recognizing the generic features embedded in the Gospels is crucial for deciding for which audience or readership the Gospels were written.

2. "By Committees, for Communities, about Theological Ideas"

Therefore, before we can identify the Gospels' intended audience, we have to discover what kind of books they might be. Traditionally, the Gospels were viewed as biographies of Jesus. Thus they were used as "windows" onto Jesus, written for those who wanted to know about him. Even with the development of literary and historical critical studies, the quest for the historical Jesus still used the Gospels as a basis to discover information about Jesus' life, teaching, and death.

During the nineteenth century, biographies began to explain the character of a great person by considering his or her upbringing, formative years, schooling, psychological development and so on. The Gospels began to look unlike such biographies. During the 1920s, scholars like Karl Ludwig Schmidt and Rudolf Bultmann rejected any notion that the Gospels were biographies: the Gospels appear to have no interest in Jesus's human personality, appearance, or character, nor do they tell us anything about the rest of his life, other than his brief public ministry and an extended concentration on his death. Instead, the Gospels were seen as popular folk literature, collections of stories handed down orally over time. Far from being biographies of Jesus, the Gospels were "unique" forms of literature, *sui generis,* and this approach dominated Gospel studies for the next half century or so.[3]

This meant that the Gospels were now less seen as windows onto the historical Jesus and more as windows onto the historical early church. One of the key arguments put forward by K. L. Schmidt for the uniqueness of the Gospels' genre was their community setting: the Gospels are "not the product of an individual author, but a folk-book,

3. See Burridge, *What Are the Gospels?* 3-13.

not biography, but cult-legend."[4] A basic tool of the form critics was to seek to discover the *Sitz im Leben* of any saying or pericope — its setting within the life of the early Christian communities. At this point there was little attempt to define these early Christian communities; they were simply seen in a generalized or typical way. The crucial implication for our purpose here is that the stress on the oral tradition meant that there was no author to speak of, no individual mind behind the text. The evangelists were seen as merely stenographers at the end of the oral tunnel, stringing together the pearls of wisdom composed by various early preachers. This is thus authorship by committee, with notes from a secretary. Finally, the subject of the Gospels is not Jesus, but the kerygma, the preaching of the early faith of the church. Thus our three basic questions about the Gospels of author, subject, and audience can be answered as "by committees, for communities, about the faith."

However, the rise of redaction criticism and the development of new literary approaches led to the writers of the Gospels being viewed as both theologians and conscious literary artists. This reopened the questions of the genre, authorship, and audience of the Gospels, and their place within the context of first-century literature.

The pioneering work of Bornkamm on Matthew, Marxsen on Mark, and Conzelmann on Luke directed attention to the particular theological interests of each evangelist. Composition by committee was replaced by deliberate selection of material on the part of the Gospel writers; once redaction critics attributed shaping of the material to the evangelists as well, then issues of authorship were bound to arise. This led quickly on to the question of the communities. If the form critics were interested in the general *Sitz im Leben* in which this or that kind of pericope might be used, the redaction-critical stress on the particular

---

4. "Nicht individuelle Schriftstellerleistung, sondern Volksbuch, nicht Biographie, sondern Kultlegende," K. L. Schmidt, "Die Stellung der Evangelien in der allgemeinen Literatur-geschichte," in *EUCHARISTERION: Studien zur Religion und Literatur des Alten und Neuen Testaments,* ed. Hans Schmidt (Göttingen: Vandenhoeck und Ruprecht, 1923), 2:50-134; quotation from 76.

theology of each Gospel led to an attempt to define the community interested in those aspects or affected by the situations envisaged to require that teaching. Thus the word *community* itself begins to appear regularly in titles of studies that attempt to reconstruct the group or church behind each of the Gospels — the so-called Matthean or Johannine community.[5] A good example is the way in which R. E. Brown and J. L. Martyn see theological issues, especially that of Christology, as defining the various stages of the development of the Johannine community and the parallel multiple editions of the Fourth Gospel.[6] Thus the Gospel writers have begun to be seen as theologians, while the subject matter has moved from the basic kerygma to the particular concerns of the writer's community; the audience is therefore defined very specifically as the church within which and for which this Gospel was written. The text is thus a window for the modern critic onto the ancient communities.

These approaches were refined still further by the development of approaches using the social sciences. In many respects, the search for the evangelists' communities followed the model of reconstructing the Pauline communities to which his various epistles were addressed. It is no coincidence that Wayne Meeks, who wrote the excellent introduction to sociological analysis of the Pauline churches in his *The First Urban Christians,* should also consider the question of Johannine sectar-

5. See for example, Stephenson H. Brooks, *Matthew's Community: The Evidence of His Special Sayings Material,* Journal for the Study of the New Testament Supplement Series 16 (Sheffield: Sheffield Academic Press, 1987); David L. Balch, ed., *Social History of the Matthean Community: Cross-Disciplinary Approaches* (Minneapolis: Fortress, 1991); J. A. Overman, *Church and Community in Crisis: The Gospel According to Matthew* (Valley Forge, Penn.: Trinity Press International, 1996); Howard Clark Kee, *Community of the New Age: Studies in Mark's Gospel* (Philadelphia: Westminster, 1977); Philip Francis Esler, *Community and Gospel in Luke-Acts: The Social and Political Motivations of Lucan Theology,* Society for New Testament Studies Monograph Series 57 (Cambridge: Cambridge University Press, 1987); Raymond E. Brown, S.S., *The Community of the Beloved Disciple* (London: Geoffrey Chapman, 1979).

6. J. L. Martyn, *History and Theology in the Fourth Gospel,* 2d ed. (Nashville: Abingdon, 1979); R. E. Brown, *John,* Anchor Commentary, 2 vols. (New York: Doubleday, 1966, 1970); Brown, *Community of the Beloved Disciple.*

ianism.[7] Over recent years, all four Gospels have been subjected to such sociological analysis, and many different reconstructions of their communities have been hypothesized. Unlike the historical approach's concept of the "window" onto the early communities, such studies prefer to see the community as "reflected" in the text, preferring therefore the image of the text as a mirror.[8]

The problem with both the redactional and the sociological reconstructions of the evangelists' communities is the variety of conflicting versions produced from so little evidence. While we might marvel at the complexity of the different stages of the development of the Johannine community according to Brown or Martyn's model, few Gospel scholars are prepared to accept that all these details can be reconstructed from the hints "reflected" in the text. The problem is even more acute with the reconstruction of hypothetical communities from the redaction of hypothetical documents, as in the work on the different periods of the so-called Q-community![9] While it is possible that the Gospel texts may reflect periods of change and development in the early church, the lack of scholarly agreement about the supposed reconstructions suggests that this is an impossible task. Equally, as Stephen Barton shows elsewhere in this volume, there are similar problems of both agreement over multiple reconstructions and methodology

7. Wayne A. Meeks, *The First Urban Christians: The Social World of the Apostle Paul* (New Haven: Yale University Press, 1983); "The Son of Man in Johannine Sectarianism," *Journal of Biblical Literature* 91 (1972): 44-72.

8. For a full discussion and critique of such approaches, see Stephen Barton's chapter, "Can We Identify the Gospel Audiences?" in this book.

9. See the different reconstructions offered by J. S. Kloppenborg, *The Formation of Q: Trajectories in Ancient Wisdom Collections* (Philadelphia: Fortress, 1987), and M. Sato, *Q und Prophetie: Studien zur Gattungs- und Traditionengeschichte der Quelle Q,* Wissenschaftliche Untersuchungen zum Neuen Testament 2.29 (Tübingen: Mohr-Siebeck, 1988); see also *Semeia 55: Early Christianity, Q and Jesus,* ed. J. S. Kloppenborg (Atlanta: Scholars/Society of Biblical Literature, 1992); other Q-scholars are less sanguine about such "stratification" of Q and its community, see E. P. Meadors, *Jesus the Messianic Herald of Salvation,* Wissenschaftliche Untersuchungen zum Neuen Testament 2.72 (Tübingen: Mohr-Siebeck, 1995), 17-35, and D. R. Catchpole, *The Quest for Q* (Edinburgh: T. & T. Clark, 1993), esp. 188.

with the sociological approaches to the Gospels' communities. The fact that, whatever genre the Gospels may be, they are at least different from Pauline epistles (which are written for the most part to specific communities) must cast doubt on these reconstructions.

Thus if the Gospels cannot be used as a window onto the early Christian communities, nor even as a mirror to reflect them, it should be no surprise that some recent literary approaches have given up on the original audience completely. According to these, since we know nothing of the author, nor his community or context, the communication model of author-text-reader cannot be used: we just have texts and readers. While some forms of reader-response criticism do try to reconstruct the "implied reader" — the reader implied by or "in" the text with the necessary amount of competence to recognize the reading encoded in the text — more extreme versions suggest that the reader is "over" the text and able to impose any reading he or she wishes upon it.[10] At this point the text has become a completely silvered mirror, in which all we can see is our own present reflection — but behind which we cannot penetrate at all. This means that such approaches must abandon any attempt to outline the communities or audience for whom the Gospels were originally written, and concentrate instead on how we find them.

This brief survey of the last century of Gospel studies has thus demonstrated that the issues of author, subject, and audience are bound up with the question of genre. The form-critical understanding of the Gospels as unique products of the oral tradition suggested that they were written for early communities about the faith by committees in the tradition. Redaction critics began the rehabilitation of the evangelists as authors, while defining the communities in terms of the specific issues of content found in each Gospel; however, the lack of attention to the genre of the Gospels and to the question of

10. For discussion of reader-response approaches, see *Semeia* 31: *Reader Response Approaches to Biblical and Secular Texts*, ed. R. Detweiler (Decatur: Scholars/Society of Biblical Literature, 1985) and Stephen D. Moore, *Literary Criticism and the Gospels: The Theoretical Challenge* (New Haven: Yale University Press, 1989).

whether they were the kind of texts that would allow such analysis raises questions about this enterprise. Sociological studies have also produced benefits, but the treating of the Gospels as though they shared the same genre as Pauline epistles compounds the problem. Finally, to take refuge in extreme reader-response approaches concerned only with present readings is a counsel of despair, giving up completely on the original audience for whom the Gospels were written. Therefore, we need a better understanding of the genre of the Gospels in order to illuminate their intended audience or readership.

3. "About a Person" — Subject

Many attempts to deal with the subject of the Gospels fail because they do not consider the issue of genre. Thus Perrin says that "the nature of a Gospel is not the ministry of the historical Jesus, but the reality of Christian experience."[11] This is typical of the general approach taken by form critics to the genre and content of the Gospels, but it will not stand closer analysis. Paul also writes about "the reality of Christian experience," but he is writing in a different genre (epistles) with different subject material and for different specific communities.[12]

The form-critical idea that the Gospels are unique is nonsense from the point of view of genre. Something totally novel from the point of view of genre could not be written, since all communication is produced within a context of other communication; furthermore, even if it were possible to compose something unique, it would not be able to be communicated to others, since genre plays the crucial part in interpretation of meaning.[13] In recent years, many genres have been proposed for the Gospels, but increasingly they have been again seen

11. N. Perrin, *What Is Redaction Criticism?* (London: SPCK, 1970), 75.

12. See further Burridge, *What Are the Gospels?* 256-57.

13. Eliseo Vivas, "Literary Classes: Some Problems," *Genre* 1 (1968): 103.

as biography. The work of Charles Talbert[14] and David Aune[15] has contributed greatly to this development, while my own work has attempted to give a detailed argument combining literary theory and classical studies with Gospel scholarship.[16]

a. The Generic Features of the Gospels Compared with Biography

A generic comparison of a group of different works from different authors will illustrate the nature of any genre. I undertook this exercise with ten examples of ancient biography: Isocrates' *Evagoras,* Xenophon's *Agesilaus,* Satyrus's *Euripides,* Nepos's *Atticus,* Philo's *Moses,* Tacitus's *Agricola,* Plutarch's *Cato Minor,* Suetonius's *Lives of the Caesars,* Lucian's *Demonax,* and Philostratus's *Apollonius of Tyana.* This is a diverse group deliberately chosen to include the origins of biography in fourth-century B.C. rhetorical encomia through to third-century A.D. forerunners of the novel and hagiography. This shows that "Lives" form a diverse and flexible genre, yet still one with a recognizable family resemblance in both form and content. They were known in the ancient world as "lives," βίοι or *vitae;* the word *biography* itself does not appear until the fifth-century work of Damascius, preserved in the ninth-century writer Photius. Bultmann's statement that the Gospels are not biography was a result of comparing them with modern examples and ideas of biography. This is a category error; when using the word *biography* of both the Gospels and ancient Lives, we must avoid modern connotations and compare them with one another to ascertain their shared generic features.

14. Charles H. Talbert, *What Is a Gospel? The Genre of the Canonical Gospels* (Philadelphia: Fortress, 1977; London: SPCK, 1978); "Once Again: Gospel Genre," *Semeia* 43 (1988): 53-73.

15. David E. Aune, *The New Testament in Its Literary Environment* (Philadelphia: Westminster, 1987; Cambridge: James Clarke & Co., 1988); Aune, ed., *Greco-Roman Literature and the New Testament: Selected Forms and Genres,* Society of Biblical Literature Sources for Biblical Study 21 (Atlanta: Scholars, 1988).

16. The following two subsections summarize the main argument of my book, *What Are the Gospels?* 109-239.

From the formal or structural perspective, they are written in continuous prose narrative, between 10,000 and 20,000 words in length — the amount on a typical scroll about 30-35 feet long. Unlike modern biographies, Greco-Roman lives do not cover the whole life in strict chronological sequence, complete with detailed psychological analysis of the subject's character. Often, they have only a bare chronological outline, beginning with the birth or arrival on the public scene and ending with the death; the intervening space includes selected stories, anecdotes, speeches, and sayings, all displaying something of the subject. Against this background, the Gospels' concentration on Jesus' public ministry from his baptism to death does not seem very different.

The content of Greco-Roman biographies also has similarities with the Gospels. They begin with a brief mention of the hero's ancestry, family, or city, followed by his birth and an occasional anecdote about his upbringing; usually we move rapidly on to his public debut later in life. Accounts of generals, politicians, or statesmen are much more chronologically ordered when recounting their great deeds and virtues, while lives of philosophers, writers, or thinkers tend to be more anecdotal, arranged around collections of material displaying their ideas and teachings. While the author may claim to provide information about his subject, often his underlying aims may include apology (to defend the subject's memory against others' attacks), polemic (to attack his rivals), or didactic (to teach his followers about him). Similarly, the Gospels concentrate on Jesus' teaching and great deeds to explain the faith of the early Christians. As for the climax, the evangelists devote between 15 and 20 percent of the Gospels to the last week of Jesus' life, his death, and the resurrection; similar amounts are given over to their subject's death in biographies by Plutarch, Tacitus, Nepos, and Philostratus, since in this crisis the hero reveals his true character, gives his definitive teaching, or does his greatest deed.

Therefore marked similarities of form and content can be demonstrated between the Gospels and ancient biographies.

b. The Subject of the Gospels

It was suggested above that form critics proposed a wide variety of subjects for the Gospels such as the Kingdom of Heaven, the kerygma, faith, discipleship, and so forth, while redaction critics see the subject matter as closely connected with the particular concerns of the specific community within which and for which the Gospel was written. However, detailed analysis of the verbal structure of the Gospels and ancient biographies demonstrates another generic connection. Every sentence in English and in ancient languages must have a subject — the person or thing doing the action of the verb. Analysis of the subjects of the verbs can be extended from one sentence to a paragraph and then across a whole work. Most narratives, ancient or modern, have a wide variety of subjects, as different people and things come to the fore at different times. It is a peculiar characteristic of biography that the attention stays focused on one particular person. My analysis has demonstrated that it is quite common in ancient biography for around a quarter or a third of the verbs to be dominated by one person, the hero; furthermore, another characteristic is that another 15 to 30 percent of the verbs can occur in sayings, speeches, or quotations from the person.[17] So too in the Gospels: Jesus is the subject of a quarter of the verbs in Mark's Gospel, with a further fifth spoken by him in his teaching and parables. Matthew and Luke both make Jesus the subject of nearly a fifth of their verbs, while about 40 percent are spoken by him. About half of John's verbs either have Jesus as the subject or are on his lips. Thus we can see clearly that, just like other ancient biographies, Jesus' deeds and words are of vital importance for the four evangelists as they paint their different portraits of Jesus.

c. The Implications of the Biographical Hypothesis

Thus the Gospels are a form of ancient biography, and we must study them with the same biographical concentration upon their subject to see the particular way each author portrays his understanding of Jesus.

17. For diagrams of all this data, see *What Are the Gospels?* App. 261-74.

The Gospels are neither a clear glass window onto the historical Jesus or the early communities, nor a polished mirror in whose reflection we can see anything we happen to place before them. They are more like a piece of stained glass *through which* we can catch the occasional glimpse of what is behind them and *in which* we sometimes mistake our own reflection from in front of them, but *upon which* the main picture has been assembled using all the different colors of literary skill — and it is the portrait of a person. The historical, literary, and biographical methods combine to show us that the Gospels are nothing less than Christology in narrative form, the story of Jesus.

The implications of this biographical hypothesis is that the Gospels are about a person, not about theological ideas. Therefore the hermeneutical key for understanding them is not to be found in presumed problems or difficulties in their hypothetical communities, but rather in their Christology. Every passage and pericope must be interpreted in the light of the biographical genre of the whole: in interpreting them, we need to ask what this story or incident is designed to tell us about the author's understanding of Jesus. This christological approach can be illustrated easily by considering a notorious problem in Gospel studies, namely Mark's depiction of the disciples as slow to understand and lacking in faith. Despite the suggestion that the disciples are given the secret (μυστήριον) of the Kingdom of God (Mark 4:11), they fail to understand, and Jesus gets increasingly frustrated with them especially in the three boat scenes (Mark 4:40-41; 6:50-52; 8:14-21); James and John want the best seats in heaven (10:35-45), while they all fail to understand the Passion predictions (8:32-33; 9:32; 10:32-41). Eventually, they fall asleep in Gethsemane and desert Jesus, leaving Judas to betray him and Peter to deny him (14:37-50, 66-72). Not only do modern scholars find this picture rather harsh, but so do Matthew and Luke, who "improve" it, so that Matthew turns Mark's "no faith" (Mark 4:40) into "men of little faith" (Matt. 8:26), while in Luke the disciples ask Jesus, "increase our faith" (Luke 17:5).

A redaction-critical approach that sees the Gospels as written for specific communities seeks to solve this problem by relating it to certain groups or leaders in the early church. Thus, Weeden's account is actually entitled *Mark: Traditions in Conflict;* he sees the slow-witted disciples as standing for other leaders, particularly those with a *theios aner* Christology to whom Mark is opposed.[18] Quite apart from the fact that there are problems over the concept of *theios aner,* such an approach does not do justice to the positive material about the disciples in Mark: Jesus continues to explain things to them (e.g. 7:17-23; 8:34-38; 10:23-31; 11:20-25; 13:5-37); he has pity on their exhausted sleep (14:38); and Peter has at least followed Jesus into danger after the others fled, as he promised (14:29). If the disciples represent the wrong leaders, why does Jesus promise to meet them in Galilee (14:28; 16:7)? Once we stop seeing the Gospels as written about certain problems for specific communities and read them instead as belonging to the genre of ancient biography, then the christological key can be used to interpret such passages. The point of each passage is not to tell us about the disciples, but to indicate something about the biography's subject — namely, Jesus of Nazareth — in this case, that he is someone who is hard to understand and tough to follow. Given both the positive and the negative aspects of the disciples' portrayal, the readers should not be surprised if they find discipleship difficult; yet it is such struggling disciples whom Jesus calls and teaches, despite the difficulties.

Thus, interpreting the Gospels in the light of their biographical genre, as being about a person rather than about community ideas or problems, has some immediate benefit in their interpretation.

4. "By People" — Author

We argued above that the form-critical approach developed by K. L. Schmidt and Rudolf Bultmann placed the creative process for the Gospels firmly within the oral tradition. The evangelist was merely the person who wrote down what came to him from the oral tunnel and is therefore a servant of the community with no personal identity; we cannot talk of an "author," nor do issues connected with authorship arise. The creation of material and the transmission of existing stories all arise from the early communities and serve their needs.

18. T. J. Weeden, *Mark: Traditions in Conflict* (Philadelphia: Fortress, 1971).

The development of redaction criticism, however, enabled us to see how each evangelist has shaped material to suit his purposes. Careful Synoptic parallel criticism reveals the particular vocabulary, interests, and ideas of each writer. Once redaction critics directed our attention towards the personal creativity of the evangelists as theologians, then issues about authorship were bound to follow. However, redaction criticism was also responsible for refining the idea of the evangelists' specific communities. Although the evangelist may be seen as a creative theologian, the driving force behind his creativity is understood to be the particular needs of his narrowly defined community. Thus the depiction of "the Jews" in the Fourth Gospel and the ἀποσυνάγωγος material (John 9:22; 12:42; 16:2) reflect actual events which happened to or in the Johannine community, according to Brown and Martyn,[19] rather than having anything to do with the author's personal interests or understanding of Jesus as his subject.

However, too much stress on events or issues in the evangelists' communities as determining the Gospels' special interests or theologies turns the writers back into the stenographer model, with the form-critical oral tunnel replaced by the redaction-critical community. There is also a circularity inherent in interpreting the texts in the light of hypothetical communities, the nature of which has already been deduced solely from the texts! The biographical genre for the Gospels argues against too much community emphasis; the evangelists' selection of previous material and their treatment of their sources, plus their own special material, all imply the creative personality of an author. Literary theory, not just of biography but of most genres, suggests that committees and communities do not write books — or at least, not books as interesting as the Gospels, which do not read like turgid committee reports or community minutes.

Unlike static communities, authors move around, collecting ideas and developing their understanding. Their ideas get refined by wider experience and by the collection of source material. This process is acknowledged by Luke in the preface to his Gospel (1:3). While authors may write for groups of people or communities, this is better

19. See note 6.

seen as their response to the needs or desires of perceived markets or audiences.

Furthermore, the rise of narrative criticism of the Gospels has demonstrated how each Gospel tells the story of Jesus in a particular and coherent way. If the form critics concentrated on individual pericopae, "cut around" (περι-κόπτω) from their contexts, and the redaction critics were interested in the different versions of each section, narrative critics have redirected our attention back to the story as a whole. Studies such as those by Rhoads and Michie on Mark, Kingsbury on Matthew, Tannehill on Luke-Acts, and Culpepper on John have analyzed the plotlines throughout each Gospel, looking at how the characters develop, how repetition and reference back or forward in the narrative can lead to irony, and how the main themes come to a climax or are resolved.[20]

Curiously, such studies have tended to ignore the issue of genre. The biographical hypothesis leads us to expect the depiction of one person, the subject, as understood by another person, the author. If we read the Gospels as *bioi,* then this is exactly what we find. Instead of a form-critical approach to the Gospels as Passion narratives preceded by disjointed pericopae strung together, narratological readings show how each evangelist fits the Passion to the themes of his Gospel.

Thus Mark depicts Jesus as someone who appears fully grown almost from nowhere (1:9) and then rushes around everywhere "immediately," εὐθύς. He is misunderstood by everybody, including his family and friends and the authorities (3:19-35). The interlude of chapters 8–10 shows that Jesus is the enigmatic wonder-worker who

20. David Rhoads and Donald Michie, *Mark as Story: An Introduction to the Narrative of a Gospel* (Philadelphia: Fortress, 1982); Jack Dean Kingsbury, *Matthew as Story,* 2d ed. (Philadelphia: Fortress, 1988); Robert C. Tannehill, *The Narrative Unity of Luke-Acts: A Literary Interpretation,* 2 vols. (Philadelphia and Minneapolis: Fortress, 1986 and 1990); R. Alan Culpepper, *Anatomy of the Fourth Gospel: A Study in Literary Design* (Philadelphia: Fortress, 1983). See also Mark Stibbe, *John as Storyteller: Narrative Criticism and the Fourth Gospel,* Society for New Testament Studies Monograph Series 73 (Cambridge: Cambridge University Press, 1992); Mark Allen Powell, *What Is Narrative Criticism? A New Approach to the Bible* (Minneapolis: Fortress, 1990; London: SPCK, 1993).

binds people to secrecy, the eschatological prophet who will die in Jerusalem, the Messiah who will suffer, both Son of God and Son of Man. Rather than seeking to explain any conflict between such titles as deriving from different historical traditions or problems in the Markan community in the manner of Weeden's study discussed above, a biographical narrative approach holds them together as the text does — in a complementary tension. This is borne out by the final section as Jesus comes to find Jerusalem and the temple as barren as the fig tree and prophesies that they will face the same destruction (chaps. 11-13). He suffers and dies all alone in dark desolation: "My God, my God, why have you forsaken me?" (15:34). The Passion narrative thus brings to a climax all Mark's themes throughout the Gospel. Even the ending is full of enigma, fear, and awe (16:1-8).

Matthew, however, has a rather different atmosphere. We begin with Jesus' Jewish background, genealogy and birth (chaps. 1-2). When he begins his ministry, Jesus is another Moses, who teaches from mountains (5:1) and fulfills the law and the prophets, giving his teaching in five great blocks, which may remind the reader of the Pentateuch (5–7, 10, 13, 18, 24–25). Unfortunately, this brings him into conflict with the leaders of Israel. While Matthew includes practically all of Mark's Passion, he gives it a more awesome atmosphere: the cry of abandonment is answered by an earthquake and resurrections; no wonder that unlike Mark's lone centurion, here *everyone* realizes this was truly the Son of God (27:51-54, cf. Mark 15:39). Finally, the resurrection continues this supernatural atmosphere with further divine earthquakes and a new Israel on a mountain to receive Jesus' commission to go to the Gentiles (28:1-20).[21] Again, the climax resolves all the themes of the Gospel.

Luke begins with a Greek periodic preface to make clear Jesus' universal significance (Luke 1:1-4). He sets his account of Jesus within the historical perspective of both Israel's history and contemporary Roman rule (1:5-80; 2:1; 3:1) and gives it a geographical structure with

21. For a good comparison of Matthew with Mark, see J. L. Houlden, *Backward into Light: The Passion and Resurrection of Jesus According to Matthew and Mark* (London: SCM, 1987).

the journey from Galilee to Jerusalem (9:51–19:28). Throughout Luke's narrative, Jesus is concerned for the poor, the lost and unacceptable, outcasts, women, Samaritans, and Gentiles. He is also the man of prayer (11:1-4). Thus the Passion narrative shows him concerned for the women of Jerusalem (23:27-31) and praying for forgiveness for the soldiers and the penitent thief (23:34, 43), and committing himself in trust to his Father (23:46). After the resurrection, history and geography run the other way, from Israel's past to the world's future, moving away from Jerusalem (24:44-47). The Gospel ends as it began "in Jerusalem with great joy, in the Temple blessing God" (24:51-52, cf. 1:5-23). Such a clear overall and balanced biographical narrative reflects a single author, not a community's interests.

John begins not with Jesus' baptism, nor his birth, but before all time, in the beginning, with God (John 1:1-18). Jesus is constantly center stage and he is characterized, as in most ancient writing, by indirect means as the author interweaves "signs" and discourse, revealing the effect of meditation and theological reflection upon the person of Jesus: he is the Son, equal with the Father (10:30), yet totally dependent on him (5:19). Opposition from "the Jews" develops through the first half (2–12); as the tension comes to a climax, Jesus gathers his disciples to his breast, washes their feet, and explains what will happen (13–17). The hour of glory is also the Passion: throughout, Jesus is serenely in control, directing events (19:11), organizing his mother and disciple (19:26-27), fulfilling Scripture (19:28) until finally "it is accomplished" (19:30). After the resurrection he appears as he wishes to comfort Mary (20:14), challenge Thomas (20:26), and restore Peter (21:15-19). Once again, we have a clear portrait of the subject running through the ministry of Jesus to culminate in the account of his death and resurrection.

These four individual accounts, each concerned with the resolution of their particular themes,[22] suggest that they have been composed, not by communities, but by four single writers each of whom wants to portray a particular view of Jesus in his Gospel in the manner of

22. For a fuller of account of such christological readings, see Richard A. Burridge, *Four Gospels, One Jesus? A Symbolic Reading* (Grand Rapids: Eerdmans; London: SPCK, 1994).

ancient biography — as is suggested by Justin Martyr's reference to the "memoirs" of the apostles (ἀπομνημονεύματα τῶν ἀποστόλων, *Ap.* I.67.3; cf. also, I.66.3, and *Dial.* 106.3). If we see the Gospels as the products of four creative authors rather than produced by and for four separate communities, this helps to explain how the fourfold canon came to be used and preserved so quickly by the time of the early fathers like Irenaeus (*Adversus Haereses* III.11.8-9). This is particularly striking since whereas one Gospel would fit onto one scroll, keeping four Gospels together required the development of the codex.[23] If the Gospels were written solely within and for small communities, how did they come to be collected together and used in plurality for the wider church? Furthermore, the plurality of the Gospels' witness was a problem for the fathers — and a gift to opponents like Celsus, Porphyry, and Julian. This problem could easily have been solved by choosing one to be "the authorized biography" (as Marcion did with Luke) or by combining them into a mixed narrative (as Tatian did with the *Diatessaron*).[24] The fact that the fathers chose to keep four separate accounts, despite the problem of plurality and possible conflict, demonstrates that they recognized that these works were coherent single accounts of Jesus written by four individual authors for a much wider audience than just four specific communities.

5. "For People" — Audience

We have seen that interpreting the Gospels as ancient biographies means that they are not to be understood as written by committees within the

23. See C. H. Roberts and T. C. Skeat, *The Birth of the Codex* (Oxford: Oxford University Press, 1987).

24. For the fourfold canon and plurality, see T. C. Skeat, "Irenaeus and the Four-Fold Gospel Canon," *Novum Testamentum* 34, no. 2 (1992): 194-99, and Oscar Cullmann, "The Plurality of the Gospels as a Theological Problem in Antiquity" in his collection, *The Early Church: Studies in Early Christian History and Theology,* ed. A. J. B. Higgins (Philadelphia: Westminster, 1956), 37-54, translated from the original German article in *Theologische Zeitschrift* i (1945): 23-42; see also Richard A. Burridge, *Four Gospels, One Jesus?* 25-27, 164-79.

oral traditions about theological concepts for particular communities, but by authors about a person for other people. Therefore we must turn at last to this third element of communication theory, the intended audience or readership. In fact, the application of the biographical hypothesis to the questions of subject and author has already raised doubts about the assumption that the Gospels were written within and directed at four specific small communities.

We have argued that genre is essentially a social construct that functions as an agreement between authors and readers to provide a conventional set of expectations to guide both the composition of a text and its later interpretation. This is why it is vital to compare the Gospels with other texts from their own period, rather than attempting to compare them with modern concepts of biography or apply the standards of accurate news-reporting to them. The main problem is that we have no evidence outside the Gospel texts themselves about their sociological setting, the contexts within which and for which they were written. A comparison with other Greco-Roman biographies may help us to reconstruct possible audiences or markets for the Gospels, as well as illuminate how and why these lives were written, published, or circulated.

a. Comparable Communities or Audiences for Other Bioi

New Testament scholars often assume that the Gospels were written within the context of a community and produced specifically for that community. In fact, these are two separate issues, since it is possible for a work to be written within one group but aimed at people outside that community, or conversely, to be directed at a community by an individual writing from outside it. If the Gospels are indeed a form of Greco-Roman biography, we should consider whether there is any evidence that Lives functioned in such a community-based way in the ancient world. Given the plurality of the Gospels just noted, it would be particularly interesting if we could find any parallels for groups of Lives about one person in any other Greco-Roman social grouping.

If by "community" we mean a tightly defined group or school, then the nearest parallel may be the philosophical schools of the fourth and third centuries B.C. According to the stories, Aristoxenus, annoyed because Theopompus was preferred over him as Aristotle's successor, went off in a huff to write a *bios* of Socrates to show all his faults! We know of many *bioi* of various philosophers from this period, although since the works themselves are not preserved, we cannot be sure how fully they fit the genre.[25] However, this does at least show that *bioi* can be written for people outside the author's own group.

Closer in time to the Gospels, we have the sequence of "Cato literature": accounts of Cato the Younger as the last great Republican were written by both sides in the civil war at the end of the Roman Republic and on into the Empire. Thus, Cicero wrote a panegyric, the *Cato,* to which Caesar replied with the *Anti-Cato.* This led into a succession of works by Brutus, Hirtius, Augustus, and Thrasea Paetus as "Catonism" became "an ideological hallmark of the Early Principate."[26] However, this was more of a sequence of Lives issuing from groups of people sharing ideas at a similar time, rather than actual "schools"; there was no "Cato community." Furthermore, Plutarch showed that it was possible to write a life of Cato without taking part in this political debate when he composed his *Cato Minor.*

Something similar can be seen with regard to Tacitus's life of his father-in-law, Agricola, who was governor of Roman Britain from 77 to 84 A.D., after which he was recalled by the emperor Domitian to Rome, where he spent a quiet retirement and died. Tacitus meanwhile continued his political career, being nominated by Domitian for the consulship. One interpretation of the *Agricola* is that it was written

25. See Fritz Wehrli, *Die Schule des Aristoteles,* 10 vols. (Basel: Schwabe & Co., 1967-69) for the fragments; for further discussion of the schools, see A. Momigliano, *The Development of Greek Biography* (Cambridge, Mass.: Harvard University Press, 1971), 66-79; and for a comparison of Hellenistic school biographies with Acts, see L. C. A. Alexander, "Acts and Ancient Intellectual Biography," in *The Book of Acts in Its First Century Setting,* vol. 1 of *The Book of Acts in Its Ancient Literary Setting,* ed. B. W. Winter and A. C. Clarke (Grand Rapids: Eerdmans, 1993).

26. J. Geiger, "Munatius Rufus and Thrasea Paetus on Cato the Younger," *Athenaeum* 57 (1979): 48-72, quotation from 48.

after Domitian's fall as a political apology for people like Tacitus and Agricola who held positions under the tyrant: Tacitus deliberately uses Agricola as an example that it is possible for good men to work with evil emperors, *"posse etiam sub malis principibus magnos viros esse,"* and argues that this is better than courting an ostentatious martyrdom of no use to the republic, *"in nullum rei publicae usum ambitiosa morte"* (42.4) — a sideswipe at people like Thrasea Paetus and Helvidius Priscus.[27] Clearly, this suggests that the book is written within one group (Tacitus and his family) while being aimed at others involved in Roman politics. This is a long way from talking of a "Tacitean community" within which and for which the book is written. Tacitus is directing his work at anybody who wishes to know about his father-in-law; in biographies, the portrait of the subject matters more than the readership.

This is true of most ancient biographies. Even when there is a particular point being made about the subject, as with Socrates, Cato, or Agricola, the books are intended for wider circulation. Therefore this should cause us to hesitate about using "community-talk" for the Gospel audiences. This concept may be helpful in Pauline studies, where letters are clearly written to specific communities and include particular greetings or messages for named persons. Without such names or external evidence for the "Matthean" or "Johannine" communities, we cannot assume that reconstructions like those of Brown or Martyn are valid. If Greco-Roman *bioi* are not written solely for specific communities, then interpreting the Gospels as *bioi* provides a critique of much community-based sociological analysis of the Gospel audiences.

The above examples suggest that the writers had certain types of people in mind when writing for wider circulation, which is more like our modern concept of "market," rather than just one narrow community. By comparing Mark's Gospel with the genre of "popular litera-

27. See H. Furneaux, *Cornelii Taciti, Vita Agricolae* (Oxford: Clarendon, 1898), 10-15; also Dorey, " 'Agricola' and 'Domitian' " in his *Tacitus* (London: Routledge & Kegan Paul, 1969), 1-18; Syme, *Tacitus* (Oxford: Oxford University Press, 1958), 1:26-29, 125-31.

ture," Mary Ann Tolbert has suggested that Mark was written for a wider readership among both Christians being persecuted and for others interested in the faith.[28] Similarly, Mary Ann Beavis has argued for a "more general audience of early Christian missionary teaching/preaching."[29] Interpreting the Gospels as ancient *bioi* confirms that this development towards the "audience" implied within each Gospel is more helpful than imagined hypothetical communities.

b. Genre as a Clue to Social Function

Genre can sometimes be a clue to both the social context and the function for which a work was composed. For example, *encomia* were speeches to be delivered on certain specific social occasions (for someone entering public office, or at funerals or memorials) with the social function of praising the individual — and *psogos* had the opposite function. Shuler argued that encomium biography existed as a separate genre to which the Gospels belonged; this provides the clue to their social function — praise of Jesus. In fact, the rhetorical purpose of praise of an individual is rather different from the praise given by Gospel writers to Jesus, as even Shuler himself is aware,[30] and there are grave doubts about whether this genre existed at all.[31]

The problem with the biographical hypothesis for the Gospels is that there were a variety of functions for ancient *bioi,* and different lives appear to have been used in different ways — including praise and blame (Xenophon's *Agesilaus*), but also for exemplary, moral purposes (Plutarch), for didactic purposes or information (Satyrus), to preserve the memory of a great man (Tacitus's *Agricola*) or even, in the case of

28. Mary Ann Tolbert, *Sowing the Gospel: Mark's World in Literary-Historical Perspective* (Minneapolis: Fortress, 1989); see esp. 59-79 and 303-6.

29. Mary Ann Beavis, *Mark's Audience: The Literary and Social Setting of Mark. 4.11-12,* Journal for the Study of the New Testament Supplement Series 33 (Sheffield: Sheffield Academic Press, 1989), 171.

30. Philip L. Shuler, *A Genre for the Gospels: The Biographical Character of Matthew* (Philadelphia: Fortress, 1982), 105-6.

31. See Burridge, *What Are the Gospels?* 86-89, for a fuller critique.

Lucian or Philostratus, simply to entertain.[32] Therefore, putting the Gospels into this genre does not automatically answer all our questions about purpose and social function within a community setting.

However, one possible similarity for the Gospel communities arises from the social functions of apologetic and polemic. We saw these functions at work in the early *bioi* written in the philosophical schools after Aristotle and Aristoxenus, and through the various examples of the Cato tradition. It is also the case that *bioi* were used in this way for debate between Christians and pagans at the end of the third and early fourth centuries A.D. with lives like Porphyry's *Plotinus* and Eusebius's *Origen*.[33] We have noted that Weeden has argued that Mark is to be understood in terms of conflict between different understandings of Jesus;[34] Johannine scholars also point to apologetic and polemic in the Fourth Gospel and the Johannine epistles directed not only at the synagogue, but also at other Christian groups, with suggestions of these writings being both pro- and anti- either Gnosticism or Docetism.[35]

However, this function of apologetic and polemic suggests a wider audience for a work than merely the community within which it was written. After all, there is no point in defending oneself against opponents' attacks or criticizing them, if one does not intend the work to be read by both the opponents and a wider audience not yet committed to either side. A better concept is that of "social legitimation," whereby an author seeks to explain or justify the position taken by

32. For a fuller list of the functions of *bioi*, see Burridge, *What Are the Gospels?* 149-52 and 185-88; also C. H. Talbert, "Biographies of Philosophers and Rulers as Instruments of Religious Propaganda in Mediterranean Antiquity," *Aufstieg und Niedergang der römischen Welt* II.16.2 (1978): 1620-23.

33. See Patricia Cox, *Biography in Late Antiquity: A Quest for the Holy Man* (Berkeley: University of California Press, 1983), especially 135.

34. T. J. Weeden "The Heresy That Necessitated Mark's Gospel," *Zeitschrift für die neutestamentliche Wissenschaft* 59 (1968): 145-58, and *Mark: Traditions in Conflict.*

35. See for example, Rodney A. Whiteacre, *Johannine Polemic: The Role of Tradition and Theology,* Society of Biblical Literature Dissertation Series 67 (Chico, Calif.: Scholars, 1982), or B. Lindars, *John* (Sheffield: Sheffield Academic Press, 1990), 46-62.

himself or his social grouping. Thus, the lives of Cato can be seen as legitimating narratives for the opposing views being taken towards the empire by its supporters and by Republicans; Nero certainly seems to have read Thrasea Paetus's account of Cato in this way, which is why he reacted by ordering Paetus to commit suicide (see Tacitus *Annals* XVI.34). While most classicists are not prepared to see the *Agricola* as simply a political apology for those who held office under Domitian,[36] passages such as 42.4, already noted above, can be read as Tacitus's legitimation of the behavior of people like himself and his father-in-law, as opposed to the pointless vain-glorious gestures of people like Thrasea Paetus, who only succeeded in getting himself killed. Once again, we must be wary of "community-language": in these cases, the group being legitimated are people like the author, or those who might agree with him, rather than a specific community — and the intended audience is a wider readership.

Referring to my suggestions about apologetic and polemic in *bioi*, Graham Stanton has declared that "this is precisely the social function I envisage for Matthew's βίος of Jesus" and he goes on to argue for a wider audience than just one single "Matthean community."[37] Similarly in Luke-Acts, we have the constant declaration of the "innocence" of Jesus (by Pilate, 23:4, 14-15, 22, and also in Luke's redaction of the centurion in 23:47), and this is then repeated frequently of the early church leaders like Peter and Paul in Acts. This implies that the author envisaged a wider public, aiming to legitimate the church in the eyes of contemporary society. Brown argues that the Fourth Gospel's portrayal of "the Jews" and the references to being put out of the synagogue (9:22; 12:42; 16:2) suggest that conflict is taking place between the

36. "The Agricola is, then, neither a political pamphlet nor a personal apologia," Ogilvie in *Cornelii Taciti de vita Agricolae*, ed. R. M. Ogilvie and I. Richmond (Oxford: Oxford University Press, 1967), 19.

37. Graham N Stanton, "Revisiting Matthew's Communities," *Society of Biblical Literature Seminar Papers 1994*, ed. E. H. Loverington (Atlanta: Scholars, 1994), 9-23, quotation from 10; see also Stanton, *A Gospel for a New People: Studies in Matthew* (Edinburgh: T. & T. Clark, 1992), 70, also 104-7 and 378-79 for more on legitimation, and 232-55 for the use of Matthew in early Christian-Jewish polemic and apologetic.

"Johannine community" and the synagogue.[38] However, this would have been happening all over the ancient Mediterranean, rather than in just one city, such as Ephesus. The evangelist writes his account of the *bios* of Jesus in terms of growing conflict in order to legitimate this separation from the synagogue and to help similar groups in similar situations across the whole Jewish-Christian world.

Thus even the social functions of apologetic and polemic suggest that the Gospels, like other *bioi,* are written for wider audiences than just single communities. This result is confirmed by a brief consideration of the other social functions and purposes of ancient biography. Both Luke (1:3-4) and John (20:30-31) suggest that informing their readers about Jesus was part of their purpose, and this can be compared with statements from Philo (*Moses* I.1) and Philostratus (*Apollonius of Tyana,* I.2-3) about correcting people's ignorance concerning their subjects. Similarly, the didactic function of biography is seen in Philo's desire to teach what sort of life Moses lived (τοιοῦτος μὲν ὁ βίος, II.292) and his discussion of his subject's teachings; Lucian says much the same of Demonax (ὁποῖος ἐκεῖνος ἀνὴρ ἐγένετο, *Dem.* 67) and both he and Philostratus include their subject's teaching. The amount of Jesus' teaching included in the Gospels, especially by Matthew and Luke, demonstrates a similar aim. Furthermore, we must not forget that much ancient biography was written to entertain the audience, which is best exemplified by the anecdotes about Euripides preserved in Satyrus, or by the satirical undercurrents included by Lucian, who was a professional entertainer, in his *Demonax,* not to mention the literary skill of Plutarch's or Tacitus's writings. While the evangelists may not have made this their top priority, Beavis points out that their accounts had to be sufficiently interesting to hold the audience's attention,[39] while Luke's literary skill can be seen in the variations of his Greek from the Semitic opening chapters to the more Greek style employed as the narrative gets closer to Athens and Rome.

Thus comparing the Gospels with other ancient biographies allows us to see a variety of social functions directed at wider audiences than the "community hypothesis" usually suggests.

---

38. See Brown, *The Community of the Beloved Disciple,* 40-43, 66-69.
39. Beavis, *Mark's Audience,* 124-30.

c. Social Levels

One of the interesting things about the New Testament from a classicist's perspective is that it contains material of a different social level from that of most surviving classical texts, which tend to originate from the literate and ruling elites. Dibelius, K. L. Schmidt, and Bultmann all used the distinction between *Hochliteratur* (formal conscious literary works) and *Kleinliteratur* (oral and popular storytelling) as a further reason for the Gospels' uniqueness and why they cannot be compared with ancient genres.[40] In fact, writing takes place at many different levels in Greco-Roman society, and questions of genre, conventions, authorial intention, and reader expectation can — and must — be asked of them all. It is just an accident of history that the majority of surviving classical texts come out of the social top drawer. However, we know of material that reached right across the social spectrum. There is no reason to suppose that the New Testament writings are particularly unique, any more than we should consider New Testament Greek special because it is different from classical or literary prose. Analysis from the work of Deissmann onwards of first-century letters and papyri written in the same popular, common (Koiné) style as much of the New Testament has shown the fallacy of such assumptions.[41]

Here then is another area where the biographical hypothesis might help to illuminate the question of the audience for which the Gospels were written. While it is the case that most surviving *bioi* do come from the literary and ruling elites, we know of a range of titles of *bioi* across a wider spectrum;[42] furthermore, biographical stories and anecdotes were used even in primary education or in the home for moral instruction — providing the paradigm to follow or the wretched ex-

40. M. Dibelius, *From Tradition to Gospel* (London: James Clarke, 1971), 1-2; Schmidt, "Die Stellung der Evangelien," 76 and 82; R. Bultmann, *The History of the Synoptic Tradition* (Oxford: Blackwell, 1972), 371-72.

41. A. Deissmann, *Light from the Ancient East,* trans. L. Strachan, 4th ed. (Grand Rapids: Baker Book House, 1965).

42. See K. Berger, "Hellenistische Gattungen im Neuen Testament," *Aufstieg und Niedergang der römischen Welt,* II.25.2 (1984): 1031-1432; see his list on 1231-36.

ample to avoid. When we turn to specific examples, we can see differences in their social settings; compare, for instance, the politically charged atmosphere of Greek (the *Evagoras* or *Agesilaus*) or Roman *(Agricola)* ruling groups with Plutarch's "salon society." Despite the dedication of his work to a *Roman,* Q. Sosius Senecio, and the various people mentioned by name at the start of his works, Plutarch aimed for a wider distribution of his *Lives* outside that actual circle; he explains Roman institutions and words, suggesting that he wants to inspire his *Greek* compatriots to take part in public life.[43] Whatever we are to make of Philostratus's claims to have been commissioned by the Empress Julia Domna to write about Apollonius for her circle, both his expressed desire to correct widespread ignorance about the sage (I.2-3) and the style suggest a wider readership than the imperial court.[44] Certainly, works of writers like Satyrus and Lucian seem aimed beyond an elite readership to a moderately educated popular audience.

Loveday Alexander's study of the Lukan preface has led her to compare it with those found in scientific and technical treatises in the ancient world. This suggests that Luke's "social matrix" belongs in an intermediate zone between the upper literary classes and the lower social levels.[45] Luke's dedication of his work to Theophilus "does not mean that it is a private communication for one reader only; dedication is a widely recognized literary courtesy."[46] We might compare it with the dedications by Plutarch and Philostratus mentioned above.

---

43. See C. P. Jones, *Plutarch and Rome* (Oxford: Clarendon, 1971), 39-64, and Philip A. Stadter, "The Proems of Plutarch's Lives," *Illinois Classical Studies* 13 (1988): 275-95.

44. See Graham Anderson, *Philostratus: Biography and Belles Lettres in the Third Century A.D.* (London: Croom Helm, 1986), 4-7.

45. L. C. A. Alexander, *The Preface to Luke's Gospel: Literary Convention and Social Context in Luke 1.1-4 and Acts 1.1,* Society for New Testament Studies Monograph Series 78 (Cambridge: Cambridge University Press, 1993); see chapter 8 on "The Social Matrix of Luke's Preface," 168-86; also Alexander, "Luke's Preface in the Context of Greek Preface-Writing," *Novum Testamentum* 28 (1986): 48-74.

46. Alexander, *The Preface to Luke's Gospel* 187; 187-200 consider Theophilus in more detail.

This all suggests an intended social level for the Gospels' audiences in the middle of the scale, rather than the old rigid distinction of *Hoch-* and *Klein-literatur*. This is what we should expect as a result of Hellenistic education across the ancient world; its very success in the Jewish world can be deduced from the response by conservative Jews from the period of the Maccabees onwards to set up their own schools to counteract this influence. The language of the New Testament may be simpler than Plutarch's, but it still implies education and some rhetorical knowledge: Luke is clearly aware not just of conventions (like prefaces) but also of literary motifs from Homer onwards (like the storm-tossed travelers in Acts 27). The elements of surprise and irony, tragedy and comedy in the Fourth Gospel, together with the multilevel functioning of its text, also imply sophisticated literary knowledge and usage.[47]

Thus comparison of the Gospels with *bioi* and other middle-range works like monographs or treatises proves illuminating for the evangelists' social settings and levels. The wider circulation of such works around the ancient Mediterranean beyond their dedicatees or author's immediate circle again suggests that the Gospels were intended for a wider audience than just a single community.

d. Social Setting of Delivery and Publication

Another area where hypothetical sociological reconstructions are traditionally deduced from the Gospels' texts concerns how they were produced and used. It is often assumed that they were designed to be read in church, either in worship (hence the various lectionary hypotheses) or for instruction (hence suggestions about manuals of teaching).[48] This takes us straight into questions about the production and publication of ancient texts and the extent to which people were able to read them. Although we

---

47. See Stibbe, *John as Storyteller,* esp. 13-22.

48. For worship, see M. Goulder, *The Evangelist's Calendar: A Lectionary Explanation of the Development of Scripture* (London: SPCK, 1978); see also Mary Ann Beavis's comprehensive discussion of proposals for Mark's audience in terms of worship (*Mark's Audience,* 46-50) and teaching (50-66).

do have references in first-century poets to their manuscripts being copied and put out for sale in book shops, it is probably not the case that the evangelists' "target market" was the bookstore in the chariot stop on the main highway out of Rome, nor the best-seller lists! However, this does not mean that the Gospels were community-specific documents, written to and published or circulated within only one specific social group. Even Paul's letters, which were written to specific communities, seem to have been passed around to others to read aloud — and they were then preserved in collections for further reading. We might compare the collections of letters by Cicero, or the Roman governor Pliny, who considered his correspondence with the emperor Trajan about very specific (and often mundane) matters in his province still publishable and of interest to others — but this does not require us to postulate a "Pliny community."

Reading aloud was one of the main ways of "publication" in the ancient world, often as entertainment after dinner. To this extent we can see a "communal setting" (rather than the tighter definition of a sectarian community) as a frequent feature of ancient literature. The *Agricola* contains many *sententiae,* pithy little maxims which conclude each section with a rhetorical flourish — allowing a "pause for applause." Similarly, the style of Lucian's *Demonax* lends itself to oral delivery, with space for audience reaction (even laughter?) after each anecdote. Lucian, and other traveling sophists, could deliver such works in public as they went from city to city.

One of the reasons for the division of ancient works into "books" is that one scroll is about the amount which can be delivered in one "sitting" — with allowance for comfort breaks! The average length of a book of Herodotus or Thucydides is about 20,000 words, which would take around two hours to read. After the Alexandrian library reforms, an average 30-35 feet scroll would contain 10,000 to 25,000 words — exactly the range into which both the Gospels and many ancient *bioi* fall.[49] We

---

49. Scrolls tended to be 8-12 inches high and 30-35 feet long; columns were 2-4 inches wide, with 18-25 letters per line and 35-45 lines per column; see F. G. Kenyon and C. H. Roberts, "Books, Greek and Latin" in *The Oxford Classical Dictionary,* 2d ed. (Oxford: Oxford University Press, 1970), 172-75; on the relative lengths of different genres, see Burridge, *What Are the Gospels?* 118-19.

are so used to hearing the Gospels in lectionary use in small sections of twelve to twenty verses or studying individual pericopes that we forget that the entire text can be read out aloud in a couple of hours. It is significant that Alec McCowen's dramatic solo rendition of Mark's Gospel (in the King James Version) has been an evening's entertainment on stage on both sides of the Atlantic; the video recording of his performance runs for only 105 minutes in total.[50] Christopher Bryan's *A Preface to Mark* provides an interesting study of that Gospel as a Hellenistic life designed to be read aloud.[51]

Consideration of how *bioi,* like those of Tacitus and Lucian, were read aloud or performed can benefit Gospel studies, illuminating how they may have been read, not just in one community, but in many different groups across a wide geographical area. Although Harris's work has noted the limits of literacy in the ancient world, he points out the importance of someone reading aloud for the benefit of a less literate person or group, and uses the church as an example: "in the second century the scriptures were normally *heard.*"[52] He further suggests that the need to read Gospels and epistles as sacred Scripture may have contributed to the spread of literacy in the ancient world.[53] Early Jewish Christians would also be familiar with the readings of Scripture in synagogues. However, the comparison of the Gospels with ancient biographies allows for their reading in much larger blocks than is usually suggested by liturgical or lectionary hypotheses for their genre. One can imagine illiterate or semiliterate groups gathering to hear (dra-

50. The video of Alec McCowen's solo performance of Mark's Gospel is produced by Arthur Cantor Films, 2112 Broadway, Suite 400, New York, NY 10023.

51. Christopher Bryan, *A Preface to Mark: Notes on the Gospel in Its Literary and Cultural Settings* (Oxford: Oxford University Press, 1993).

52. William V. Harris, *Ancient Literacy* (Cambridge, Mass.: Harvard University Press, 1989), 305, his italics.

53. Harris, *Ancient Literacy* 220-21; see also *Literacy in the Roman World,* ed. Mary Beard *et al., JRA* Supplementary Series 3 (Ann Arbor, Mich.: Journal of Roman Archeology, 1991), especially Mary Beard's chapter "Ancient Literacy and the Function of the Written Word in Roman Religion," 35-58, and Nicholas Horsfall's treatment of the evidence for literacy in the church, "Statistics or States of Mind?" 59-76.

matic?) readings as a form of entertainment, in the way lecture tours flourished in the pretelevision age. Downing has argued that literary and cultural awareness was mediated down the social scale through public debates and speakers, but also through after-dinner entertainment, with the lower classes listening in while serving or attending, so that "there is no sign of a culture-gap between the highly literate aristocracy and the masses."[54] The comparison between an after-dinner reading for the guests with servants listening in and a meeting for worship in a house including readings at the Eucharistic meal again suggests a wider audience for the Gospels than just one community.

Thus viewing the Gospels as ancient biographies can liberate us from the circularity of deducing the communities from the text and then interpreting the text in light of these (deduced) communities. Instead, this generic comparison provides external evidence of social groupings and levels in which *bioi* functioned. Rather than the very specific communities posited by redaction critics, these comparisons suggest that our modern concept of "target audience" or "market niche" is better. Thus Tacitus writes for anyone interested in the events under Domitian, particularly as they affected his father-in-law Agricola, probably with half an eye on those who might criticize him for working with the tyrant. Such people are likely to have come from the Roman ruling classes, probably senatorial, but they do not comprise a "Tacitean community." The idea of the "implied reader" of the Gospels is thus more useful than speculations about their communities. Therefore it is reasonable to assume that Matthew has as his target audience Christians from a Jewish background who have a high regard for the Mosaic law and who have suffered antagonism or persecution from other Jews, perhaps around the time of the separation of the church from the synagogue in the later years of the first century. On the other hand, Luke is more likely to be aiming to explain Jesus' life and teaching for a Gentile market niche. Instead of looking at the archeological and literary evidence about Antioch (as a possible site for the Matthean

54. F. Gerald Downing, "A bas les aristos: The Relevance of Higher Literature for the Understanding of the Earliest Christian Writings," *Novum Testamentum* 30 (1988): 212-30.

community) or Ephesus (for the Johannine) and then interpreting the Gospels in that light, we would do better to imagine people all over the Mediterranean world who might fit each evangelist's projected readership, rather than just a small group of people in one specific community. Matthew's Gospel might well appeal to Christians who were from Jewish backgrounds, while Luke appealed to those of Gentile origin, but they could well be members of the same church congregation. The Gospels would then be functioning and circulating in a very similar way to other ancient biographies.

6. Conclusions and Implications

This chapter has argued that the scholarly stress on the evangelists' communities as both the context *within which* the Gospel was composed and the audience *for whom* it was written has arisen from a misunderstanding of the genre of the Gospels. Behind the recent consensus has been the supposition that the Gospels are unique forms of literature (genre), composed by many different people through the oral tradition and written down by a scribe (authorship) for the benefit of a specific community (audience) to inform them about various theological issues (subject). On the other hand, a realization that the genre of the Gospels is actually a form of ancient biography has liberated all three aspects of the communication model. The essentially person-centered nature of biography reminds us that *bioi* are works written by people for people about people. The *content* of the works concerns the subject of Jesus; the *author* is a particular writer with a view of Jesus he wishes to communicate; and the intended *audience* is more likely to include various groups and individuals across the Mediterranean world interested in Jesus, probably both inside and outside the churches. Of course, people are to be found in communities, and none of this argument should detract from the communal or ecclesial nature of the early church groups. However, like other ancient biographies, the Gospels are written to explain the person of Jesus to individuals and groups in many places, rather than just one specific sectarian community in one city. This is after all the function that they have performed, certainly since the time of Irenaeus and the development of the fourfold canon in the second century, right through to today. New Testament critics should not expect them to have functioned differently or to have been more narrowly defined in the first century. The Gospels are for all Christians — and even beyond the church for all those who want to know about Jesus of Nazareth.

John for Readers of Mark

RICHARD BAUCKHAM

I

Most of the discussion of the relationship between the Fourth Gospel and Mark's Gospel[1] has been orientated to the source-critical question of whether the fourth evangelist, in writing his Gospel, was *dependent* on Mark. Even the view that he did not use Mark as a source, but knew Mark, so that reminiscences of Mark's text sometimes appear in his Gospel, is usually formulated as an answer to the question of the independence of John's traditions in view of the close verbal resemblances to Mark in a few passages of the Gospel. The recent popularity of the view that John is wholly independent of Mark, such that he had presumably never even read Mark's Gospel, has coincided with the growing popularity of the view that, since the Fourth Gospel is so distinctive among the Gospels, the community in which it took shape and to which it was addressed must have been largely out of touch with the rest of the early Christian movement, developing in some isolated context where Mark's Gospel was not known. Since even the strongest advocates of the consensus view that each Gospel was written for the evangelist's own community usually agree that Mark's Gospel must have

---

1. For a full account of the discussion, see D. M. Smith, *John Among the Gospels: The Relationship in Twentieth-Century Research* (Minneapolis: Fortress, 1992).

circulated quite widely among the churches by the time that the final form of the Fourth Gospel was completed, only the view that this Gospel's community, to which it was addressed, was both idiosyncratic and isolated can make it plausible that neither the fourth evangelist (or whatever sequence of Johannine authors and editors is postulated) nor his readers/hearers knew Mark's Gospel. Conversely, the popularity of the source-critical opinion that John (unlike Matthew and Luke) is independent of Mark has probably helped to reinforce the view that the Johannine community and its Gospel existed and developed in splendid isolation. What was once a question purely of the independence of John's Gospel traditions has now become inseparable from the question of the isolation of the Johannine community from the rest of the early Christian movement.

The thesis of the present volume enables a fresh approach to the question of the relationship of John to Mark. On the hypothesis that all of the Gospels, including John, were written not for the evangelist's own community in particular but to circulate around the churches generally, the fourth evangelist must have expected most of his readers to know Mark.[2] We need not suppose that Mark was being read by every Christian community without exception when the Fourth Gospel was completed and began to circulate. The evangelist could have hoped his Gospel would be read in some communities that did not use Mark, but he must have expected the majority of his readers/hearers to know

2. On the assumption that Matthew and Luke used Mark, I think we can assume that Mark had circulated widely by the time John wrote, but not necessarily that Matthew and Luke had circulated widely. We do not have adequate evidence to establish the chronological sequence in which Matthew, Luke, and John were written, still less to be sure that one of these had already circulated widely enough for the author of another of them to expect many of his readers to know it. All three of these Gospels may well have been written within a very short chronological span late in the first century. Only if John's dependence on Matthew or Luke could be demonstrated, as I do not believe it can be, would it be possible to be sure that John wrote subsequently to either of these Gospels. The habit of regarding John as certainly the latest of the four Gospels is a relic of (1) the nineteenth-century view, held now by very few scholars, that John is dependent on all three Synoptic Gospels, and (2) the view that John is more theologically advanced than Matthew and Luke and therefore also later (a non sequitur).

148

Mark. It therefore makes sense to ask whether the Fourth Gospel is written in such a way as to accommodate such readers/hearers. Does it ignore the fact that many of the readers/hearers know Mark, or does it in any way presuppose their knowledge of Mark? This is a different question from the question of whether the Fourth Gospel is dependent on Mark. The evangelist could have used Mark as a source or could have been influenced by Mark without expecting his readers/hearers to know Mark. But if he did expect many of his readers/hearers to know Mark, this could be apparent in features of the Gospel other than those that are usually the focus of attention when the source-critical question is asked. So, instead of approaching the question of John's relationship to Mark from a source-critical perspective, we shall approach it here from the perspective of John's implied readership. If the consensus in Johannine scholarship, according to which the Gospel is addressed to the Johannine community, is correct, the Gospel should show evidence that its implied readership can be expected already to know many of the peculiarly Johannine Gospel traditions which it contains. But if the thesis of this volume is correct, the Gospel's implied readership cannot be expected already to know any peculiarly Johannine traditions but might be expected to know Mark. If the evangelist could expect a majority, but not necessarily all of his readers to know Mark, he could not write in a way that would be unintelligible to those who did not know Mark, but he might nevertheless find ways of enabling the majority of his expected readers to relate their knowledge of Mark to his own narrative. If we find evidence that the Gospel is designed to accommodate such readers, while not excluding others, and if there is no similar evidence that a readership already familiar with specifically Johannine Gospel traditions is in view, this will be a significant confirmation of the argument that John was written, not for the "Johannine community," but to circulate generally among the churches.

To some extent our agenda requires a return to questions that were most discussed in the period when it was generally believed that John was dependent on all three Synoptic Gospels.[3] The prevalent nineteenth-century view was that the fourth evangelist intended his

3. See Smith, *John Among the Gospels*, chap. 1.

Gospel to supplement the Synoptics, while Hans Windisch in 1926 argued that he intended his Gospel to displace and replace the Synoptics.[4] Such questions have subsequently been generally marginalized[5] by the discussion about whether John knew any of the Synoptics at all, as well as by the rise of theories about the Johannine community and the stages of composition of the Gospel in relation to the history of the community. If the thesis of this book is correct, the questions discussed in the older scholarship need now to be taken up again, though primarily in relation to Mark, rather than in relation to all three Synoptics. Without nineteenth-century scholarship's confidence in John's dependence on Matthew and Luke, we cannot think it likely that John could expect many of his readers to know either of those Gospels. But if the Fourth Gospel does show evidence that many of its readers are expected to know Mark, then we also need to consider whether this evidence is such as to indicate that the Gospel is intended to replace Mark or to be read in addition to Mark.

II

A characteristic feature of the Fourth Gospel is the large number of parenthetical explanations it contains. They take many different forms and perform various different functions.[6] We should not suppose that all of the implied readers are expected to need all of these explanations. For example, the translations of the words "Rabbi" and "Messiah" (1:38, 41) are unlikely to have been needed by any Jewish reader/hearer, even in the diaspora, but their presence in the Gospel does not indicate that only Gentile readers/hearers are expected. They are included for the sake of those readers/hearers who may need them. In this chapter

---

4. H. Windisch, *Johannes und die Synoptiker: Wollte der vierte Evangelist die älteren Evangelien ergänzen oder ersetzen?* Untersuchungen zur Neuen Testament 12 (Leipzig: Hinrichs, 1926).

5. An exception is B. de Solages, *Jean et les Synoptiques* (Leiden: Brill, 1979).

6. G. Van Belle, *Les parenthèses dans l'Évangile de Jean*, Studiorum Novi Testamenti Auxilia 11 (Leuven: University Press/Peeters, 1985), esp. 106-12.

we shall argue that two of John's parenthetical explanations (3:24; 11:2) are intended specifically for readers/hearers who also knew Mark's Gospel. The functions of these two explanations, which are otherwise very difficult to understand, become clear when they are recognized as indications of the way readers/hearers who also know Mark's Gospel are to relate John's narrative to Mark's. One of these explanations (3:24) serves to relate John's chronological sequence to Mark's; the other (11:2) serves to identify a named character in John as one already known anonymously to readers of Mark. Using each of these parenthetical explanations as a starting point, we shall also explore the way in which two aspects of the Fourth Gospel relate to Mark: its narrative sequence and its characters. For readers/hearers of John already familiar with Mark's Gospel, these would be perhaps the most obvious and important ways in which they would need to relate the two Gospels as they read or heard John. Both Gospels, after all, are narrative accounts of broadly the same sequence of events: the ministry, death, and resurrection of Jesus. As Richard Burridge argues elsewhere in this volume, both would have been most easily understood by their first readers/hearers as *bioi* of Jesus. For readers/hearers already familiar with the narrative sequence and characters of one of these *bioi* of Jesus, the differences and overlaps in narrative sequence and characters between the two *bioi* would strike them much more immediately than the resemblances and differences in theological interpretation, especially as the differences both in narrative content and in prominent characters in the two Gospels are very striking. If the fourth evangelist expected such readers/hearers, he may well have provided some assistance for them in relating his own narrative sequence and characters to Mark's.

Van Belle's exhaustive study of the parentheses in John has shown the extent to which, in both style and content, they are homogeneous both with each other and with the rest of the Gospel.[7] The habit of

---

7. Van Belle, *Les parenthèses,* esp. 113-55, 206-10; see also the supplementary study which updates his work: G. Van Belle, "Les parenthèses johanniques," in *The Four Gospels 1992: Festschrift F. Neirynck,* ed. F. Van Segbroeck, C. M. Tuckett, G. Van Belle, and J. Verheyden, Bibliotheca Ephemeridum Theologicarum Lovaniensium 100 (Leuven: University Press/Peeters, 1992), 3:1901-33.

critics, prior to recent literary studies, of attributing many of them to later redactors or glossators is unjustified. The presence of explanatory parentheses of various kinds in the Gospel is not evidence of redactional processes in the history of the composition of the Gospel or of later additions to the text of the Gospel, but is simply a characteristic literary feature of the Fourth Gospel as such.[8] The parentheses in general must be regarded as integral to the Gospel, and to treat any particular parenthesis as a gloss requires a very good argument in that particular case if it is to be convincing. However, since both 3:24 and 11:2 have not infrequently been regarded as glosses, which could therefore tell us nothing about the implied readership of the Gospel in the form in which it first began to circulate, we shall offer in each case reasons for treating the parenthesis as integral to the Gospel. In the case of 3:24 (οὔπω γὰρ ἦν βεβλημένος εἰς τὴν φυλακὴν ὁ Ἰωάννης), several points can be made: (1) οὔπω is characteristic of the vocabulary of the Gospel.[9] (2) οὔπω is especially characteristic of the parentheses in John (6:30; 7:8, 30, 39; 8:20; 11:30; 20:17; cf. οὐδέπω in 7:39; 20:9). (3) Three other parentheses begin in the same way as 3:24 (7:39: οὔπω γὰρ ἦν; 20:9: οὐδέπω γάρ; 20:17: οὔπω γάρ). (4) The resumptive use of οὖν in 3:25 is an instance of a very common usage after parentheses in John (van Belle lists 51 cases).[10] Thus we can safely treat 3:24 as integral to the Gospel and proceed to investigate its function for the implied readers of the Gospel.

In 3:23 the evangelist introduces John the Baptist for the first time since John's testimony to Jesus in 1:36. He describes a period, following Jesus' first visit to Jerusalem (2:13–3:21), in which Jesus and his disciples were baptizing in Judea (3:22), while John continued his own ministry of baptism (1:23). The evangelist adds the parenthetical explanation: "For John had not yet been thrown into prison" (3:24).

8. See also the important study by C. W. Hedrick, "Authorial Presence and Narrator in John: Commentary and Story," in *Gospel Origins and Christian Beginnings,* ed. J. E. Goehring, C. W. Hedrick, J. T. Sanders, and H. D. Betz, J. M. Robinson Festschrift; Forum Fascicles 1 (Sonoma, Calif.: Polebridge, 1990), 74-93.

9. New Testament usage: Matthew 2; Mark 5; Luke 1; John 11; Paul 2: Hebrews 2; 1 John 1; Revelation 2. Cf. also οὐδέπω: John 3; Acts 1.

10. Van Belle, *Les parenthèses,* 119.

As an explanation purely of what the text of the Gospel has said, this explanation seems ludicrously redundant. If John was still baptizing, of course he could not yet have been imprisoned. It might be supposed that the evangelist wished in this way to convey to his readers that John's ministry was going to be brought to an end, in order to prepare for 3:30 ("He [Jesus] must increase, but I [John] must decrease") and 5:35 (which presupposes that John's ministry — if not his life — had by then come to an end). But 3:24 would be a very odd way in which to do this. It refers to John's imprisonment as though it were something already known to the readers/hearers and as though a chronological point were at issue.

To understand the reason for the explanation, we are obliged to postulate implied readers/hearers who know more than the Gospel itself has told them. They seem to be expected already to know that John's ministry came to an end when he was imprisoned, but even this knowledge is not sufficient to account for the explanation. Whether or not readers/hearers already know that John was imprisoned, they do not need to be told the obvious: that he was not yet imprisoned when he was still baptizing. Most commentators are therefore obliged at this point to refer to Mark 1:14 (par Matt. 4:12), where, following the account of Jesus' baptism and period in the wilderness, Mark recounts the beginning of Jesus' ministry in Galilee: "Now after John was arrested, Jesus came to Galilee, proclaiming the good news of God." If readers/hearers of the Fourth Gospel (or at least those of them for whom the parenthetical explanation in 3:24 is intended) can be presumed to know this Markan account, then the reason for the explanation becomes clear. It serves, not to make a point about the ministry and fate of John the Baptist for their own sake, but to make a point about the chronological relationship of Jesus' ministry to John's. The evangelist is pointing out that this period of Jesus' ministry in Judea preceded the beginning of the Galilean ministry as recounted by Mark, since the former preceded John's imprisonment, while the latter, as Mark 1:14 states, succeeded it. It is not very likely that readers/hearers of the Fourth Gospel would be expected to know from oral Gospel traditions that Jesus' Galilean ministry followed the imprisonment of John. The chronological sequence in Mark 1:14 (followed by Matt. 4:12, but not by Luke 4:14) is more likely to be Markan than traditional. But even if it could have been known from oral tradition, we should still need to explain why the fourth evangelist takes the trouble to make this kind of explicit connection of his own narrative with it. This, as we shall see, is more explicable if his intention is to relate the whole of the first part of his Gospel narrative to the sequence of events in Mark's account of the beginning of Jesus' ministry.

John 3:24 has sometimes been understood as an explicit correction of Mark:[11] whereas Mark dates the beginning of Jesus' ministry after the end of the Baptist's, John depicts a period in which Jesus' ministry was contemporaneous with the Baptist's. In fact, however, the beginning of the public ministry of Jesus in Galilee, which Mark 1:14 dates after the imprisonment of John, does not occur in the narrative of the Fourth Gospel until 4:43-45. In 2:1-12 there is no reference to a public ministry in Galilee: the miracle at Cana is witnessed only by Jesus' disciples.[12] Ministry in Jerusalem (2:13–3:21), Judea (3:22–4:3), and Samaria (4:3-43) follows. Not until 4:45 does the fourth evangelist indicate a public role for Jesus in Galilee. The function of 3:24, for readers/hearers of Mark, is therefore not to correct Mark's chronology, but to place the events of John 1:19–4:43 between Mark 1:13 and Mark 1:14. To readers/hearers of Mark it will already have been clear that the Fourth Gospel's narrative begins after Mark 1:13, since the baptism of Jesus is not narrated but presupposed. On the second day of the Fourth Gospel's narrative, John the Baptist refers back to it — or at least to the descent of the Spirit in the form of a dove, which in Mark 1:10 occurs at the time of Jesus' baptism — as an event in the past (John 1:32), preceding the point at which the Fourth Gospel's narrative began. John 3:24 enables readers/hearers familiar with Mark's narrative to continue to place John's narrative in correct relationship to it, by indicating that they are still in the period between Mark 1:13 and Mark 1:14.

The function of John 3:24 is not, therefore, merely that of pre-

11. E.g., de Solages, *Jean et les Synoptiques*, 182-83.
12. This is confirmed by 4:45: when Jesus returns to Galilee, the Galileans know him, not from his earlier reputation in Galilee, but from Jerusalem.

cluding the impression that John's narrative is at this point inconsistent with Mark's.[13] It also serves to make quite clear the way in which the narrative of John's first four chapters is designed to dovetail into Mark's, such that John 1:19–4:43 fits into a putative gap that readers/hearers of John who also know Mark are obliged by John to postulate between Mark 1:13 and Mark 1:14.

This rather explicit indication of the way in which John's narrative relates chronologically to Mark's would encourage readers/hearers of John who also knew Mark to correlate the rest of the two Gospel narratives in a similar way. Modern scholars rarely notice the ease with which this, for the most part, can be done. This is no doubt partly because they have been preoccupied with the issue of John's possible dependence on Mark, rather than with the way in which John's narrative would be read/heard by an audience very familiar with Mark. Probably also a suspicion of the kind of harmonization associated with traditional harmonies of the Gospels has led scholars to read the two different sequences of events in Mark and John as alternative and incompatible rather than as complementary accounts. Our purpose now is not to return to a traditional form of harmonization, but to suggest that for the most part (not, as we shall see, in every detail) readers/hearers of John who were already familiar with Mark could easily have read the two narratives as complementary.

For such readers/hearers, the feeding of the five thousand and the walking on the water (John 6:1-21; Mark 6:31-53), which are the only events narrated by both evangelists prior to Jesus' final week in Jerusalem, divide the Galilean ministry narrated by Mark into two parts. To the first part, prior to these events (Mark 1:14–6:13), there corresponds in John only the healing of the official's son at Capernaum (John 4:46-54). For such readers/hearers, then, John takes Mark's account of this first part of the Galilean ministry as read, supplementing it with just one miracle story. Even this story could easily be presumed, by

---

13. So R. Bultmann, *The Gospel of John*, trans. G. R. Beasley-Murray (Oxford: Blackwell, 1971), 171 and n. 2; B. Lindars, *The Gospel of John*, New Century Bible (London: Marshall, Morgan, and Scott, 1972), 165; R. E. Brown, *The Gospel According to John*, Anchor Bible 29-29A (New York: Doubleday, 1966), 153.

readers/hearers familiar with Mark, to have taken place before Mark's account of the Galilean ministry begins. It takes place when Jesus, traveling north from Samaria, is in Cana (John 4:46), before he reaches the Sea of Galilee (Mark 1:16).

It is notable that this first part of the Galilean ministry in Mark includes the appointment of the twelve (Mark 3:13-19), to which John 6:67-71 can refer back as an event that has already occurred, even though the Fourth Gospel itself has not narrated it, just as John 1:32 refers back to the descent of the Spirit at Jesus' baptism. Readers/hearers of John who were also familiar with Mark might notice two further correlations between John 5: the visit of Jesus to Jerusalem, which John places immediately before the feeding of the five thousand, and the narratives that immediately precede the feeding of the five thousand in Mark. First, Mark narrates what the twelve did when Jesus sent them out on mission (6:7-13, 30), with no indication of what Jesus himself did meantime, whereas John narrates a visit of Jesus to Jerusalem in which no mention is made of the disciples (John 5). Secondly, during this visit to Jerusalem, Jesus refers to John the Baptist's ministry as now past (John 5:33-35), while the death of the Baptist, which this reference most naturally presupposes, is an event of which readers of Mark have been informed precisely at the corresponding point in Mark's narrative, immediately prior to the feeding of the five thousand (Mark 6:13-29). Although these correlations are not important enough for John to make them explicit, they could easily be seen by readers/hearers of John who were familiar with Mark's narrative, especially since many such readers/hearers are likely to have been very familiar indeed with the narrative sequence of the only written Gospel they had previously known.

The second part of the Galilean ministry in Mark (6:54–9:50), following the feeding of the five thousand and the walking on the water, is summarized by John in a single sentence (7:1a), which very clearly implies a significant period of ministry left wholly unnarrated by John. According to John's explicit chronology (6:4; 7:2) a period of six months[14] in Galilee is here left entirely unnarrated by John. No clearer

---

14. This is as long as the period in which all the events John narrates from 7:2 to the end of his Gospel take place.

indication would be needed for readers/hearers who knew Mark to understand this period as that narrated by Mark in chapters 7–9. After John 7:1-9 John's Jesus is never again in Galilee (until after the resurrection) but visits Jerusalem for the Feast of Booths (7:10–10:21), is still there at the Feast of the Dedication (10:22-39), engages in ministry beyond the Jordan (10:40-42), visits Bethany (11:7-44), and goes into hiding in Ephraim (11:54), before returning to Bethany (12:1-8) at the beginning of his final week in Jerusalem. For readers/hearers of John who were also familiar with Mark, what John narrates in 7:10–10:39 would fill out Mark's mere indication that, at the conclusion of his Galilean ministry, Jesus "left that place [Capernaum] and went to the region of Judea" (Mark 10:1a), while the account of Jesus' ministry in the region "beyond the Jordan" (Mark 10:1) which follows in Mark (10:1-31) would be summarized by John's brief reference to this period (John 10:40-42). Such readers/hearers would then have to insert the events of John 11 between Mark 10:31 and Mark 10:32.

A final, impressive instance of the way John's narrative seems designed to dovetail into Mark's occurs in John 18:13-28. According to Mark 14:53, Jesus was taken from Gethsemane "to the high priest (ἀρχιερέα]," with whom the Jewish ruling group ("all the chief priests [ἀρχιερεῖς] and the elders and the scribes") was assembled. The high priest is not named by Mark. John's narrative involves two high priests: Caiaphas, the reigning high priest, and Annas, who, as a powerful ex-high priest, can still be called high priest (John 18:19), one of the group known as "the chief priests" (where the distinction between "high" and "chief" is made only in English translations, not in the Greek). In John Jesus is first interrogated by Annas and then taken to Caiaphas. For readers/hearers of John who were also familiar with Mark, John makes quite clear that the interrogation before Annas is not the trial before the high priest and the ruling group that Mark records, but precedes it. According to John 18:13, "they took [Jesus] first to Annas," who is then distinguished from Caiaphas, identified as the reigning high priest ("who was high priest that year"). Readers/hearers of John who also knew Mark would therefore realize that it is Caiaphas, not Annas, whom Mark calls the high priest, and in relating the two narratives they would interpose the interrogation by Annas in John

157

before the trial before the high priest in Mark. John's later information that "Annas then sent him bound to Caiaphas the high priest" (18:24) would be the indication for them that John's narrative joins Mark 14:53 only at this point. Such readers/hearers of the Gospel, unlike those who know only the Fourth Gospel, would not have to wonder what happened when Jesus was brought before Caiaphas, about which John is completely silent (18:24, 28a). For them this is another case where John supplies what Mark lacks (the interrogation by Annas), while taking as read what Mark recounts (the trial before Caiaphas and the ruling group, as well as the meeting of the whole council which followed: Mark 15:1). John's continuing narrative in fact presupposes that the Jewish ruling group ("the Jews": 18:31) have considered Jesus' case along with Caiaphas, since it is "they" (unexplained at first) who take Jesus from Caiaphas to the praetorium (18:28) and hand him over to Pilate (18:28-31). It is not strictly necessary to suppose that their charge against Jesus ("he ought to die because he has made himself the Son of God": 19:7) presupposes Mark's account of the trial before the high priest (Mark 14:61-64), since Jesus' claim to be the Son of God and the Jewish ruling group's judgment that this deserves death have already occurred at earlier points in John's narrative (5:17-18; 8:49-59; 10:24-39). But readers/hearers of John who also knew Mark would readily connect this charge with Mark's narrative of the trial before the high priest.

The evidence we have discussed, of the way in which John's narrative can be read as complementing Mark's, does not, for the most part, *require* readers/hearers of John to know Mark in order to understand John. Though John's narrative is at times explicitly selective (7:1 refers to a ministry in Galilee of which nothing at all is narrated; 18:24 refers to an appearance of Jesus before Caiaphas while giving no indication at all of what happened), the reader who cannot supply these gaps is not impeded from understanding John's own narrative, which makes its own sense as a self-contained narrative. Even at a few points where events not narrated in the Gospel are presupposed (1:32; 6:70), independent knowledge of these events by the implied reader is not absolutely necessary, and could be available from oral tradition as well as from Mark. To describe John's narrative as a supplement to Mark's would be therefore misleading. It has its own integrity, with powerful narrative logic and development of its own. But at the same time it is so written that, for readers/hearers who are also familiar with Mark, it rarely repeats and largely complements Mark's narrative, and in such a way that chronological dovetailing of the two narratives can easily be accomplished. As a narrative of the Gospel story, the Fourth Gospel is no mere supplement to Mark, but nor does it compete with Mark's narrative. Its implied readers need not know Mark, but if they do they will find that John's narrative sequence relates to Mark's in a largely complementary way. At one point (3:24), however, John provides a parenthetical explanation whose whole purpose must be to aid such readers/hearers who do know Mark to relate his narrative to Mark's. At this point, the intertextual relationship with Mark is made as explicit as it can be, short of reference to another Gospel writing as such. In the light of 3:24 there can be no doubt that the other evidence of the complementary relationship of John's narrative to Mark's belongs to the deliberate design of the Fourth Gospel, and that the Gospel presupposes that many of its readers/hearers will know Mark and will expect to be able to relate John's narrative to Mark's.

It is worth comparing John's relationship to Mark, in this respect, with Matthew's and Luke's relationships to Mark. Matthew and Luke, who repeat most of Mark's narratives, effect considerable changes in their order, while John, who repeats few of Mark's narratives, complements Mark's overall narrative in a way that can leave Mark's sequence of events for the most part intact. However, there are two major points at which John must be read as correcting Mark's chronological sequence.

Two of the Markan narratives John repeats — the "cleansing" of the temple and the anointing at Bethany — are moved from their place in Mark's sequence to an earlier point. The "cleansing" of the temple (Mark 11:15-18; John 2:14-22) is placed by Mark on the second day of the only visit to Jerusalem by Jesus that Mark recounts, whereas John places it in the visit to Jerusalem which in his Gospel inaugurates Jesus' public ministry, preceding the beginning of the Galilean ministry as recounted by Mark. At this point, for readers/hearers who know Mark, it must be clear that John corrects Mark. He makes it clear that in this difference of narrative sequence from Mark, it is his own sequence that is to be taken seriously as chronology, since he dates the "cleansing" of the temple, not only relatively to other events in his narrative of Jesus, but also absolutely. John 2:20 would provide a date for those who knew some Judean history, but even for those who did not it would indicate that the Johannine chronology is seriously intended to place the events of the Gospel in accurate historical time (whereas Mark offers no such precise chronological indication). Moreover, John 12:36b indicates that Jesus' public ministry ended with the first day of his last visit to Jerusalem, the day of the triumphal entry (John 12:12-36), contradicting, in this respect, not only Mark's placing of the "cleansing" of the temple on the following day (Mark 11:12, 15-18), but also Mark's account of Jesus' public teaching in the temple on the subsequent day (Mark 11:27–12:40). Thus readers/hearers of Mark who learn from the Fourth Gospel that Jesus visited Jerusalem several times prior to the only visit they knew from Mark would also learn from John that some of the events in Jerusalem that Mark placed in the only part of his Gospel in which Jesus is in Jerusalem could with greater chronological accuracy be placed in the earlier visits which Mark does not record.

The anointing at Bethany is precisely dated by John (12:1) several days before it occurs in Mark's narrative sequence (Mark 14:1, 3-9).[15] This precise dating once again makes the difference of narrative sequence (the anointing precedes the triumphal entry in John, but follows it in Mark) more than a matter of literary presentation. For readers/hearers of John who also know Mark, John's narrative sequence claims chronological accuracy in preference to Mark's, just as it does in the case of the "cleansing" of the temple. So, just as for the most part John enables his readers/hearers to relate his narrative sequence to Mark's in a way that leaves the latter undisturbed, so in these two cases

15. A third case where John may be understood as correcting Mark's narrative sequence is rather different. John's narrative of the way Andrew and Peter became disciples of Jesus, which he places precisely within the tight chronological sequence of the first week of his Gospel narrative (1:35-42), is not only thus placed much earlier than Mark's account of the call of Andrew and Peter (Mark 1:16-18) but is also a very different story. Readers/hearers who knew both Gospels might understand John to be correcting Mark, but equally they might read the two narratives as accounts of two different events.

he enables them to relate his narrative sequence to Mark's in a way that requires a reordering of Mark's narrative sequence.

III

We turn to the second explanatory parenthesis which, we shall argue, is directed at readers/hearers of John who already know Mark's Gospel: John 11:2. John 11:1-2 reads: "Now a certain man was ill, Lazarus of Bethany, of the village of Mary and her sister Martha. ²Mary was the one who anointed the Lord with perfume and wiped his feet with her hair; it was her brother Lazarus who was ill."

Most commentators have found the reference to Mary's anointing of Jesus awkward, since John does not narrate this event until 12:1-8. The most popular explanation of the difficulty has been to regard verse 2 as a later gloss.[16] However, there are quite decisive arguments against this view of verse 2, which have been strangely overlooked: (1) If verse 2 is removed, then it is not until verse 19 that readers/hearers discover that Lazarus is the brother of Martha and Mary. The abrupt introduction of this information in verse 19 would be very odd, as would be the absence of any indication of the relationship between Lazarus and the two sisters in the early part of the story, which clearly presupposes some kind of close relationship. It cannot be that knowledge of the relationship is assumed, since it is generally agreed that verse 1 introduces Lazarus for readers/hearers who have not necessarily heard of him before. Thus, in addition to whatever other function it may have, verse 2 performs an essential role in the narrative in explaining that Lazarus was the brother of Martha and Mary. (2) Just as Luke 10:38-39 refers first to Martha and then to her sister Mary, so John 11:5 refers to "Martha and her sister," and 11:19 to "Martha and Mary." The indications are that Martha was the elder sister, who would usually be named

16. E.g. J. H. Bernard, *A Critical and Exegetical Commentary on the Gospel According to St. John,* International Critical Commentary (Edinburgh: T. & T. Clark, 1928), 372; Bultmann, *The Gospel of John,* 396 n. 1; Lindars, *The Gospel of John,* 387; Brown, *The Gospel According to John,* 423.

before her sister. Furthermore, Martha plays a more prominent role than her sister in the narrative of John 11. The fact that verse 1 refers to "the village of Mary and her sister Martha" therefore requires explanation. If verse 2 belongs to the original text, there is an obvious explanation. Of the three persons introduced in verse 1, Mary is the one whose identity the evangelist can go on to elucidate by reference to a story about her which his readers/hearers can be expected to know. Mary is named before Martha in verse 1 because her identity is to be explained in verse 2. (3) The form of verse 2a ("Mary was the one who anointed the Lord . . .": ἦν δὲ Μαριὰμ ἡ ἀλείψασα τὸν κυρίον . . .) is parallel to other explanatory parentheses in the Gospel which begin ἦν δὲ + a proper name (1:44; 3:23; 11:18; 18:14, 40), and is even more precisely parallel to that of another parenthetical explanation of the identity of a person in 18:14: "Caiaphas was the one who advised the Jews . . ." (ἦν δὲ Καιάφας ὁ συμβουλεύσας τοῖς Ἰουδαίοις . . .). These two explanations (11:2; 18:14) differ in that 11:2 refers forward to an event still to be narrated (12:1-8), while 18:14 refers backward to an event already narrated (11:49-53), but the precise linguistic parallel indicates common authorship. Commentators who attribute 11:2 to a glossator are inconsistent in not treating 18:14 in the same way. It is easier to attribute both parenthetical explanations to the evangelist. (4) The way in which the end of verse 2 (ἧς ὁ ἀδελφὸς Λάζαρος ἠσθένει) picks up what was said in verse 1 (Ἦν δέ τις ἀσθενῶν, Λάζαρος) is characteristic of the way Johannine narrative resumes after a parenthesis,[17] as is the resumptive use of οὖν in verse 3.[18] (5) The observation that 11:2 is un-Johannine because the evangelist avoids referring to Jesus as ὁ κύριος in narratives set before the resurrection (unlike postresurrection narratives: 20:25; 21:7, 12) does not present a real difficulty. Precisely the character of 11:2 as a parenthetical explanation distinguishes it from references to Jesus in narrative. It is a remark made from a temporal perspective outside the narrative time either of chapter 11 or of 12:1-8. As in the parentheses in general, the author adopts the post-Easter temporal standpoint of himself and his

17. Van Belle, *Les parenthèses,* 119, 122-23.
18. Van Belle, *Les parenthèses,* 119-20 (he lists 51 cases).

readers/hearers at the time of writing and reading/hearing.[19] (If the last three words of 6:23 [εὐχαριστήσαντος τοῦ κυρίου] can be regarded as original, they provide a parallel instance. The textual evidence for omitting them is weak, and the use of κύριος should not, for the reasons just given in relation to 11:2, be held to count against their originality.)

These arguments show conclusively that verse 2 is not a later gloss. How then is it to be understood as part of the original text of the Gospel? As an explanation of the identity of a character by referring forwards to that character's appearance later in the Gospel narrative, verse 2 is unique in the Gospel. It is not therefore likely that it is an explanation intended for second- or third-time readers/hearers of the Gospel who will remember the story of John 12:1-8 from their previous hearing or reading of the Gospel. In that case, we should expect more examples of the same phenomenon. Moreover, what needs to be understood is not only the fact that the way in which Mary is identified is unique, but also the fact that, of the three characters introduced in verse 1, it is only Mary whose identity is explained in this way. If the explanation in verse 2 were intended for members of the Johannine community who already knew the story of John 12:1-8 from its oral telling prior to its incorporation in the Gospel, it would be inexplicable why these members of the Johannine community should be expected to have heard already of Mary, but not of Lazarus and Martha. If specifically Johannine traditions were already known as oral traditions to the implied readers/hearers of the Gospel, then these traditions would have featured all three of the Bethany family, who are all equally important in the Gospel's narratives.

The narrative functions performed by verses 1-2 together are two: (1) They introduce three important characters, who enter the Gospel's narrative at this point, by identifying one of them, Mary, as the woman about whom hearers/readers already know the story of her anointing of Jesus, and the others as her siblings. (2) They distinguish the Bethany where the three reside from the other Bethany in the Fourth Gospel, "Bethany beyond Jordan" (1:28), where Jesus is at this point in the

19. Cf. Van Belle, "Les parenthèses," 1915-16.

narrative (10:40-42). The knowledge presupposed in the implied readers/hearers by these two functions is knowledge that readers/hearers of Mark have: they know of a woman who anointed Jesus in the Bethany that is near Jerusalem (Mark 14:3-9; cf. 11:1, 11). Readers/hearers of Luke would not have the required knowledge, since it is not the sisters Martha and Mary (Luke 10:38-42, not located in Bethany) of whom readers/hearers of John 11:1-2 are expected to have heard, but a woman who anointed Jesus in Bethany near Jerusalem.[20] Luke has such a story (7:36-50) but does not locate it in Bethany.[21] Of course, a story of a woman who anointed Jesus in Bethany could have been known from oral tradition. But the fact that John 11:1-2 presupposes that (at least a large proportion of) its readers/hearers know precisely this information, while not expecting them to have heard either of Lazarus or of the sisters Martha and Mary, makes it likely that readers/hearers who knew Mark's Gospel well are implied. If the fourth evangelist wrote for the those churches (the "Johannine community") in which he himself was a well-known teacher, he would expect them to know of Lazarus, Martha, and Mary from his own telling of the Gospel traditions which he put into his Gospel, if not from those earlier forms of Johannine Gospel traditions that Johannine scholarship is in the habit of postulating. However, if he wrote his Gospel for general circulation around the churches, he would not be able to rely on the readers/hearers' knowledge of any particular items (other than the most important) of oral Gospel tradition, which would vary from place to place. But he would be able to expect that most readers/hearers would know Mark's Gospel, which he would know had already circulated very widely by the time he wrote.

20. R. A. Culpepper, *Anatomy of the Fourth Gospel* (Philadelphia: Fortress, 1983), 215, is inaccurate in stating, "Lazarus must be introduced, but Martha and Mary are known (11:1)." This ignores the fact that verse 1 is written with verse 2 in view. From verse 2 it is clear that only one of the two sisters is expected to be already known, and not necessarily by name.

21. The issue here is not, of course, the much debated one of the relationship between the traditions used by John, Mark, and Luke in their stories of the anointing, but the quite different issue of the prior knowledge of such a story which John 11:2 presumes in its readers/hearers.

The description of Mary's anointing of Jesus (11:2: "anointed the Lord with perfume and wiped his feet with her hair") closely echoes the narrative in John 12:3 and differs, of course, from Mark 14:3, where the act of wiping Jesus' feet with her hair is not mentioned. However, it is entirely natural that John should echo his own version of the story rather than Mark's, and readers/hearers who knew Mark's Gospel would not be impeded by the unfamiliar detail from recognizing the story they already knew from Mark. In fact, John 11:2 actually differs less from Mark 14:3 than John 12:3 does, in that the object of the anointing — the head of Jesus in Mark 14:3, the feet in John 12:3 — is in John 11:2 specified no more closely than as "the Lord." Thus, while John 11:2 unmistakably refers to the Johannine version of the story, it does so in a way that permits identification with the Markan version a little more easily than the Johannine story itself does.

Our study of John 11:1-2 can lead to the hypothesis that readers/hearers of John may be expected already to know those characters in the story who appear also in Mark's Gospel, but not other characters — an hypothesis that we can now test against other evidence. There are several characters in the Fourth Gospel who are both introduced, as though not already known to the readers/hearers, when they first appear in the narrative, and are also, on subsequent appearances in the narrative, identified by reference back to their first appearance. This is true of Lazarus, introduced in 11:2, and subsequently twice reintroduced with the words: "whom [Jesus] raised from the dead" (12:1, 9). Such identification within such a short space of text may seem unnecessary, and probably in 12:9 the point is not to identify Lazarus so much as to explain the crowd's interest in Lazarus. But first-time readers/hearers might need to be reminded who characters were, especially if the Gospel would not always be read as a whole in a continuous reading but also in short sections spread over time. The same technique of reminding readers/hearers of the identity of a character is therefore used also in the case of Nicodemus, who is carefully introduced for the first time in 3:1 and then identified by means of a reference back to this first appearance on both of his subsequent appearances (7:50; 19:39; cf. 3:2). In addition, it is used in the case of the beloved disciple, introduced in 13:23, reappearing in 19:26; 20:2, but reintroduced with

165

a reminder of his first appearance in 21:20 (cf. 13:23-25). Admittedly, such cross-references to the earlier appearances of characters may sometimes serve specific literary purposes. For example, 13:23-25 and 21:20-23 form an *inclusio,* which indicates the beginning and the end of the Fourth Gospel's story of Peter and the beloved disciple as a parallel and contrasting pair of disciples. But not all such cross-references have such specific purposes, and their full range is difficult to explain if all readers/hearers are expected to be already familiar with these Gospel characters. The three just mentioned are all uniquely Johannine characters, the last undoubtedly already well known in the churches in which the Fourth Gospel originated (21:23). They are characters "Johannine Christians" ought already to know, but readers/hearers elsewhere could not necessarily be expected to know, especially if Mark's Gospel functioned for the evangelist as the indication of what he could reasonably expect most of his readers/hearers already to know.

A final example of a character in the Fourth Gospel who is both identified on his first appearance in the narrative and then, on a subsequent appearance, identified with a reminder of his first appearance, is the high priest Caiaphas (11:39; 18:13-14, cf. 24). He is also a character who, like the woman who anointed Jesus, appears anonymously in Mark (14:53, 60-64) but is given a name in John. For readers/hearers of Mark, the description "Caiaphas, who was high priest that year" (John 11:49; 18:13) would serve on both occasions to identify the man called high priest by Mark, while on the second occasion it ensures at the same time that such readers/hearers do not mistakenly identify Annas with the man called high priest by Mark.

Thus with regard to peculiarly Johannine characters (including those who are anonymous in Mark but named in John) our hypothesis seems to be confirmed. Readers/hearers are not expected to know them already; the "Johannine community" would, but readers/hearers elsewhere could not necessarily be expected to. However, it is by no means so clear that the implied readers/hearers of John are expected already to know characters who appear in Mark. For example, while John's identification of Barabbas (18:40) is less full than Mark's (15:7), it is an adequate explanation for readers/hearers who have not previously heard of Barabbas. Readers/hearers of John who were already familiar with Mark would know Joseph of Arimathea (Mark 15:43), whom John introduces as though not already known to his readers/hearers (19:38). But here it is clear that John wishes to stress information about Joseph that Mark does not give: "a disciple of Jesus, though a secret one because of his fear of the Jews." This puts him into the category John has described in 12:42. Probably John intends us to see Joseph, like Nicodemus, as a member of the Jewish ruling group, some of whom, according to 12:42, secretly believed in Jesus. Readers/hearers who already knew Joseph from Mark would be more easily able to place him in this group than those who met Joseph for the first time in John 19:38.

There are a few characters in the Fourth Gospel whom the implied readers/hearers seem expected to know already. First, the account of John (the Baptist, but not so called in the Fourth Gospel) in 1:19-28, despite the introduction of him in Old Testament narrative style in 1:6, would probably be somewhat puzzling to readers/hearers who had never heard of him. They have not been told that John baptized people until his interlocutors ask why he does so (1:25). Second, the introduction of Andrew as "Simon Peter's brother" (1:40; cf. also 6:8, on Andrew's second appearance in the Gospel) may presume that Simon Peter, if not Andrew, is already known to the readers/hearers, though the phrase also serves to anticipate the following narrative (1:41-42). In this case there is nothing not intelligible to readers/hearers who have not previously heard of Simon Peter. Third, "the twelve" as a specific group among Jesus' disciples appear in 6:67-71 (cf. 20:24) as though readers/hearers will already have heard of this group. Fourth, Judas Iscariot's act of betrayal of Jesus is mentioned on several occasions where Judas appears in the narrative prior to the betrayal itself (6:71; 12:4; 13:2; 18:2). These forward references, especially in 6:71 and 12:4, appear to presume that readers/hearers already know the story of Judas' betrayal of Jesus.[22] Fifth, Pilate appears without explanation of his identity

---

22. References to disciples other than Peter and Judas Iscariot (Andrew [1:40; 6:8; 12:22]; Philip [1:44; 6:5; 12:21; 14:8]; Nathanael [1:45; 21:2]; Thomas [11:16; 14:5; 20:24; 21:2]; the other Judas [14:22]; Mary Magdalene [19:25; 20:1]; the sons of Zebedee [21:2]) show no pattern or consistency in the

(18:29). The knowledge of these four individual characters and of "the twelve" that appears to be expected of the implied audience could, of course, be presumed in an audience familiar with Mark's Gospel, but it could probably also be presumed in almost any Christian readers/hearers who knew any version of the Gospel tradition. Mark's Gospel itself identifies Judas as "Judas Iscariot, who betrayed him" (3:19), presumably expecting readers/hearers already to know the story, and, like the Fourth Gospel, it introduces Pilate without explanation (15:1; contrast Matt. 27:2; Luke 3:1). Paul, reporting tradition, refers to "the twelve" (1 Cor. 15:5).

Thus it is only in 11:2 that the Fourth Gospel introduces a character in a way that is unequivocally addressed to readers/hearers who already knew Mark. In some other cases where a character seems to be already known to the implied readers/hearers, this character would have been known to readers/hearers of Mark, but would probably also have been known to most Christian readers/hearers from those oral Gospel traditions that could be presumed to be more or less universally known throughout the early Christian movement. But in no case does the Fourth Gospel appear to presuppose prior knowledge of a character who could not have been known from Mark's Gospel. Such peculiarly Johannine characters as Nicodemus, Lazarus, Annas, and the beloved disciple are introduced as fully as any reader/hearer who had never heard of them could wish and in a way that it is impossible to explain on the view that the Fourth Gospel was addressed to the evangelist's own community alone. Thus the evidence outside 11:2 is consistent with the implication of that verse that at least many of the implied

---

way these characters are introduced or identified, but it is always clear at least from the context that they are disciples of Jesus. Nothing can be confidently concluded as to whether the implied readers/hearers are expected already to know them. (Culpepper, *Anatomy,* 214-15, is rather more — but not completely — confident that they are.) Only Judas Iscariot (6:71) and Thomas (20:24) are explicitly said to be members of the twelve, while it is implied that Simon Peter is (6:67-68). Readers/hearers of John who know only this Gospel could not confidently tell whether any of the other named male disciples are members of the twelve, unless 6:66-67 is taken to mean that from this point in the narrative Jesus' only disciples are the twelve.

readers/hearers could be expected to know Mark's Gospel, and, like 11:1-2, it is entirely inconsistent with the view that the Gospel was addressed to the "Johannine community," which would already be familiar with specifically Johannine Gospel traditions.

IV

We have not attempted in this chapter a complete account of the way in which readers/hearers of John who already knew Mark could be expected to relate the two Gospels. In a fuller investigation, it would be important to ask how far such readers would be able to see John's theological interpretation of his Gospel narratives as having points of connection with Mark. For example, in one of the few Markan narratives that John also tells, John, like Mark, has Jesus say, "It is I" (i.e., "I am" [ἐγώ εἰμι]; Mark 6:50; John 6:20). In John this becomes the second of the Gospel's theologically potent series of seven absolute "I am" sayings (4:26; 6:20; 8:24, 28, 58; 13:19; 18:5, 6, 8). For readers/hearers of Mark, this series would not only develop the christological significance of the "I am" saying they already knew in Mark 6:50 but also inform their understanding of the "I am" saying in Mark 14:62. In ways such as this, it would be possible to argue that John provides readers/hearers who already know Mark with a much fuller and more developed christological and soteriological interpretation of the Gospel story, but one which had clear continuity with the Markan Christology and soteriology they already knew. They would not perceive John's interpretation of Jesus as correcting or invalidating Mark's, but as extending and deepening it. With their understanding of Jesus enhanced by John's more reflective treatment, they could read not only John, but also Mark from a Johannine theological perspective. With the benefit of John's explicit interpretations of the few "signs" of Jesus which he has carefully chosen for his highly selective Gospel narrative, they could also read with fresh perception the "many other signs" (John 20:30) that Mark records. While the fourth evangelist surely meant to lead his readers further and deeper into the significance of Jesus and his story than Mark's Gospel had done, he need not have intended them henceforth to leave Mark aside and to read only his own Gospel. He did not aim to replace Mark, but to write a different kind of Gospel: one which, by selecting far fewer traditions, left space for the reflective interpretation that is the distinctive characteristic of the Fourth Gospel.

The chapter has focused on narrative sequence and characters because these would be the most immediately significant respects in which readers/hearers of John who also knew Mark would feel the need to relate the two Gospel narratives. We have shown that, in two of his parenthetical explanations (3:24; 11:2), John has provided explicit help for such readers/hearers, while other features of his narrative sequence and his identification of characters would also enable such readers/hearers readily to relate the events and the characters of the two Gospel narratives. It is a notable, though generally unnoticed, feature of John's narrative sequence that it is both largely compatible with Mark's while also largely avoiding repetition of Mark's narrative. While going its own way, it intersects with and leaves space for Mark's, in a way that makes the two Gospel narratives complementary. The nineteenth-century view that John wrote to *supplement* the Synoptics certainly does not do justice to the relationship of John's narrative to Mark's. It is not a mere series of additions to Mark's narrative. It has a narrative integrity of its own. It makes both narrative and theological sense in its own terms, quite independently of Mark. But for readers/hearers of John who also knew Mark, John's narrative can be read as *complementing* Mark's, just as Mark's can be read as complementing John's. The two narratives, each complete in its own terms, intersect with only a minimum of events in common and only a minimum of contradiction in sequence.

It seems unlikely that such a result is accidental, and the value of the two parenthetical explanations we have studied (3:24; 11:2) is that they are points where the text of the Gospel virtually requires to be understood as inviting readers/hearers who also know Mark to relate the two Gospel narratives in a complementary way. We have also seen that the way the Fourth Gospel introduces its characters is entirely inconsistent with the view that it was addressed to the evangelist's own community, but requires its implied readers/hearers to know only those Gospel characters who appear in Mark or in the most widespread of oral Gospel traditions. The material we have studied and the conclusions reached provide a strong case for the view that the Fourth Gospel was written, not for a Johannine community isolated from the rest of the early Christian movement, but for general circulation among the churches in which Mark's Gospel was already being widely read.

Can We Identify the Gospel Audiences?

STEPHEN C. BARTON

I

In recent years, an immense amount of scholarly energy has been directed at the question: To what kinds of audiences, groups of people, or churches were the Gospels written? One of the main assumptions behind the question is that a key to understanding the differences between the Gospels lies in the differences between the audiences to which they were addressed. In effect, the Gospels are read by analogy with the letters of Paul. Just as Paul wrote to (say) the house churches in Corinth to provide guidance and instruction in doctrinal and moral matters and to settle conflicts between factions, so too the evangelists "tailored" the Jesus tradition in order to allow it to speak in ways relevant to the needs of their respective communities. Furthermore, just as Paul's letters to the Corinthians provide vital clues to the history of early Christianity, the social identity of converts, and the beliefs, rituals, and patterns of life which they adopted, so too the Gospels are read with an eye to what they might disclose, not only about the mission of Jesus, but also about the life and social location of the post-Easter communities from which or to which they were written.

It could be said that the results of this kind of approach to the Gospels have significantly advanced our imaginative grasp both of the social and cultural horizon within which the Gospel texts took shape and of the history of earliest Christianity in general. We are more aware than ever before of the communal dimension, not only of the world portrayed within the Gospels, but also of the world of which the Gospels were a part.[1]

Nevertheless, perhaps it is time to take stock and to ask to what extent the assumptions on which this work proceeds are well founded. In particular, how valid are the attempts made by redaction and social-scientific criticism over the past three or four decades to identify the social location of the Gospel audiences? We will proceed, first, by raising some general issues of ideology and method in current Gospels interpretation. Then we will turn to questions that are pertinent for scholarly work on each of the four Gospels. A brief conclusion will draw the threads together.

II

There are a number of ideological and methodological problems that often lie hidden behind attempts to reconstruct the Gospel communities. I wish to draw attention to three problems in particular.

1. The first is the very use of the term *community*. As is recognized widely in the social sciences — but perhaps not sufficiently in New Testament studies — this is a notoriously ambiguous, even "loaded," term. Social anthropologist Anthony Cohen makes the point thus:

> "Community" is one of those words — like "culture," "myth," "ritual," "symbol" — bandied around in ordinary, everyday speech, apparently intelligible to speaker and listener, which, when imported into the discourse of social science, however, causes immense difficulty . . . perhaps for the simple reason that all definitions contain or imply theories, and the theory of community has been very contentious.[2]

1. For one recent survey, see S. C. Barton, "The Communal Dimension of Earliest Christianity," *Journal of Theological Studies* 43 (1992): 399-427.
2. A. P. Cohen, *The Symbolic Construction of Community* (Chichester, U.K.: Ellis Horwood, 1985), 11.

The candid recognition that definitions of the word *community* contain or imply theories is salutary. For New Testament interpretation, it raises a question: What theoretical load does *community* carry in the attempt to define the social location of the respective Gospels? Has study of the Gospel communities gained such a strong momentum because the word *community* conceals as much as it reveals? In Cohen's view, *community* is itself a verbal symbol that people use in various ways to express their sense of similarity and difference, of relationship and boundary.[3] Applied to the relatively recent vogue among Gospel scholars for reconstructing the Matthean community, the Markan community, and so on, it seems legitimate to ask whether or not *community* is being used to advance the symbolic or other interests of particular groups of scholarly interpreters as much as to elucidate the Gospels in their historical contexts.

In other words, the quest for the Gospel communities, like the quest for the historical Jesus, which it has displaced to some extent, is not a neutral exercise and is likely to be prone to the same dangers.[4] Therefore, in the hope of stimulating further debate, the following three sets of questions — rather bluntly put — may be worth raising. First, is it coincidental that so much of this work has taken place in the individualist, yet highly conformist, cultural context of secular modernity, where alienation from the traditional church is strong and, simultaneously, nostalgia for a sense of community long since lost is so pervasive? Related to this, how much of the current interest in "community" has its roots in the quest for new forms of community in the 1960s, with added impetus coming from the communitarian movements of the 1990s?

Second, is it coincidental that "sociological exegesis" aimed at defining the social location of the Gospels has arisen, not only on the back of the establishment of university sociology departments, but also in a period when the (confessional) biblical theology movement of the

---

3. Cohen, *Community,* 12-15.

4. On how this applies to the quest for the historical Jesus, see especially L. T. Johnson, *The Real Jesus: The Misguided Quest for the Historical Jesus and the Truth of the Traditional Gospels* (San Francisco: HarperCollins, 1996).

postwar period was in decline? So has sociological inquiry replaced theological inquiry, even to the point of becoming (implicitly or explicitly) antitheological: God is out, community is in? Or, in circles still religiously inclined, perhaps it is more the case that the God of existentialist hermeneutics is out and a more social conception of faith is in, from which an interest in the social location of early Christianity would follow naturally.

Third, is it possible that attempts to define as precisely as possible the putative Gospel communities are part of a (not sufficiently acknowledged) attempt to do ecclesiology by another name — to get behind the (conservative) church to the (more radical) primitive Gospel communities, or alternatively to trace the decline from the originality and radicalism of Jesus to the power politics of the post-Easter churches? This is a clear tendency in a number of strains of New Testament scholarship: liberal Protestantism, liberation theology, and charismatic and house-church theology, to mention a few.

Each of these questions requires elaboration and refinement, no doubt, and none of them admits of a simple answer: for it could in principle be the case that the kinds of contemporary factors just mentioned are a source of insight into the Gospels and not a barrier at all. Nevertheless, it is important in the interests of hermeneutical integrity that these kinds of questions are asked. The hermeneutics of suspicion has to be used of the interpreters of the Gospels, not just of the Gospels themselves, particularly when we are dealing with such a slippery, ideologically "loaded" word as *community*.

2. A second problem, this time of a more methodological kind, has to do with the basis on which the reconstruction of the Gospel communities is carried out. In effect, the history of the Gospel tradition, traced by means of form and redaction criticism, becomes the basis for describing the history of the Gospel community. Warrant for this is found in the sociology of knowledge and the sociology of literature,[5] according

5. See the accounts in J. G. Gager, *Kingdom and Community* (Englewood Cliffs, N.J.: Prentice-Hall, 1975), 9-14; and P. F. Esler, *Community and Gospel in Luke-Acts* (Cambridge: Cambridge University Press, 1987), 16-23.

to which it is possible to make correlations between the form and content of the text and the shape of the community on the axiomatic grounds that a group will receive, preserve, and transmit traditions that sustain and advance its particular needs and concerns. In effect, the text becomes "transparent" to the social realities lying behind it; or, to use another popular metaphor, the text serves as a mirror of the community. It does so because the meaning of the text lies, sociologically speaking, less in what the author meant than in how the text functions to legitimate the interests of the community.

Thus, for example, the emphasis on rigorous observance of the law in Matthew betokens a community in competition with Pharisees and at risk from Gentile antinomians; the "messianic secret" theme and the pervasive apocalyptic strain in Mark mirror the interests of an early Christian eschatological sect; the hostility to wealth and the exaltation of the poor in Luke reflect a community made up of people from the margins of society; and the vilification of "the Jews" in John is a literary antidote to the hostility of the synagogue to the members of the Johannine community.

However, it is now increasingly recognized that this way of proceeding, prone as it can be to a rather crude functionalism whereby the text is little more than the "product" of a hidden substructure of sociological factors and forces, is strongly reductionist in its handling of the meaning of the text.[6] Although it is by no means necessarily the case, such approaches tend to draw attention away from the original participants' ways of seeing things, play down the individual and particular in favor of what is judged as typical for the group, and redefine the personal, spiritual, or mystical dimension in terms of the political and communal. Bengt Holmberg's critical comments on Theissen's reading of the Gospels[7] as a cipher of the post-Easter Palestinian Jesus movement are directly relevant:

6. See especially the sobering essay by S. K. Stowers, "The Social Sciences and the Study of Early Christianity," in *Approaches to Ancient Judaism*, ed W. S. Green (Missoula, Mont.: Scholars, 1985), 5:149-81.

7. G. Theissen, *The First Followers of Jesus: A Sociological Analysis of the Earliest Christianity* (London: SCM, 1978).

The postulate of complete and positive correlation between a text and the social group that carries and receives it is implausible. To read the Gospel narratives as if they were uniformly allegories of early church life is, if nothing else, somewhat unimaginative. A text can just as well be standing in a negative correlation to the situation of the receivers. . . . And the uncertainty concerning what type of correlation we encounter applies especially where the texts use symbolic language, which often is a kind of double talk that has metaphorical and distant references, or may be charged with irony. In practice this means that one should at least ask oneself if the correlation between the analyzed text and its social situation is complete or partial, positive or negative. . . . And as the process of correlation very likely is a dialectical one, this increases the impossibility of concluding to the social situation from the end result. One original social situation can lead to several different results, because the intervening interactive factors need not be the same. And the same end result can, at least in theory, have been reached by several different routes. It seems inevitable that once we leave the primitive idea of strong, direct correlation between ideas and social basis of an almost deterministic kind, we are bereft of the possibility to say anything much about correlations at all.[8]

3. This leads naturally to a third point, also of a methodological kind. Given the problems associated with attempting to draw correlations between a Gospel text and a social location extrinsic to the text, may it not be the case that social-scientific exegesis is more appropriately directed at clarifying the contours of the various groups, communities, and societies portrayed within the text? This would do more justice to the nature of the Gospel texts as (for want of a better phrase) kerygmatic biography, thus allowing the insights of literary criticism to be taken more seriously.[9] It would also lessen the danger, so strong in positivist

8. B. Holmberg, *Sociology and the New Testament: An Appraisal* (Minneapolis: Fortress, 1990), 124-25, 139.
9. For one attempt to combine sociological exegesis and literary criticism in a reading of the Gospels, see S. C. Barton, *Discipleship and Family Ties in Mark and Matthew* (Cambridge: Cambridge University Press, 1994).

historical criticism and functionalist sociology, of distracting attention away from the text towards what the ingenious scholar can show lies behind or beneath the text.

Identifying more precisely and more vividly the social location of the beliefs and behaviors of the characters and groups presented in the Gospel narratives allows the text itself and the author implied in the text to be understood with ever deeper levels of appreciation.[10] The potential then is for interpretation of the Gospels to run with rather than against the grain of the text, since the meaning of the text is not being constantly subverted by a hermeneutic of suspicion and a rather superficial kind of sociological allegorization.

III

Having opened up some problems of a general ideological and methodological kind in current study of the putative Gospel communities, I wish now to draw attention to issues that can be raised in the interpretation of each of the four Gospels which are relevant to the present inquiry. This analysis will, of necessity, be brief and suggestive, looking at representative examples of scholarly work. It is intended only to show that there are good grounds for doubting aspects of the current consensus and for considering more sympathetically the view that the Gospels were written for a wide readership rather than for a particular group, "the evangelist's community." This will open up a related question of great importance that appears to have become sidelined: whether or not the Gospels were written as much for unbelievers as for believers.

10. For recent collections of essays on the Gospels along these more promising lines, see D. L. Balch, ed., *Social History of the Matthean Community: Cross-Disciplinary Approaches* (Minneapolis: Fortress, 1991); and J. H. Neyrey, ed., *The Social World of Luke-Acts: Models for Interpretation* (Peabody, Mass.: Hendrickson, 1991).

1. Matthew

It is striking that the attempt to identify "the Matthean community" has produced such a variety of suggestions. This itself gives reason to pause and think again. According to Stendahl and subsequently Orton, the interpretation of the Scriptures and other redactional features in Matthew give grounds for describing the Gospel as the product of an early Christian "school";[11] Schweizer reconstructs Matthew's community as charismatic and itinerant;[12] Kingsbury, Riches, and others (contrariwise) read the Gospel as addressed to a community that is settled, urban, and becoming more conservative;[13] Overman and Stanton argue for a model of the community as "sectarian," sharing many of the characteristics of the late-first-century Jewish sectarianism with which Matthew is embroiled;[14] Crosby sees Matthew through the prism of the household, as written to Christian house churches in Antioch;[15] and Carter thinks that the evangelist is trying to encourage a fairly settled, urban church in a more "liminal" direction, their households less compromised by the hierarchical and androcentric structures of the surrounding society.[16]

11. K. Stendahl, *The School of St. Matthew,* 2d ed. (Lund: Gleerup, 1967); D. E. Orton, *The Understanding Scribe* (Sheffield: Sheffield Academic Press, 1989).

12. E. Schweizer, "Observance of the Law and Charismatic Activity in Matthew," *New Testament Studies* 16 (1969-70): 213-30.

13. J. D. Kingsbury, "The Verb *Akolouthein* ('To Follow') as an Index of Matthew's View of His Community," *Journal of Biblical Literature* 97 (1978): 56-73; J. Riches, "The Sociology of Matthew: Some Basic Questions Concerning Its Relation to the Theology of the New Testament," *Society of Biblical Literature 1983 Seminar Papers* (Chico, Calif.: Scholars, 1983), 259-71.

14. J. A. Overman, *Matthew's Gospel and Formative Judaism* (Minneapolis: Fortress, 1990); G. N. Stanton, *A Gospel for a New People* (Edinburgh: T. & T. Clark, 1992), esp. 85-107; and G. N. Stanton, "The Communities of Matthew," *Interpretation* 46 (1992): 379-91, esp. 386-87.

15. M. H. Crosby, *House of Disciples: Church, Economics, and Justice in Matthew* (Maryknoll, N.Y.: Orbis, 1988).

16. W. Carter, *Households and Discipleship: A Study of Matthew 19–20* (Sheffield: Journal for the Study of the Old Testament Press, 1994).

There is also divergence between those who interpret Matthew as directed to a church dominated by concerns external to it (coming from "the synagogue across the street"), and those who see Matthew as a critical response to problems of an intramural kind (like false prophets and charismatic antinomians).[17] The fact that the same text can produce such various (although sometimes overlapping) reconstructions of the Matthean community shows how difficult is the attempt to make a direct correlation between the Gospel and a specific social-historical location.

These and other considerations lend weight to the view that we should think of Matthew's "audience" or "readership" rather than his "community." The question of genre is obviously relevant; and many have commented on the difference between a Gospel, with a relatively open horizon, and a letter, with a considerably more restricted horizon. This point applies to all four Gospels. Concerning Matthew in particular, the recent comments of Graham Stanton are pertinent:

> A gospel is not a letter. Since letters do not always provide a clear window onto the social circumstances of the recipients, we must be even more careful with gospels. The examples of Paul, the author of I Peter, and of Ignatius raise two further points which must be considered. Perhaps Matthew did not have first hand information about the circumstances of *all* the Christian communities for which he wrote. Perhaps, like the author of I Peter, the evangelist wrote for a loose network of communities over a wide geographical area. If this suggestion is plausible, an important corollary follows: Matthew's gospel should not be expected to provide us with *detailed* information about the social setting of the first recipients. I am convinced that Matthew's choice of literary genre and the evidence of the text of the gospel itself both point in this direction. . . . We should stop supposing that the gospel reflects the evangelist's close relationship with one group of Christians in one house church in one particular urban geographical location. . . . Surely Matthew's carefully crafted, very full account of the βίος of Jesus was not written

---

17. See R. H. Smith, "Matthew's Message for Insiders: Charisma and Commandment in a First-Century Community," *Interpretation* 46 (1992): 229-39.

for such a small group of people: surely we should envisage a loosely linked set of communities over a wide geographical area.[18]

Stanton's position on Matthew reflects a shift in interpretation from reconstructing one community to reconstructing a "set of communities" behind the text. It could be argued, however, that this modification is only a strategic retreat in order to allow investigation to continue on basically the same terms, and that the seriousness of the problems to which the modification is a response has not been faced up to. We are still left with a sociological, mirror-reading approach that inclines the interpreter from the start to look for the telltale clues of communal apologetic and self-definition. It is as if the mystery of Jesus' divine sonship has become the mystery of the hidden community or communities! The text as revelatory testimony potentially open to readers of all kinds (believers and unbelievers) seems to shrink to the status of "foundation document" of "minority Christian communities over against both Judaism and the Gentile world at large."[19] If this suggestion has any merit, then it needs to be asked whether a different model of Matthew's Gospel and its audience is required.

2. Mark

In recent redaction-critical and social-scientific interpretation of Mark, the assumption that the Gospel was written for a particular community — variously located in Rome or Galilee or Syria (the range and disparity of suggested geographical locations are telling!) — is all-pervasive. In his influential monograph of 1977, Howard Kee argues on the basis of a sociology of knowledge approach that the Markan community is a missionary sect whose ethos is markedly at odds with dominant social mores and whose worldview is apocalyptic and esoteric.[20] Along similar

18. G. N. Stanton, "Revisiting Matthew's Communities," *Society for Biblical Literature 1994 Seminar Papers* (Atlanta: Scholars, 1994), 9-23, at 11-12.
19. Stanton, "Revisiting Matthew's Communities," 10.
20. H. C. Kee, *Community of the New Age* (London: SCM, 1977).

lines, Joel Marcus sees Markan epistemology, like that of the Qumran community, as apocalyptic in nature, arising out of a context of a community suffering persecution.[21]

Interestingly, it may be worth noting in passing that both scholars (and many others with them) find in the writings of the Qumran sect the closest analogies to the themes and perspectives of the Gospel. This may well be so at the level of ideas: but whether the analogies remain strong at the level of social identity and organization is perhaps open to question. Just because we can speak in some meaningful sense of "the Qumran community" (whose remains, both literary and archeological, continue to attract enormous attention), it does not follow that it is meaningful also to speak of "the Markan community" as if one day we might be able to sift through its remains as well! There is an implicit historical positivism here of which we need to be wary.

Yet the assumption that it is meaningful to speak of Mark's community in this way is strong, and mirror-readings of the Gospel have become common, in spite of John Riches's warning that: "Remarkably little can be inferred from the text [of Mark] to the form of the community."[22] Thus, Mark is read commonly as a polemical, inner-Christian text written to correct christological heresy within the community or to counteract the influence of Christians outside the community. A case in point is the view of T. J. Weeden, J. D. Crossan, and others[23] that Mark's hostile portrayal both of the twelve disciples and of the family of Jesus reflects hostility in Mark's own day towards the leadership of the Jerusalem church, prominent among whom were Jesus' mother and especially

21. J. Marcus, "Mark 4:10-12 and Marcan Epistemology," *Journal of Biblical Literature* 103 (1984): 557-74, esp. 572-73.

22. J. Riches, "The Synoptic Evangelists and Their Communities," in *Christian Beginnings: Word and Community from Jesus to Post-Apostolic Times,* ed. J. Becker (Louisville: Westminster/John Knox, 1993), 213-41, at 221.

23. T. J. Weeden, *Mark — Traditions in Conflict* (Philadelphia: Fortress, 1971); J. D. Crossan, "Mark and the Relatives of Jesus," *Novum Testamentum* 15 (1973): 81-113; cf. also J. B. Tyson, "The Blindness of the Disciples in Mark," *Journal of Biblical Literature* 80 (1961): 261-68; W. Kelber, *The Kingdom in Mark: A New Place and a New Time* (Philadelphia: Fortress, 1974); E. Trocmé, *The Formation of the Gospel According to Mark* (London: SPCK, 1975), esp. 130-37.

James, the Lord's brother. The Gospel, in other words, mirrors the intramural politics of the early Christian churches.

But there are good reasons for rejecting this hypothesis.[24] First, if Mark sets out to write what he calls "the Gospel of Jesus Christ" (Mark 1:1), it is *a priori* far more likely that he is concerned to pass on the tradition in a way that will summon his readers to faith and instruct them in the way of true discipleship rather than to engage in acts of subtle literary character assassination designed to undermine the leaders of neighboring churches. Second, the hypothesis is dependent on a thematic linking of Jesus' relatives and the disciples, both viewed negatively. However, Mark 3:31-35 and 6:1-6 are set in narrative contexts that portray the disciples in a positive light over against his kinsfolk (see respectively 3:13-19 and 6:7-13). Following on from this, the portrayal of the disciples is not consistently negative by any means. Indeed, 14:28 and 16:7 clearly imply the enlightenment and rehabilitation of the disciples after the resurrection. Fallible the disciples may be, but consistent failures they are not. So the disciples and the family of Jesus are poor material for a hostile polemic against the apparently hated leaders of the Jerusalem church. Third, if stories about the family of Jesus are meant to evoke the leadership of James, the Lord's brother, at Jerusalem, we might expect him to be singled out, in the way Peter is, for example. But this does not occur (cf. Mark 6:3).

On these grounds, therefore, Mark's account of Jesus, his disciples, and his kinsfolk ought not to be interpreted as a kind of allegory of ecclesiastical politics in the post-Easter period. Such interpretations positively distract our attention from the plain sense and the clear rhetorical goal of the text, which have to do with the revelation of the hidden messiahship of Jesus and the summons to cross-bearing discipleship.[25] This is a message whose relevance cannot be reduced to the needs of a single "community" somewhere in Rome or Syria. Nor can

24. See further Barton, *Discipleship and Family Ties,* esp. 82-85.
25. See C. D. Marshall, *Faith as a Theme in Mark's Narrative* (Cambridge: Cambridge University Press, 1989); also M. A. Tolbert, "How the Gospel of Mark Builds Character," *Interpretation* 47 (1993): 347-57.

its significance be restricted to believers only. If Mark's Gospel has a pastoral intention, which there is good reason to accept, there is no good reason to deny that it has an evangelistic or "propagandistic" intention as well.[26] So we would do better to speak of Mark's audience rather than Mark's community.

This conclusion finds a considerable measure of support in the recent monograph of Mary Ann Beavis, significantly entitled *Mark's Audience*. On the basis of a study of the likely social and literary location of Mark 4:11-12, she concludes that Mark's Gospel was intended for a quite mixed audience — although (perhaps inconsistently) she still considers it appropriate to speak of "the Marcan sect" and "Mark's church." She says:

> [T]he question should be seriously considered whether Mark was directed not only to the evangelist's church, but to the more general audience of early Christian missionary teaching/preaching; as noted earlier, in Mark, διδάσκειν and κηρύσσειν are synonyms, and early Christian meetings could be open to unbelievers (1 Cor. 14.23). We have seen that, rhetorically, the Gospel is framed in a manner that would have been attractive to and understood by a first century audience, and, as V. K. Robbins has shown, the portrayal of Jesus as suffering teacher-king would also have been admired. Mark's teaching may thus have been directed not (or not only) to converts, but to *potential* converts. . . . We should not, however, make too sharp a distinction between Christian and non-Christian audiences; the evangelist may well have had both in mind as he composed his Gospel. . . . Our revival of the hypothesis that Mark's Gospel is indeed εὐαγγέλιον, information about Jesus to be used in missionary preaching (cf. Mk 14.9), is quite radical in the face of the critical consensus that the Gospels were written for Christian audience [*sic*] only, and warrants further discussion and testing.[27]

Beavis's final point here is worth noting. Once sufficient doubt is cast on the grounds for positing the Markan (Matthean, etc.) commu-

26. Cf. Riches, "The Synoptic Evangelists and Their Communities," 216-17.
27. M. A. Beavis, *Mark's Audience: The Literary and Social Setting of Mark 4.11-12* (Sheffield: Sheffield Academic Press, 1989), 171, 172, 176.

nity, it is surely a logical next step to ask whether the evidence points beyond a single "community" to a much wider potential audience, an audience likely to include outsiders as well as insiders.[28]

3. Luke

Three essays on the quest for "the Lukan community," taken in chronological order, point in the same direction. In his essay of 1979, "On Finding the Lukan Community,"[29] Luke T. Johnson makes a number of important points. First (making a point with which we are now familiar), not even in the interpretation of Paul's letters — Romans, for example — has there been unqualified success in drawing inferences about the social location of his addressees, since "not every element in the document is determined by the place, the people, or the occasion."[30] Second, how justified is the assumption that the pastoral and theological concerns of a Gospel writer are determined by a situation of crisis among his readers? As Johnson says, "Reading everything in the Gospel narratives as immediately addressed to a contemporary crisis reduces them to the level of cryptograms, and the evangelists to the level of tractarians."[31]

28. A significantly different reconstruction of the Markan audience to that of Beavis is Richard L. Rohrbaugh's essay, "The Social Location of the Markan Audience," *Interpretation* 47 (1993): 380-95. Rohrbaugh moves Mark (or at least Mark's readers) well down the social scale and out of an urban environment, and assumes that Mark's audience matches the social profile of a rural peasant village. He then shows how well the characters in Mark match the social stratification of agrarian society in Galilee, Syria, or Transjordan. On this basis, he argues that the Gospel is likely to have been written with such an audience in view. But the problem of circularity in this construction is endemic (see esp. 393-94) — though this does not mean that Rohrbaugh's interpretation is false, just that it cannot be proven. But the difference between his mirror-reading and that of Beavis shows again how uncertain the quest for the evangelist's community must be.

29. L. T. Johnson, "On Finding the Lukan Community: A Cautious Cautionary Essay," *Society for Biblical Literature 1979 Seminar Papers* (Missoula, Mont.: Scholars, 1979), 1:87-100.

30. Johnson, "On Finding," 89.

31. Johnson, "On Finding," 90.

In regard to Luke-Acts in particular, Johnson argues that the difficulties of mirror-reading are even more acute: the author's identity is unknown; the named addressee is an individual, not a church; due weight has to be given to the influence of the tradition and to Luke's professed intention to write an historical account; due weight has to be given also to the differences between Luke's two volumes, which complicate attempts to "read off" the community from the text; and there is the additional complicating factor of the evidence of literary artifice in Luke's writing: "Given a fairly intricate and intelligible literary structure . . . our *first* assumption with regard to individual parts within that structure should not be that they point to a specific community problem, but that they are in service to the larger literary goal of the author."[32]

A second essay along these lines is Dale Allison's more recent piece of 1988, "Was There a 'Lukan Community'?"[33] If anything, he is more doubtful of the possibility of finding Luke's community than Johnson, and he justifies his doubt on five considerations: (1) The reticence of scholars to say what they mean by "community" means that we do not really know what we are looking for. (2) If the author of Luke-Acts was the companion of Paul, as early tradition attests (Col. 4:14; 2 Tim. 4:11), it is likely that his identity was not bound up with any one church but instead with the church universal, a supposition that fits well with the ecumenical outlook of Luke-Acts itself. (3) We cannot safely assume that Luke belonged to one group in particular if he was an itinerant missionary; and Luke's thorough-going interest in journeys and itinerant preachers suggests that he was. (4) Luke's prologue (1:1-4) makes no mention either of a particular community or of a communal crisis that explains why Luke has written. On the contrary, it is formulated in "frustratingly general terms" and gives good reason for inferring that "its author anticipated that Luke-Acts would enjoy wide circulation" beyond the bounds of any single audience.[34] (5) Related to the preceding, the difficulty of establishing Luke's purpose and the diversity

---

32. Johnson, "On Finding," 92.

33. Dale C. Allison, "Was There a 'Lukan Community'?" *Irish Biblical Studies* 10 (1988): 62-70.

34. Allison, "Lukan Community?" 66.

of scholarly proposals about it may be indicative of the writer's translocal concerns and his relative independence of any particular Christian group.[35]

The third and most recent essay is that of Halvor Moxnes on the social location of Luke, which begins with the following pertinent observation:

> How can we move from the text of Luke's Gospel to the social situation of his first readers? This problem in Gospel research has so far not been solved. . . . The Lukan text creates a narrative world, and it is this world we examine as we analyze the social relations, ethos, and symbolic universe of Luke. Still, this does not mean that we now have a "window" that opens onto the social situation of Luke's historical community.[36]

Here, Moxnes articulates very clearly the methodological difficulties identified earlier in correlating symbolic and social structures. In fact, in spite of this opening statement, Moxnes does then attempt to delineate the social situation of the historical Lukan community! What is noteworthy about his attempt, however, is the degree of generality and tentativeness of his conclusions. Like Stanton on Matthew, he is uncertain (rightly) whether to speak of "community" or "communities." As with many interpreters of the other Gospels, he is unwilling (justifiably) to situate "Luke's location" in any one city, such as Ephesus or Antioch, and opts instead for "an urban setting in the eastern parts

35. Cf. also Riches, "The Synoptic Evangelists and Their Communities," 233-34: "Luke's work raises a fundamental question as to whether we should relate the Gospel and its author to a particular congregation or indeed to a particular place. The preface, with its address to Theophilus, suggests that in fact it was not addressed to a particular congregation, and though it may well be that some of the traditions special to Luke have a particular local provenance, there is nothing to Luke's presentation of his story to link it with any particular congregation or place. . . . Luke's parish seems to be a wider one than that of either of the other two Synoptic evangelists, and his concerns are those of the emerging church with its various settlements scattered across the empire."

36. H. Moxnes, "The Social Context of Luke's Community," *Interpretation* 48 (1994): 379-89, at 379.

of the Mediterranean."[37] He also recognizes that the peculiar "tensions" in Luke-Acts "are so general in character that they can be found in a number of Hellenistic cities in the eastern part of the Roman Empire."[38] And he concludes (unsurprisingly, given what we know about ancient city life) by inferring that Luke's "empirical readers" constituted "a group of nonelite persons who are culturally and ethnically mixed but who also include among them some who come from the elite periphery. Their life together centered on a meal that served as a means of integration, not just of Jews and non-Jews but also of members from various status groups and social positions. . . ."[39]

What Moxnes does offer is interesting and important background on Mediterranean urban life and culture that helps us enter the narrative world of Luke-Acts more sensitively.[40] But his inability to sketch more than the most general outline profile of Luke's likely readers appears to reinforce the position of those who argue that the Gospels were not written for particular "communities" at all.[41]

4. John

It is probably in Johannine studies that the quest for the evangelist's community has been pursued with the greatest vigor and imagination. Because of its widely acknowledged significance in breaking new ground, the following comments will focus on the seminal essay of

37. Moxnes, "Social Context," 380.

38. Moxnes, "Social Context," 381.

39. Moxnes, "Social Context," 387.

40. See also Moxnes's essay, "Social Relations and Economic Interaction in Luke's Gospel," in *Luke-Acts: Scandinavian Perspectives,* ed. P. Luomanen (Göttingen: Vandenhoeck & Ruprecht, 1991), 58-75.

41. Of course, a number of Lukan scholars think otherwise — for example Philip Esler, in his ground-breaking monograph *Community and Gospel in Luke-Acts: The Social and Political Motivations of Lucan Theology* (Cambridge: Cambridge University Press, 1987). Cf. S. C. Barton, "Sociology and Theology in Acts," in *The Theology of the Book of Acts,* ed. I. H. Marshall and D. Peterson (Grand Rapids: Eerdmans, forthcoming).

Wayne Meeks entitled "The Man from Heaven in Johannine Sectarianism," first published in 1972.[42] Here Meeks argues that the distinctiveness of John — in particular, its persistently riddling, symbolic, and mythological language — is best explained by sociological factors to do with the kind of community to which the Gospel is addressed. The meaning of the language is related to its social function for an alienated sect. Meeks sums up his thesis thus:

> *The book functions for its readers in precisely the same way that the epiphany of its hero functions within its narratives and dialogues.* . . . In telling the story of the Son of Man who came down from heaven and then re-ascended after choosing a few of his own out of the world, the book defines and vindicates the existence of the community that evidently sees itself as unique, alien from its world, under attack, misunderstood, but living in unity with Christ and through him with God. It could hardly be regarded as a missionary tract, for we may imagine that only a very rare outsider would get past the barrier of its closed metaphorical system. It is a book for insiders.[43]

Meeks is not alone in his view that the Fourth Gospel betrays a sectarian, "in-group" consciousness. Among others who take this view we may cite J. Louis Martyn, Raymond Brown, Fernando Segovia, and David Rensberger.[44] In spite of the strength of the scholarly consensus,

42. W. A. Meeks, "The Son of Man in Johannine Sectarianism," in *The Interpretation of John,* ed. J. Ashton (Philadelphia: Fortress; London: SPCK, 1986), 141-73.

43. Meeks, "Son of Man in Johannine Sectarianism," 162-63 (Meeks's emphasis).

44. D. Moody Smith ("Johannine Christianity: Some Reflections on Its Character and Delineation," *New Testament Studies* 21 [1975]: 224-48, at 223-24) reflects a widely held consensus when he says: "it can probably be agreed that on any reading of the Gospel and Epistles there appears a sectarian consciousness, a sense of exclusiveness, a sharp delineation of the community from the world. . . . Comparisons with community consciousness in Qumran, which is likewise related to a fundamental dualism, are entirely apposite and to the point." Cf. J. Louis Martyn, *History and Theology in the Fourth Gospel,* 2d ed. (Nashville: Abingdon, 1979); R. E. Brown, *The Community of the Beloved Disciple* (London: Geoffrey

however, grounds for doubt remain. There is, for example, the persistent problem, not at all unique to the interpretation of John (as we have seen already), of drawing sociological inferences from a very small literary deposit, even if we include the Johannine epistles as well. Meeks's claim — extended to a fantastic degree by Raymond Brown in his elaborate reconstruction of the stages of development of *The Community of the Beloved Disciple* (1979) — that the story of the Johannine Jesus correlates in a quite direct manner with the history and sociology of the putative Johannine community runs too great a risk of finding what is not there or what, by the nature of the evidence, cannot be found.[45]

Certainly, the evidence is ambiguous, and that alone should give us reason for caution. Meeks makes a lot, for example, of the sectarian, "us-versus-them" consciousness that can be read off the encounter between Jesus and Nicodemus in John 3.[46] But it may be questioned whether Nicodemus is cast unambiguously in the outsider role that Meeks attributes to him; whether also he plays the role of an uncomprehending fool any more, say, than the Samaritan woman or Thomas or Peter; and whether what is being conveyed in the dialogue is only that Jesus is incomprehensible, as Meeks claims. A more sympathetic reading is certainly possible, as others have shown;[47] and if it is, then a crack begins to appear in Meeks's reconstruction of the audience of John as a sect alienated from the world. Even Raymond Brown, who

---

Chapman, 1979); F. F. Segovia, *Love Relationships in the Johannine Tradition* (Chico, Calif.: Scholars, 1982); D. Rensberger, *Johannine Faith and Liberating Community* (Philadelphia: Fortress, 1988). For a useful survey and critical evaluation, see T. L. Brodie, *The Quest for the Origins of John's Gospel* (New York: Oxford University Press, 1993), 15-21.

45. See further the sharp attack of Frederik Wisse, "Historical Method and the Johannine Community," *Arc* 20 (1992): 35-42.

46. Meeks, "Son of Man in Johannine Sectarianism," 147-52.

47. See, e.g., J. M. Bassler, "Mixed Signals: Nicodemus in the Fourth Gospel," *Journal of Biblical Literature* 108 (1989): 635-46, esp. 639-42. In addition, note now the quite different construction advanced in Richard Bauckham's essay, "Nicodemus and the Gurion Family," *Journal of Theological Studies* 47 (1996): 1-37, esp. 29-32.

is at most points sympathetic to Meeks's approach, says of Nicodemus something much more literal and traditional: "[his] role is not to illustrate or personify the attitudes of a contemporary group in the Johannine experience, but to show how some who were attracted to Jesus did not immediately understand him."[48]

Doubt may also be cast on Meeks's claim that the Fourth Gospel shows all the signs of being a "book for insiders," since "only a very rare outsider would get past the barrier of its closed metaphorical system." This is surely a *tour de force*. On this view, it is a wonder that anyone made it into the Johannine "community" at all! Is it really the case that metaphors like light, bread, water, wine, shepherd, way, vine, temple, Logos, Son of God, and so on — each of them with deep roots in the biblical and Jewish traditions and not without a certain currency in the wider Hellenistic milieu either — are as opaque and hermetic as Meeks makes them out to be?[49] May it not be the case that the metaphorical, parabolic, and symbolic language of the Gospel represents an invitation to the reader/hearer — outsider as well as insider, non-Johannine as well as Johannine — to explore further and go deeper, beyond the level of surface appearance? Why should riddling language appeal only to members of John's own circle?[50] If the function of such language is only to leave someone like Nicodemus floundering in the epistemological dark, is it not surprising that he does not pass permanently from the scene after that first, difficult encounter? If questions like these have any force at all, then a further crack appears in Meeks's social-functionalist edifice.

Overall, Meeks's interpretation maps only one possible social location for John's Gospel. However, there is no necessary correlation between the dualism of John's symbolic and mythological language and any putative community. This is obvious by analogy with the fact that

48. Brown, *Community of the Beloved Disciple,* 72 n. 128.

49. For an excellent exposition, see J. Painter, "Johannine Symbols: A Case Study in Epistemology," *Journal of Theology for Southern Africa* 27 (1979): 26-41; and, from an earlier generation, C. H. Dodd, *The Interpretation of the Fourth Gospel* (Cambridge: Cambridge University Press, 1953).

50. Relevant here is Kim Dewey's essay, *"Paroimiai* in the Gospel of John," *Semeia* 17 (1980): 81-99.

in our own day this same Gospel is the favorite both of exclusive fundamentalist churches for whose self-understanding John 14:6 is central, and of much broader, ecumenical churches for whom John's narrative of the Word made flesh, or the prayer for unity in chapter 17, are at the heart of things. Furthermore, the approach advocated by Meeks remains equivocal at two important points. It is unable to distinguish in a stable way one community from a number of communities (plural); and it is equivocal about whether the Gospel reflects the mentality of the community(ies) from which it comes or the community(ies) to which it is addressed. Finally, Meeks's position so strongly emphasizes the role of the community that it is in danger of losing sight of the role of the evangelist as one of the most creative individual theologians of earliest Christianity.[51] Nor should it be forgotten that the evangelist's own testimony to the purpose of his Gospel (20:30-31) resists any simple identification of his intended audience as one community or many, believers or unbelievers.[52]

IV

In relation to the question which forms the title of this essay, the cumulative force of the preceding arguments is that the Gospels themselves do not allow us to identify, beyond a high level of generality, the audiences for which they were written. Certainly, interpretation of the Gospels as if they were directed only to one specific community (house

51. Note, e.g., Meeks's statement (in "Son of Man in Johannine Sectarianism," 145): "Nevertheless, it has become abundantly clear that the Johannine literature is the product not of a lone genius but of a community or group of communities that evidently persisted with some consistent identity over a considerable span of time." Contrast the conclusion of Martin Hengel, *The Johannine Question* (London: SCM, 1989), 104: "Here, then, was a towering creative teacher who ventured with reference to the acitivity of the Spirit Paraclete to paint a quite different picture of the activity and proclamation of Jesus from that which we can see in the Synoptic tradition."

52. Cf. D. A. Carson, "The Purpose of the Fourth Gospel: John 20:31 Reconsidered," *Journal of Biblical Literature* 106 (1987): 639-51.

church? group of house churches?) appears now to be highly question-able. As with the quest for the historical Jesus, the quest for the Mat-thean (Markan, etc.) community and attempts to trace its history can be undertaken only with a much greater caution and modesty. Ideo-logically, the (Protestant, Catholic, or secular) liberal nostalgia for "com-munity" makes many interpreters prone to look for what may not be accessible or what they think they know already before coming to the Gospels themselves.

This does not mean that the quest for the Gospel *audiences* and their social location(s) is illegitimate. On the contrary, it is an important act of the historical and social-scientific imagination. One positive consequence of it is that we are more aware than ever before of (what we might refer to broadly as) the social dimension of the reality of the Gospels — whether of the world behind the Gospels, or of the world within them, or of the world in front of them which we inhabit as interpreters.[53] It would be a serious mistake, however, if this relatively new awareness tempted us to reduce the Gospel texts from their role as primary witnesses to God-in-Christ to the status of incidental by-products of something putatively more fundamental, "the community" — especially if one of the corollaries is that we foreclose prematurely on the possibility that the Gospels are open texts intended, not only for audiences of believers, but for audiences of unbelievers as well.

---

53. So also, W. A. Meeks, "A Hermeneutics of Social Embodiment," *Har-vard Theological Review* 79 (1986): 176-86.

Toward a Literal Reading of the Gospels

FRANCIS WATSON

Richard Bauckham's paper on the readership for which the Gospels were intended belongs within the scholarly genre of the "challenge to a consensus." In order to work, an argument along these lines must show both that a consensus on a particular issue actually exists and that it is vulnerable to criticisms that attack its very foundations. The challenge to a consensus has a vested interest in emphasizing both the virtual unanimity of existing opinion and the seriousness of its own criticisms; and in both respects it may easily succumb to the temptation to exaggerate. The "general consensus" may prove to be no more than a fairly widespread assumption; and the criticisms that are proposed may necessitate a few revisions of the thesis in question (or of certain versions of it), but not its outright abandonment.

In my view, Bauckham's attack on the consensus that the Gospels presuppose an initial setting within a specific community is entirely successful. The position he attacks appears to qualify as a consensus; and the criticisms he offers are fundamental enough to show that it cannot merely be restated in a slightly revised form, but that it must be abandoned. The hypothesis that the Gospels were shaped by and addressed to the problems of a specific community is not just flawed or one-sided but simply wrong. In this case, unusually, a challenge to a general consensus appears to have achieved exactly what it purports to do.

The assumption that the Gospels were written to meet the needs of specific communities is, at one level, a straightforward historical hypothesis, and it is entirely appropriate that it should be criticized on this same level. One might perhaps identify other examples of interpretative paradigms that guide the research of significant numbers of biblical scholars but which are equally vulnerable to criticism on strictly historical grounds. However the "historical-critical method" is defined, it cannot be understood as a general guarantee that the particular models employed by biblical scholarship will necessarily prove appropriate to their subject matter. A genuinely critical scholarship will be capable of criticizing not only the "results" or "findings" of particular scholarly endeavors but also the models or frameworks within which these results or findings are identifiable as such. At this point, the focus of contemporary hermeneutical discussion on the act of interpretation itself is of direct relevance even to an empirically minded scholarship which believes that it can make do with a bare minimum of serious theoretical reflection.

Yet the Gospels are more than the objects of various types of historical debate. Individually and together, they constitute the truth-claim not only that, as a matter of historical fact, there once lived a certain individual, Jesus of Nazareth, who spoke and acted in various ways and to whom various things happened, but also that this individual is the Christ, the ultimate and definitive agent of God's purposes in the world who discloses God's very being. The Gospels do not assert this truth-claim *alongside* a straightforward historical rendering of words and deeds that may be pronounced "authentic" by neutral, objective historical procedures. On the contrary, the Gospels *are* this truth-claim, and scholarly interpretation will almost inevitably imply certain provisional decisions about this truth-claim. These provisional decisions are not simply a matter of the individual's existential choice; they are embedded in the scholarly paradigms themselves. It follows that particular interpretative paradigms may be subject to criticism at the theological as well as the historical level. Despite every attempt to reconstruct biblical scholarship along "purely historical" lines, the theological and historical levels prove difficult to disentangle.

What of the claim that the Gospels, like many of the epistles, were written in response to the needs of a specific community? In principle, it would seem possible to discuss this issue as a straightforward question of fact, without reference to theology. In practice, however, tacit theological decisions of one kind or another are frequently assumed in work on the evangelists' hypothetical "communities," and if this work proves vulnerable on historical grounds it is also worth investigating the viability or otherwise of its theological concerns. A *theological* critique of theologically relevant aspects of biblical scholarship has, indeed, been very little practiced in recent years. It is customary either to ignore the theological dimension of an interpretative position or to regard it as a sign that the purity of historical study has (once again) been contaminated by theology. Yet if, because of the nature of the subject matter, the theological and historical dimensions of interpretation are closely related to one another, it is essential to attend to the former as well as to the latter.

Fundamental to recent work on the evangelists' communities is the concept of the *Sitz im Leben.* Taking Willi Marxsen's *Mark the Evangelist* (1956) as broadly representative of the way it continues to function, I shall argue that this concept is by no means the theologically neutral entity that it purports to be.[1] This becomes especially clear when Marxsen's redaction-critical application is traced back to its roots in the work of Rudolf Bultmann. With its claim that the Gospels speak primarily of the Christian community and not of Jesus himself, redaction criticism and its successors practice an *allegorical* interpretation of the Gospels. The main reason for criticizing it in some detail is to assert the theological priority of an interpretation of these texts in their literal sense.

1. *Sitz im Leben:* Analysis of a Theological Construct

Marxsen's book offers a particularly clear rationale for the application to the Gospels of a new approach, *Redaktionsgeschichte,* the aim of which

---

1. W. Marxsen, *Mark the Evangelist: Studies on the Redaction History of the Gospel* (Nashville: Abingdon, 1969). Subsequent references will be given parenthetically in the text.

would be to study the achievement of the evangelist as a creative theologian responding to the particular concerns of his own community. In this work, therefore, we lay bare one of the roots of more recent interest in the evangelists' communities.

For Marxsen, *Redaktionsgeschichte* (conventionally translated as "redaction criticism") is a natural and necessary step beyond *Formgeschichte* ("form criticism"). Form criticism investigates the history and development of the Synoptic tradition prior to its literary embodiment. It opposes the view that the Gospels represent a more-or-less transparent rendering of Jesus as a great creative personality, emphasizing instead the anonymous communal processes in which the tradition about Jesus was shaped and reshaped. Form criticism makes tradition visible as tradition; it tells us that we can have access to Jesus only indirectly, by way of his reception in the early church. It destroys the illusion of direct access. Indeed, the Gospel material is understood as *primary* evidence not of the historical Jesus but of the contexts in the early church within which it was created and handed down. The production of written texts is simply the final stage of the tradition's development, and one should not overemphasize the creative contribution of the individual evangelists. As Martin Dibelius puts it, "The literary understanding of the synoptics begins with the recognition that they are collections of material. The composers are only to the smallest extent authors. They are principally collectors, vehicles of tradition, editors" (quoted by Marxsen, 15). Far from standing out over against the church (the traditional view), the evangelists and their Gospels are absorbed back into it.

According to Marxsen, this is a one-sided picture. "Tradition is indeed the primary factor which we encounter, but it is the tradition of the evangelists, that is, the tradition laid down in the Gospels. . . . Can it then be our first task to proceed to the investigation of the material for synoptic tradition, ignoring the evangelists?" (20). If the quest for the historical Jesus (revived by Käsemann and others) studies the Synoptic material in relation to the *Sitz im Leben* of Jesus' own ministry, and if form criticism studies it in relation to its *Sitz im Leben* within the early church, there still remains a third *Sitz im Leben* to be investigated — that of the evangelist and of "the community in which the Gospels arose" (Marxsen, 24). The Gospels are primarily a source for our knowledge not of the tradition-process in general or of the historical Jesus but of the evangelist and his community. It is, Marxsen thinks, remarkable that this point has not been more clearly grasped before. It is implied as early as 1901 in W. Wrede's *Das Messiasgeheimnis in den Evangelien*. Similarly, J. Schniewind argued in 1930 that "our Gospels intend . . . to be understood as kerygma for a particular situation and task," a situation that we must determine if we are to understand them aright (quoted by Marxsen, 207). The Gospel of Mark must therefore be understood as "kerygma for a particular situation and task" — that is, in relation to its communal setting.

One of the roots of more recent interest in the original communal setting of the Gospels is therefore redaction criticism's extension of form critical concern with the *Sitz im Leben* of traditional material to the Gospel as a whole. To understand the concept of the *Sitz im Leben* within redaction criticism, we must clarify its historical and theological role within form criticism.

In his *History of the Synoptic Tradition*, Bultmann declares his agreement with Dibelius in seeing the task of *Formgeschichte* not only as the formal categorization of the various elements of the Synoptic tradition but also as the study of the *history* of the tradition in its oral phase. The tradition is to be traced back to its historical origin, on the assumption that "the literature in which the life of a given community, even the primitive Christian community, has taken shape springs out of quite definite conditions and needs from which there arise a quite definitive style and quite specific forms and categories."[2] The particular needs that give rise to the particular form constitute its *Sitz im Leben* (an expression Bultmann derives from Gunkel), which is to be understood not as an individual historical event but as "a typical situation or occupation in the life of the community" (4). Thus we move backward from the tradition's final, literary embodiment in the Gospels to the analysis of the oral, preliterary "forms" preserved there to the situation in which these forms originated. "Form" is therefore "a sociological concept and not an aesthetic one" (*History of the Synoptic Tradi-*

2. R. Bultmann, *The History of the Synoptic Tradition* (1921; Oxford: Blackwell, 1963), 4. Subsequent references will be given parenthetically in the text.

tion, 4). Unlike Dibelius, however, Bultmann believes that this connection between the forms and the life of the earliest church implies judgments about "the genuineness of a saying, the historicity of a report and the like" (5); and these judgments must very often be "skeptical" ones. But the methodological priority of the life-setting within the early church applies also to material that may provisionally be accepted as "genuine": for in inquiring about the life-setting one "is not concerned with the origin of a particular report of a particular historical happening, but with the origin and affinity of a certain literary form in and with typical situations and attitudes of a community" (40). Although "authentic" material about the historical life of Jesus is of course to be found in the Synoptic tradition, it is (for form criticism) a methodological mistake to focus on this issue at the expense of the forms and their origins in the life of the early church.

The "needs" that give rise to the "forms" are in fact sketched in a somewhat perfunctory manner. In the case of the "controversy dialogues," for example, Bultmann can only offer the generalization that these stories originated "in the apologetic and polemic of the Palestinian church," which created "imaginary scenes illustrating in some concrete occasion a principle which the church ascribed to Jesus" (*History of the Synoptic Tradition,* 40-41). Rabbinic parallels confirm that "we have to look for the *Sitz im Leben* of the controversy dialogues in the discussion the church had with its opponents, and as certainly within itself, on questions of law" (41). In the case of "biographical apothegms" such as Mark 1:16-20 (Jesus' call of the first disciples) or Mark 6:1-6 (Jesus' rejection at Nazareth), these "are best thought of as edifying paradigms for sermons," which "help to present the Master as a living contemporary and to comfort and admonish the church in her hope" (61). In practice Bultmann devotes far more attention to the "literary" aspects of form criticism than to the historical or "sociological" question of the origin of the forms in the life of the early church. Yet, however little it is invoked in practice, the concept of *Sitz im Leben* plays a crucial role in Bultmann's assertion of the relative autonomy of the Synoptic tradition in relation to the historical life of Jesus. The primary source of this tradition is the life of the community, whose internal and external needs lead it to preserve or create sayings and stories of which Jesus is the subject. A life-setting in the early church makes the hypothesis of a context in the life of Jesus redundant.

Two further examples will help to clarify this point. Outlining "The New Approach to the Synoptic Problem" in an article dating from 1926, Bultmann appeals to Wellhausen's claim that the earliest Jerusalem community was instrumental not only in preserving but also in creating *logia* ascribed to Jesus:

> In the primitive community at Jerusalem the spirit of Jesus continued to be active, and his ethical teaching was progressively elaborated and expressed in utterances which were then transmitted as the sayings of Jesus himself. Thus tradition handed down, in the form of words of Jesus, conceptions actually arising from the faith of the community, and portrayed these as regulations for church discipline and for missionary activity. . . . So far as the *logia* are concerned, this means that they are a primary source from which we can reconstruct a picture of the primitive community in which the *logia* arose. Only after we have obtained such a historical picture of the community are we in a position to attempt to reconstruct the picture of Jesus and of his preaching.[3]

Here too, the thesis of an original and primary *Sitz im Leben* within the early church serves to displace the conventional assumption that, at least at the heart of the synoptic record, we are directed to an original and primary *Sitz im Leben* in the ministry of Jesus. In a later article, Bultmann makes a similar point from the opposite direction. The work of W. Bousset, he tells us, has brought to light the Christ-cult that flourished on the soil of early Hellenistic Christianity, and that issued in a Pauline Christ-myth with little or no connection to the historical Jesus. Extrapolating back from this to the communities in which Synoptic-like tradition *was* preserved, we may conclude that even the Synoptic tradition served not historical interests but the needs of a community "assembled to worship the Lord Christ who was present

3. R. Bultmann, "The New Approach to the Synoptic Problem," in *Existence and Faith: Shorter Writings of Rudolf Bultmann,* ed. S. N. Ogden (London: Collins, 1964), 42-43.

in it."[4] Whether we approach the earliest community from the direction of the historical Jesus or from that of Hellenistic Christianity, the result is the same: the overriding concern that comes to expression in the tradition is with the *present* Christ, the Christ who is known and experienced here and now in the community of those gathered to worship him. Tradition relating to the past (the historical Jesus) is preserved and created with primary reference to the present.

References to the ongoing presence of "the spirit of Jesus" and to the "Christ-cult" imply that Bultmann acknowledges a "vertical" dimension to the creation of early Christian tradition as well as the more obvious "horizontal" dimension in which tradition in its various forms arises out of certain apologetic, polemical, or homiletical needs. Whatever the precise *Sitz im Leben* of one or other of the forms, it will necessarily include a reference to the church's living Lord, who is the true subject of the church's tradition. For Bultmann, the relative autonomy of the church and its tradition in relation to the life of Jesus does not entail a church that is left to make its way in the world out of its own resources, as it awaits a purely future eschatological event. It is the conviction that the living Lord speaks here and now that underlies the production of "new 'words of the Lord' . . . whose purpose is to decide debated questions" such as the law and the scope of the Christian mission.[5] It is in the name of the living Lord that Christian prophets utter sayings such as, "Behold, I send you out as sheep in the midst of wolves," and "Behold, I have given you authority to tread upon serpents and scorpions": a parallel may be found in the book of Revelation, where we again find "examples of Christian prophets speaking in the name of the exalted Christ" (*Theology of the New Testament*, 1.48). The fact that such prophetic utterances can be ascribed to Jesus shows that "the church drew no distinction between such utterances by Christian prophets and the sayings of Jesus in the tradition, for the reason that even the dominical sayings in the tradition were not the pronouncements of a past authority, but sayings of the risen

4. R. Bultmann, "The Christology of the New Testament" (1933), in *Faith and Understanding* (London: SCM, 1969), 271.

5. R. Bultmann, *Theology of the New Testament* (London: SCM, 1952), 1.47.

Lord who is always a contemporary for the church" (*History of the Synoptic Tradition*, 127-28). Thus, *Sitz im Leben* is not only a sociological concept, referring the Synoptic forms back to the concrete social needs in which they originated; it is also a theological concept, referring the Synoptic material to the ultimate authority of the risen, living Lord. *Sitz im Leben* marks the point of intersection between "horizontal" and "vertical" planes representing respectively the concrete needs of a particular time and place and the moment of encounter with the living Lord. In early Christian experience, it is in and through the concrete situation that the risen Christ speaks and makes himself known.

Bultmann's work on the Synoptic tradition precedes his involvement with the "dialectical theology" of Barth and Gogarten, signaled in his favorable review of the second edition of Barth's Romans commentary in 1922.[6] The historical skepticism and the emphasis on the creativity of the community derives not from theological sources but from scholars of the pre–World War I era such as Wellhausen and Wrede, Bousset and Heitmüller. Yet there is the closest possible parallel between these historical-critical emphases and the distinctive theological position that Bultmann developed during the 1920s, and this means that the concept of the *Sitz im Leben* as handed down to subsequent scholarship is marked by theological as well as historical concerns. We have seen that its role in a historical-critical context is to assert the primacy of the early church as the source of the Synoptic material; the effect of this is to make problematic the move from this material to the historical Jesus, for this material is concerned not with the historical Jesus as a figure of the past but with the present of the early church and therefore with the risen Jesus who accompanies it on its way. It is precisely this understanding of the relation of the present to the past that Bultmann also wishes to advocate on theological grounds. The concept of a life-setting for the Synoptic material *outside the life of Jesus* therefore has a crucial role to play in Bultmann's theology as well as in his historical work.

What lies at the root of Bultmann's intense antipathy towards the

---

6. R. Bultmann, "Karl Barths 'Römerbrief' in zweiter Auflage," reprinted in *Die Anfänge der dialektischen Theologie,* Teil 1, ed. J. Moltmann (Munich: Chr. Kaiser, 1974), 119-42.

"historical Jesus" of the preceding theological generations? In general terms, one may say that "dialectical theology" for Bultmann — as for the early Barth — marks a shift from a "christocentric" to a "theocentric" theology. Liberal theology attached itself to the person of Jesus, believing that in encountering him we also encounter God; dialectical theology wished to speak seriously again of God, a God who is "wholly other" and who is not to be regarded as immanent within human historical life. As Bultmann put it in 1924, "The subject of theology is *God,* and the chief charge to be brought against liberal theology is that it has dealt not with God but with man."[7] Insofar as dialectical theology continues to speak of "man," it speaks of him as "called in question by God" ("Liberal Theology," 46): "Theology speaks of God as it speaks of man as he stands before God" ("Liberal Theology," 52). Before God, man stands as a justified sinner; and this occurs in the event of the Word (i.e., Christian preaching), in which the grace and judgment of the God who justifies sinners is proclaimed and communicated. This "theocentric" theology avails itself of concepts of sin, justification, word, grace, and the cross derived from the early Luther and from Paul, and it thereby reverses the liberal Protestant subordination of the Pauline doctrine of justification to the historical Jesus of the Synoptic Gospels as the heart of the New Testament message.

From the new standpoint, the problem with theologies whose center is the historical Jesus lies in their assumption that the being and presence of God can be read directly out of the Gospel record, insofar as we expose ourselves to the overwhelming power, conviction, and holiness of the personality of which it speaks. That is, for example, the view of Wilhelm Herrmann, for whom "our certainty of God may be kindled by many other experiences, but ultimately has its firmest basis in the fact that within the realm of history to which we ourselves belong, we encounter the man Jesus as an undoubted reality" — the reality of a person who "surpassed all else that is great and noble in humanity."[8]

7. R. Bultmann, "Liberal Theology and the Latest Theological Movement," in *Faith and Understanding* (London: SCM, 1969), 29.

8. W. Herrmann, *The Communion of the Christian with God* (1892; Philadelphia: Fortress; London: SCM, 1971), 59-60.

But, as Bultmann argues in agreement with Troeltsch, historical study deals with relativities.[9] The knowledge it offers is itself relative and is liable to change as research proceeds; it can give no basis at all for a value judgment about a historical person who is said to "surpass all that is great and noble in humanity." More importantly, the historical realities studied by historical research are themselves relative, interconnected moments within the single, all-encompassing historical process. For Bultmann as for Troeltsch, it is impossible to assign absolute value to any one of these relative entities, finding in it a uniquely "firm basis" for "our certainty of God." But it is also impossible — and here Bultmann parts company with Troeltsch — to find meaning and certainty of God in one's sense of the direction of the historical process as a whole;[10] for (after the war of 1914-1918) it is no longer possible to assume that the meaningfulness of history is guaranteed by God's immanence within it. On the contrary, history is without meaning. If we are to find meaning, it must encounter us from outside the sphere of history, "vertically from above"; and that is precisely what is promised to us in the Christian concept of the Word or gospel of God's grace and judgment, disclosed in the cross of Christ. This Word is the radical divine challenge to us in our idealism or materialism, our religiosity or skepticism, or in any other of the countless ways in which we seek to bring about our own justification. The Word *judges* these futile undertakings, but it also *liberates* us from them; for it is the divine claim, whereby humans are called to the life of faith that must always be received as God's gift and God's creation.

In christological terms, this "theocentrism" — so close to that of the early Barth — entails a shift from the liberal emphasis on the *person*

9. According to Troeltsch, "The historical method must be conceived in such a way that what is relative and individual in history will come into its own as a factor that dominates history unconditionally" (*The Absoluteness of Christianity and the History of Religions* [1911; London: SCM, 1972], 30).

10. For Troeltsch, within the individual and relative phenomena that constitute history there emerge "authentic values which, in consequence of their validity, are directed towards a common goal" (*Absoluteness of Christianity*, 30-31). Bultmann finds in Troeltsch, and in liberal theology generally, a "pantheism of history" ("Liberal Theology," 32).

or personality of Jesus to an identification of the crucified and risen Jesus as the content of the divine *Word*. The Christ who is proclaimed loses his personal traits — everything that might seem to make him surpassingly "great and noble" — and, as crucified and risen, signifies the divine judgment and grace that are declared to humankind in the Word or gospel. Yet no confirmation or guarantee of the truth of the Word is to be found within history — even the history of the historical Jesus; for God is not immanent even in this history but makes himself present only in the transcendent and vertical form of the Word. It is this disjunction between history and Word that provides the theological rationale for Bultmann's antipathy towards theologies of the historical Jesus; and this theological position is of a piece with the historical conclusion that the primary focus of early Christian tradition was the living Lord, known here and now within the concrete *Sitz im Leben*, rather than the historical Jesus. The shift from person to Word corresponds to the shift in the relation of present and past. We are not to look back from our own present to a particular piece of past history, to which we vainly ascribe absolute significance; we are to listen, in our own present, for the divine Word which can only encounter us here and now, as an event, and not in the objectified fixity of past history. The concept of a *Sitz im Leben* for early Christian tradition, outside the life of Jesus, serves as a model for the situation in which — through the continuation of the tradition-process in Christian preaching — the Word encounters us here and now. Whether the *Sitz im Leben* is that of the early church or of the contemporary church, it is the living Lord with whom they and we have to do, and not with the deadness of a "Christ according to the flesh." Although history is supposed not to offer us any guarantees, in this case at least the conclusions both of history and of theology do appear to reinforce and confirm one another.

For our purposes, the significance of all this is that form criticism, together with the theology that accompanies it, makes it seem plausible and indeed necessary to postulate a life-setting for the Synoptic tradition that is basically autonomous in relation to the life and person of Jesus. It is a small step from this to the redaction-critical application of the concept of life-setting to the evangelist and the needs of his community. In both form and redaction criticism, the Gospels are *primary* sources for the early Christian community, and only secondarily — in a manner that flies in the face of their own true concerns — sources for the historical Jesus. The concept of the life-setting serves to prevent or at least to complicate the backward move from the Gospels to Jesus. It asserts that the Gospels speak not of the past but of their own present; for whatever in them derives from the past is included not as a testimony to that past but for the sake of the present. The assumption is that, despite appearances, the Gospels are *not* to be understood as speaking of Jesus of Nazareth, a figure belonging to another time and place and yet, as the Christ and the Son of God, of ultimate significance for all times and all places.

2. Against Allegorizing

As we have seen, the concept of the enclosed, autonomous life-setting originated in form criticism and is applied through redaction-critical work to the Gospel as a whole. Thus, Marxsen concludes, from Bultmann's claim that "a literary work or a fragment of tradition is a primary source for the historical situation out of which it arose," that we must therefore inquire as a matter of primary concern "into the situation of the community in which the Gospels arose" (Marxsen, 24). We have seen that the concept of "situation" or *Sitz im Leben* comprises not only a more obvious "horizontal" component — some concrete need in the life of the early church — but also a "vertical" component, arising from the church's relationship with the exalted Lord as the fundamental basis on which the concrete need is identified as such and addressed. In Marxsen's inquiry into the situation of the Markan community, these two dimensions are present especially in the emphasis on "Galilee," which, Marxsen argues, was introduced into the traditional material by the evangelist himself.

As Marxsen notes with a reference to K. L. Schmidt, form criticism assumes the secondariness and nonhistoricity of the historical and geographical framework within which the individual items of tradition are located in the Gospel of Mark. But did Mark actually intend this framework to fulfill a historical role? The alternative is that "with his outline Mark has in mind a purpose other than the historical and uses the geographical data to express it" (Marxsen, 54). On this hypothesis, ostensibly geographical data fulfill primarily theological functions. Thus, we may ask what motivates the evangelist's assertions that "Jesus came from Nazareth *of Galilee*" (Mark 1:9), that "after John was arrested, Jesus came *into Galilee,* preaching the Gospel of God" (1:14), and that he called his first disciples as he "passed along by the Sea *of Galilee*" (1:16). No doubt that was the way it was: Jesus really *did* come from Nazareth, a town of Galilee. But "is there behind the term 'Galilee' more than meets the eye?" (59). In Mark 3:7-8, we read of Jesus' withdrawing with his disciples to the Sea, followed by "a great multitude from Galilee" and "from Judea and Jerusalem and Idumea and from beyond the Jordan and from about Tyre and Sidon, a great multitude." Why? Presumably "in Mark's day Christians were living in all these places or in all these regions" (64). And, according to Mark, they have a meetingplace: the Sea of Galilee. That Galilee is for Mark "the place of Jesus' activity" coincides "with the fact that Galilee, or the Sea of Galilee, has special significance for the primitive community of Mark's day" — as the place in which it is directed to gather (64). The evangelist is motivated only indirectly by the need for historical veracity: Jesus' activity in Galilee, belonging as it does to the past, "is narrated or reported not for the sake of the past which speaks out of the tradition but for the sake of Mark's own time" (65). So direct is the relation between the pseudohistorical narration and present reality that a Galilean origin for the Gospel of Mark comes to seem a plausible hypothesis (66).

Why are Christians from places as far afield as Jerusalem and Tyre directed to gather at the Sea of Galilee? The answer is to be found in the promise of Mark 16:7 (with its backward reference to 14:28): "Go, tell his disciples and Peter that he is going before you to Galilee; there you will see him, as he told you." This verse is, Marxsen argues, a redactional addition. It is the sole basis for the tradition of resurrection appearances in Galilee that occur in the Gospels of Matthew and John. But if "we are dealing with the latest stratum reflecting the evangelist's own situation . . . , this redactional note cannot deal with an appearance of the Risen Lord awaited in Galilee; in Mark's context this passage can only refer to the expected Parousia" (Marxsen, 85, italics removed). Mark 16:7 thus explains why it is that in 3:7-8 Christians are to gather at the Sea of Galilee: for it is in Galilee that they will at last behold the return of Christ. Indeed, Christ "goes before them to Galilee"; he is there already. That means that ostensible references (in Mark 1:14, 16, 39, and elsewhere) to Jesus' historical activity in Galilee are primarily concerned with his *presence* there, shortly to be made manifest and indeed already experienced "in the proclamation" (86). "Jesus came into Galilee, preaching the Gospel of God" (1:14): and this happens *now*. In fact, it happens in and through the Gospel of Mark itself; for this text is itself proclamation. "The material deals with the earthly Jesus. But as proclamation it represents the exalted Lord whose parousia is at the door" (94). The exalted Lord is present in the kerygma.

How are we to envisage the gathering of Christians in Jerusalem and elsewhere to await the parousia in Galilee? Marxsen refers to the report of Eusebius and Epiphanius of the exodus of the Jerusalem community to Pella in A.D. 66, in response to a divine or angelic revelation. The content of this oracle cannot simply have been the command to depart: "An oracle is scarcely needed for flight from a city threatened by siege" (Marxsen, 115). The fact that Eusebius does not transmit the oracle itself is explicable if it dealt with the parousia, the non-occurrence of which would be an embarrassment. Thus, "in Mark and in the tradition underlying Eusebius and Epiphanius, we encounter a common feature traceable to the same event. The Lord orders his community to move to Galilee and repeats his command by the word of an angel" (115). The difficulty that Pella is not in Galilee is resolved if we imagine an initial move to Galilee and a subsequent move to Pella, following the non-occurrence of the parousia (115-16n). In this way, we see how the Gospel of Mark is "the evangelist's proclamation to the community of his own time" (116).

Marxsen's redaction-critical approach undoubtedly provides a much more interesting and imaginative *Sitz im Leben* for a whole Gospel than the more cautious Bultmann was able to offer for its individual components. It should be clear, however, that the basic structure of this *Sitz im Leben* is precisely that of the Bultmannian model. The Bultmannian *Sitz im Leben* is characterized, first, by a horizontal dimension, a concrete situation in the life of the early church. Here, that concrete situation is provided by the oracle that causes Christians in Jerusalem and elsewhere to gather in Galilee to await the parousia during the war of A.D. 66-70. It is characterized, second, by a vertical dimension, in the sense that the concrete situation is interpreted in the light of the church's trust in the continuing presence and guidance of the risen Lord. The risen Lord is the source of the oracle (cf. Mark 14:28); and he is secretly present in Christian proclamation, in which it is always Jesus who "proclaims the Gospel of God," especially in Galilee. It is characterized, third, by a relative autonomy in relation to the actual life of Jesus. Assertions that ostensibly refer to him as a figure of history are really and primarily about the present. And, finally, it is characterized by the assumption that this whole construct is not only appropriate to the realities of early Christian history but that it is also theologically normative. To speak of the Markan Christ as "hidden in the proclamation" is to use theological language with clear theological intent.

Marxsen's attempt to read a Gospel in the light of its supposed original communal context is naturally open to a criticism which, assuming that the project itself is viable and worthwhile, identifies problems in his execution of it. But it is not simply the execution but the project itself that is fundamentally flawed. Since this project has been enthusiastically taken up in recent scholarship, analyzing its flaws is not just a matter of a single book or the distinctive theological commitments that it reflects. Marxsen's book serves to exemplify and to focus the problem that almost inevitably recurs wherever a Gospel is interpreted in the light of its hypothetical original communal setting: in such an interpretation, an *allegorical* reading strategy is employed that systematically downplays and circumvents the *literal* sense of the text.

Despite the relativizing discovery of the role of the reader in the production of meaning, contemporary hermeneutical pluralism does not constitute a serious challenge to the concept of the *literal sense* of a text. This is presupposed in the act of translation. Although translation participates in the fluidity of all interpretation and can never provide an exact equivalence, it remains possible to distinguish a translation

210

from a mistranslation — where, for example, the translator of a New Testament text has failed to understand that the semantic range of a Greek term is quite different from that of its normal vernacular equivalent. Translation can at best provide *inexact* equivalence, which is why it can never be an adequate substitute for study of the texts in their original languages. And yet, although inexact and imperfect, it is still an *equivalence* that it offers, rather than an entirely new text. The translation presupposes and confirms the basic stability and meaningfulness of the original text; that is, it presupposes and confirms that the text has a basically stable and meaningful "literal sense."[11]

Thus the Greek words *meta de to paradothēnai ton Ioannēn ēlthen ho Iēsous eis tēn Galilaian kerussōn to euaggelion tou theou* mean "After John had been arrested, Jesus came into Galilee proclaiming the Gospel of God" (Mark 1:14). That is their literal sense, even if certain nuances have been lost and certain ambiguities left unresolved. Knowledge of the Greek or English language is, however, a necessary but not a sufficient condition for understanding this text in its literal sense. A background knowledge is also presupposed: the reader must know that "Galilee" is an actual, identifiable geographical location, and that "John" and "Jesus" denote real human beings and not fictive characters. The referential claim implied by the text is inseparable from its literal sense. This does not entail that, in any given instance, the act of reference is *successful:* Jesus (the historical Jesus) may conceivably have proclaimed the Gospel of God *before* the arrest of John, or he might have proclaimed it in Judea rather than Galilee. This does not alter the fact that the text *intends* to refer to persons, events, and places in the world outside the text, and that this intentionality is integral to its literal meaning. Equally integral to that meaning is the recognition that the particular assertion is not an isolated entity but is embedded in a narrative continuum. The assertion that one agent did something after the activity of another agent had been interrupted only makes sense in the context of a broader, diachronically unfolding narration, within

---

11. I have attempted to clarify and defend the concept of the "literal sense" in Francis Watson, *Text and Truth: Redefining Biblical Theology* (Edinburgh: T. & T. Clark; Grand Rapids: Eerdmans, 1997), 95-126.

which it marks a point of transition. It appears that we have here, as Hans Frei puts it, a "realistic" narrative in which the identities of the agents (John and Jesus) are rendered in such a way as to be "unsubstitutable"; they do not serve as ciphers or symbols for other identities or other realities.[12] The realistic narrative is the narrative that means what it says: in this case, that, after John had been arrested, Jesus came into Galilee proclaiming the Gospel of God.

But is there perhaps more to this statement than meets the eye? To raise this question is to ask about the possibility of an allegorical interpretation in which the text would mean something other *(all-)* than what it says *(agoreuein)*. Warrant for allegorical interpretation is conventionally found in the anomalies that from time to time appear to make the literal sense indecipherable; the breakdown of the literal marks the point of entry for the allegorical.[13] Thus (to recapitulate), we have in Mark 1:14 a reference to "Galilee" as the location of Jesus' activity, and we learn from Mark 16:7 that Galilee is also the place where the disciples will behold the risen Lord. Yet Mark 16:7 does not fit into its context. Its reference to the commissioning of the women ("Go, tell his disciples and Peter") contradicts the emphatic claim of the following verse that the women remained silent. It may therefore be regarded as redactional, and we may expect here a clear insight into what Mark himself wanted to say to those he is addressing. In the words ostensibly addressed by the young man to the women on behalf of the

---

12. H. Frei, *The Eclipse of Biblical Narrative: A Study in Eighteenth and Nineteenth Century Hermeneutics* (New Haven: Yale University Press, 1974); *The Identity of Jesus Christ* (Philadelphia: Fortress, 1975); G. Hunsinger and W. C. Placher, ed., *Theology and Narrative: Selected Essays* (New York and Oxford: Oxford University Press, 1993), 45-93. I have discussed Frei's work in Francis Watson, *Text, Church and World: Biblical Interpretation in Theological Perspective* (Edinburgh: T. & T. Clark; Grand Rapids: Eerdmans, 1994), 19-29.

13. "[T]he Word of God has arranged that certain stumbling-blocks, as it were, and offences and impossibilities should be introduced into the midst of the law and the history, in order that we may not . . . either altogether fall away from the true doctrines, learning nothing worthy of God, or, by not departing from the letter, come to the knowledge of nothing more divine" (Origen *De principiis*, iv.1.15; translation from *The Ante-Nicene Fathers* IV [Grand Rapids: Eerdmans, 1976]).

disciples, we really have the words of Mark, or rather of the exalted Lord, to the Christians of Mark's own time and place. Appearing to speak of a reunion between Jesus and his disciples (including Peter) shortly after the first Easter Day, this utterance actually addresses a later generation of disciples about the parousia which is shortly to occur. Mark 1:14 must therefore be reread allegorically along the same lines. The Jesus who "came into Galilee preaching the Gospel of God" is the Jesus who "goes before [his disciples] to Galilee" (16:7, cf. 14:28); the Jesus who will be visible at his parousia ("There you will see him") is therefore the Jesus who is already secretly present in the midst of the community, in the proclamation of the Gospel. The textual anomaly has proved to be a window in what had appeared to be a blank wall, through which a new story becomes visible — the story of the Markan community. Appearing to speak of the past, Mark actually speaks of the present; allegorical interpretation effaces the past for the sake of presence.

Allegorical interpretation is intended for a learned, scholarly elite that finds itself dissatisfied with the banal obviousness of the literal sense that suffices for ordinary readers. Yet, like many other scholarly constructs, it is vulnerable to the criticism that it is fundamentally *arbitrary;* that, for all its concern with textual anomalies, it actually succeeds in making a more-or-less readable and comprehensible text unreadable and incomprehensible. Allegorical interpretation may often be undone by precisely the textual anomalies to which it appeals for warrant. In the case of Mark 16:7, for example, the proposed allegorical interpretation will find it difficult to account for the reference to Peter: "Go, tell his disciples *and Peter.'* Was Peter a member of the Markan community that gathered at the Sea of Galilee to await the parousia in A.D. 66? Still harder to explain is the promise that the risen Jesus "goes before you" [*proagei humas*] to Galilee. At the parousia, the exalted Jesus becomes visible as the result of a *vertical,* downward movement (cf. 1 Thess. 4:16); but Mark 16:7 clearly speaks of a *horizontal* movement, a journey similar to the one that the Markan community is commanded to undertake. On the assumption that the verse refers to a resurrection appearance shortly after Easter, the idea of the risen Lord's journeying from Jerusalem to Galilee is comprehensible, as a comparison with Luke's Emmaus Road narrative indicates. Yet that assumption has been ruled out on the grounds that a postresurrection appearance is irrelevant to the Markan community. If, however, the hypothesis of the Markan community succeeds only in adding new anomalies to existing ones, that is a clear sign that the hypothesis is untenable. The Markan community falls victim to Ockham's Razor: for if *entia non sunt multiplicanda praeter necessitatem,* this is all the more true where the unnecessary entity in question is accompanied by new anomalies.

Allegorical interpretation subordinates the "letter" or "body" of a text to its "spirit," understanding the transition from one to the other as an *ascent* into spiritual realms that transcend bodiliness. In the case of allegorical interpretation of the Gospels, this schema will have an obvious impact on Christology. The flesh of the incarnate Word — his concrete historical existence, its contingent unfolding in the context of other contingencies — is the subject matter only of the "letter" or "body" of the text, and is held to be significant not in itself but as an indirect disclosure of the higher reality of the Word itself and its relation to the human spirit.[14] Where "the Word" does not have the historical existence of Jesus of Nazareth as its content, where it denotes an event that refers only indirectly to him, the event of the divine address occurring here and now within an enclosed and self-sufficient community, then the result is an *allegorical* interpretation in which the text's rendering of the pastness of Jesus is systematically subordinated to the pure presence it attains as the vehicle of the divine address — in and through the proclamation of the Word that lies at the heart of the community's existence. It is, however, unclear what theological basis there could be for this act of violence to the letter of the text and to the bodiliness of Jesus' existence, to which the letter of the text bears witness. Far from perpetrating any such act of violence, it is the task

---

14. "Condescending to the one who is unable to look upon the splendors and brilliancy of Deity, [the Word] becomes as it were flesh, speaking with a literal voice, until he who has received him in such a form is able, through being elevated in some slight degree by the teaching of the Word, to gaze upon what is, so to speak, his real and pre-eminent appearance'" (Origen *Contra Celsum* iv.15; translation from *The Ante-Nicene Fathers* IV). There is a clear parallel here to Origen's hermeneutic of ascent.

of Christian proclamation to assert the universal and ultimate significance, for all times and places and therefore for our own time and place,
of this particular bodily life as rendered in this particular text, in the
narrative form that so accurately reflects the historicity of human bodily
existence. The fact that, as narrated in the Gospels, this particular bodily
life ends not with death but with resurrection does not mean that its
historical particularities are taken up into the timelessness of myth and
thus always available for a purely present actualization. According to
the Gospels, it is the case not only that Jesus *was raised,* that he is alive
and not dead, but also that it is precisely *Jesus* who was raised, the name
standing for the person who is the unique and unsubstitutable subject
of the train of events from birth to death that the Gospels narrate. Any
interpretation of the Gospels that overlooks the obvious fact that the
subject of the Gospels is the particular historical existence of Jesus of
Nazareth, believed by Christians to be the Christ, the Son of God, is
simply misinterpretation. The substitution of the Word for the person,
the spirit for the body, is a simple denial that the Word became flesh
and has no place within theology or scholarship.

Wherever the evangelist's hypothetical community is made the
primary context for the interpretation of a Gospel, a substitution of
this kind is likely to occur. The Jesus of the text ceases to be the textual
embodiment of a prior bodily life. His bodiliness may be dissolved into
the divine address to the community, here and now, as in the case of
the neo-Lutheran Bultmannian theology of the Word; or it may be
replaced by a textual cipher created by the evangelist in order to communicate to the community his own understanding of its needs and
concerns. The fact that a "quest for the historical Jesus" is practiced
alongside the redaction-critical concern with the evangelists' communities does nothing to resolve this problem: for the historical Jesus and
the Markan Jesus are regarded as distinct and parallel entities, the one
a figure of past history and the other the main character in an early
Christian narrative whose subject is ultimately the present situation of
the evangelist's community. The substitution of a textual cipher for a
bodily, historical existence has as its correlate the substitution of a
bodily, historical existence that is qualitatively different from the one
rendered in the evangelist's text. In both types of scholarly endeavor, it

is taken for granted that the historical Jesus and the Markan Jesus are qualitatively different from one another; whatever the contingent links between them may be, they are therefore studied in abstraction from one another. If it is one of the functions of the hypothesis of the Gospels' communal setting to legitimate this separation between person and text, then the collapse of this hypothesis may serve as a reminder that the historical existence of Jesus is mediated in the form of the Gospel narratives, and that the sole purpose of these narratives is to mediate this particular historical existence in the light of the universal and ultimate significance that is ascribed to it.

Is it possible to envisage a future Gospels scholarship in which person and text are reintegrated? This suggestion would not entail the naive positivistic assumption that the Gospels are to be understood, so far as possible, as a direct transcript of historical reality. Like the various incompatible models of the so-called historical Jesus, the Gospels are *interpretations* of the historical reality to which they refer. The Gospels represent the early Christian *reception* of the life and person of Jesus, and the eventual emergence of the fourfold Gospel canon represents the decision that the Christian community will henceforth appeal to this complex rendering of the received reality and no other. Like other historiographical writing, the Gospels make use of formal devices such as plot that are derived from fictional texts; they assume a particular ideological stance or *Tendenz* which a representative of an alternative ideological stance might regard as "biased"; and they incorporate material of a more-or-less "legendary" character, whose role here is to testify indirectly to the universal and ultimate significance that is ascribed to the narrated life.[15] A scholarship that sought to reintegrate person and text would therefore not be a simple exercise in credulity; it would not claim to speak out of some kind of postcritical "second naivety." The faith or unfaith of the interpreter would inevitably affect the interpretation of the material (as it already does under the existing scholarly regime); but, unless faith and unfaith are understood as irrational private commitments, there is no reason why this should compromise

15. I have discussed "The Gospels as Narrated History" in *Text and Truth*, 33-70.

the "public" nature of the scholarly debate. Recognition that the nature and manner of the interpreter's faith or unfaith makes a difference to interpretation would in itself represent a major step forward from the current tendency to repress this issue, as though one could make it go away by refusing to confront it.

As an expression of Christian faith, Christian theology has a particular interest in interpreting the Gospel texts in their literal sense, in opposition to the various allegorical readings which cannot or will not understand that the primary intention of those texts is to narrate the historical life, death, and resurrection of Jesus as the unsubstitutable form of the ultimate and universal significance that Christian faith finds here. From the standpoint of Christian theology, there is every reason to welcome biblical scholarship's potential contribution to this task; and from the standpoint of biblical scholarship there is no reason to hold aloof from it. To interpret the Gospels in abstraction from the truth-claim they everywhere presuppose and intend is a sign not of scholarly integrity but of a failure to reckon with the existence of these texts in their primary, literal sense.

217

Contributors

Richard Bauckham is Professor of New Testament Studies in the University of St. Andrews, Scotland. Previously he was Reader in the History of Christian Thought in the University of Manchester. His recent publications include *Jude and the Relatives of Jesus in the Early Church* (Edinburgh: T. & T. Clark, 1990), *The Theology of the Book of Revelation* (Cambridge: Cambridge University Press, 1993), *The Climax of Prophecy: Studies on the Book of Revelation* (Edinburgh: T. & T. Clark, 1993) and *The Theology of Jürgen Moltmann* (Edinburgh: T. & T. Clark, 1995). He has also edited *The Book of Acts in Its Palestinian Setting*, vol. 4 (Carlisle: Paternoster/Grand Rapids: Eerdmans, 1995).

The Revd. Dr. **Michael B. Thompson** has been Director of Studies and Lecturer in New Testament at Ridley Hall, Cambridge, since 1995. He also teaches in the Cambridge Theological Federation and in the Divinity Faculty of the University of Cambridge. Previously he lectured in New Testament at St. John's College, Nottingham. His Cambridge doctoral dissertation was published as *Clothed with Christ: The Example and Teaching of Jesus in Romans 12.1–15.13* (Journal for the Study of the New Testament Supplement Series 59; Sheffield: JSOT Press, 1991). With Markus Bockmuehl he has edited *Vision for the Church: Studies in Early Christian Ecclesiology* (Edinburgh: T. & T. Clark, 1997).

Dr. **Loveday Alexander** is a Lecturer in New Testament in the Department of Biblical Studies, University of Sheffield. She holds her doctorate from the University of Oxford. Her publications include *The Preface to Luke's Gospel: Literary Convention and Social Context in Luke 1:1-4 and Acts 1:1* (Society for New Testament Studies Monograph Series 78; Cambridge: Cambridge University Press, 1993); she has also edited *Images of Empire: The Roman Empire in Jewish, Christian and Greco-Roman Sources* (Journal for the Study of the Old Testament Supplement Series 122; Sheffield: JSOT Press, 1991).

The Revd. Dr. **Richard A. Burridge** is Dean of King's College, London, where he also lectures in the Theology Department. He taught Classics initially, before combining theological training for ordination with a doctorate on Gospel genre. His publications include *What Are the Gospels? A Comparison with Graeco-Roman Biography* (Cambridge: Cambridge University Press, 1992) and *Four Gospels, One Jesus? A Symbolic Reading* (London: SPCK, 1994). He appears regularly on TV and other media to comment on theology and church affairs.

The Revd. Dr. **Stephen C. Barton** is a Lecturer in New Testament in the Theology Department of the University of Durham and a non-stipendiary priest of the Church of England. His publications include *The Spirituality of the Gospels* (London: SPCK, 1992/Peabody: Hendrickson, 1995) and *Discipleship and Family Ties in Mark and Matthew* (Society for New Testament Studies Monograph Series 80; Cambridge: Cambridge University Press, 1994). He has also edited *The Family in Theological Perspective* (Edinburgh: T. & T. Clark, 1996).

Dr. **Francis Watson** has taught since 1984 in the Department of Theology and Religious Studies at King's College London, London, where he is Reader in Biblical Theology. He is the author of *Text, Church and World: Biblical Interpretation in Theological Perspective* (Edinburgh: T. & T. Clark/Grand Rapids: Eerdmans, 1994) and *Text and Truth: Redefining Biblical Theology* (Edinburgh: T. & T. Clark/Grand Rapids: Eerdmans, 1997).